LYNDA BARRY

BLOOMSBURY COMICS STUDIES

Covering major genres, creators and themes, the *Bloomsbury Comics Studies* series are accessible, authoritative and comprehensive introductions to key topics in Comics Studies. Providing historical overviews, guides to key texts, and important critical approaches, books in the series include annotated guides to further reading and online resources, discussion questions, and glossaries of key terms to help students and fans navigate the diverse world of comic books today. Derek Parker Royal previously edited the series from its launch to his passing in 2019.

Series Editor: Chris Gavaler

Published Titles

Superhero Comics, Christopher Gavaler
Autobiographical Comics, Andrew J. Kunka
Children's and Young Adult Comics, Gwen Tarbox
Webcomics, Sean Kleefeld
Alan Moore, Jackson Ayres
Jewish Comics and Graphic Narratives, Matt Reingold
Manga, Shige (CJ) Suzuki and Ronald Stewart

Upcoming Titles

Queer Comics, Tof Eklund and Sam Orchard

LYNDA BARRY

A CRITICAL GUIDE

Maaheen Ahmed

BLOOMSBURY ACADEMIC
LONDON • NEW YORK • OXFORD • NEW DELHI • SYDNEY

BLOOMSBURY ACADEMIC

Bloomsbury Publishing Plc, 50 Bedford Square, London, WC1B 3DP, UK
Bloomsbury Publishing Inc, 1359 Broadway, New York, NY 10018, USA
Bloomsbury Publishing Ireland, 29 Earlsfort Terrace, Dublin 2, D02 AY28, Ireland

BLOOMSBURY, BLOOMSBURY ACADEMIC and the Diana logo are trademarks of Bloomsbury Publishing Plc

First published in Great Britain 2026

Copyright © Maaheen Ahmed, 2026

Maaheen Ahmed has asserted her right under the Copyright, Designs and Patents Act, 1988, to be identified as Author of this work.

For legal purposes the Acknowledgments on p. viii constitute an extension of this copyright page.

Cover design: Aisling Repp
Cover image: torn paper isolated © naiauss / Adobe Stock
Notebook texture © inhabitant_b / Adobe Stock
Blue Lined Paper © PTZ Pictures / Adobe Stock

All rights reserved. No part of this publication may be: i) reproduced or transmitted in any form, electronic or mechanical, including photocopying, recording or by means of any information storage or retrieval system without prior permission in writing from the publishers; or ii) used or reproduced in any way for the training, development or operation of artificial intelligence (AI) technologies, including generative AI technologies. The rights holders expressly reserve this publication from the text and data mining exception as per Article 4(3) of the Digital Single Market Directive (EU) 2019/790.

Bloomsbury Publishing Plc does not have any control over, or responsibility for, any third-party websites referred to or in this book. All internet addresses given in this book were correct at the time of going to press. The author and publisher regret any inconvenience caused if addresses have changed or sites have ceased to exist, but can accept no responsibility for any such changes.

A catalogue record for this book is available from the British Library.

A catalog record for this book is available from the Library of Congress.

ISBN: HB: 978-1-3504-5368-5
PB: 978-1-3504-5367-8
ePDF: 978-1-3504-5369-2
eBook: 978-1-3504-5370-8

Series: Bloomsbury Comics Studies

Typeset by Deanta Global Publishing Services, Chennai, India
Printed and bound in Great Britain

For product safety related questions contact productsafety@bloomsbury.com.

To find out more about our authors and books visit www.bloomsbury.com and sign up for our newsletters.

CONTENTS

List of Figures	vi
Acknowledgments	viii

Introduction		**1**
	Note on Book Structure	7
1	**Historical and Biographical Contexts**	**9**
	Growing Up	11
	Books, Comics, Graphic (Life) Narratives	32
2	**Key Texts**	**53**
	Early Comic Strips and Stories	54
	Illustrated Diaries	67
	Comics Making	79
3	**Critical Themes and Questions**	**105**
	Picturing the Invisible	106
	Writing and Language	123
	Textures	136
	Life Writing	146
4	**Social and Cultural Impact**	**155**
	Intersectional Comics	156
	Teaching Comics	172
	Expanding Comics	189
Conclusion		**197**
Bibliography		203
Index		212

FIGURES

0.1	From One Hundred Demons, 215	4
1.1	Table of Contents from One Hundred Demons	12
1.2	From Picture This, 43	16
1.3	Front matter from Everything	35
1.4	"Coping with Stress for Under One Dollar," Wimmen's Comix no. 9 (1984), 363	39
1.5	"Poodle with a Mohawk," excerpt from back cover of Big Ideas	44
1.6	Winter Issue cover, Picture This, 9	50
2.1	Violent boys from Girls and Boys in Everything, 127	56
2.2	"How to Draw Cartoons," from Girls and Boys, 6	59
2.3	"The Creation of the World," from Big Ideas, 10	62
2.4	Edna's portrait with her cousin's baby, from The Good Times Are Killing Me, 8	71
2.5	Portrait of Roberta and Cookie from Cruddy, 12	75
2.6	Barry's two-panel paintings, What It Is, 119	86
2.7	Portrait of Frasca and a variation on Giotto's Madonna and Child from What It Is, 117	87
2.8	Giotto di Bordone, Madonna and Child, 1310/1315	88
2.9	From Picture This, 10	92
2.10	"Sear's Portrait Marlys," from Picture This, 145	96
2.11	"The Hand," from Syllabus, 8	99
3.1	Impossible drawing, doodles, stain heads and the Near-Sighted Monkey with a sandwich, from Picture This, 61	109
3.2	"Head Lice" chapter separator, from One Hundred Demons, 15	116
3.3	Unpracticed drawings and a copy by Barry (top right), from Making Comics, 4	121
3.4	Fire story in the making, from Making Comics, 17	122
3.5	Second and final page of "Forestory Backward," from The Greatest of Marlys, 5	128
3.6	Second and final page of "Enjoying Anteaters," from The Freddie Stories, 147	131

3.7	*"What Is Where Is Your Imagination" collage, from* What It Is, *20*	139
3.8	*Chapter separator for "Resilience," from* One Hundred Demons, *62*	150
4.1	*"Girlness" chapter separator from* One Hundred Demons, *182*	163
4.2	*"Poems can make you see," from* Syllabus, *180*	186
4.3	*"My Favorite Doodles," from* Picture This, *124*	187
5.1	*"Why do we make comic characters?" from* Syllabus, *142*	198

ACKNOWLEDGMENTS

I would like to thank the Bloomsbury Comics Studies series editor, Chris Gavaler, for this opportunity to write about Lynda Barry. I am indebted to the fascinating and inspiring scholarship on Lynda Barry, which made this book a joy to write. A very special thank you to Susan Kirtley and Jane Tolmie for all their help with my queries. I benefited greatly from the excellent comments and suggestions from the encouraging, gentle, and generous reviewers. I hope this version lives up to their expectations.

I am very grateful to Francine Yulo at Drawn & Quarterly for granting permission to reproduce images from Lynda Barry's books. And I would like to thank the Bloomsbury editorial team, especially Aanchal Vij, Lucy Brown, and Arvind Harikumar for all their patient help.

A warm thank you to the wonderful comics studies colleagues at Ghent University and the ACME Comics Research Group, spread all over Belgium, for providing an invaluable and unique platform of exchange, inspiration, and friendship. My heartfelt gratitude also goes to the wonderfully friendly and kind group of comics studies scholars I have had the good fortune of encountering and exchanging with for over more than a decade now.

Most of the ideas fleshed out in this guide were presented on different occasions, including the Invisible Lines conference in Venice, the American Comparative Literature Association's Annual Meeting in Chicago, the International Graphic Novels and Comics Conference in Cambridge, two symposiums in Angouleme and Montpellier, the first on women in comics and the second on Lynda Barry, the Recentring Forms conference organized by the VUB in Brussels and the International AutoBiography Association's conference in Reykjavik. I am deeply grateful to the organizers of these events for the valuable opportunities to present, and to the many kind colleagues for their patient listening, pertinent questions, feedback, and encouragement.

INTRODUCTION

Born in 1956 in Richland Center, Wisconsin, Lynda Barry has a prizewinning career of making and teaching comics. She is, together with Alison Bechdel, one of the very few comics artists to receive the highly prestigious MacArthur Fellowship, also known as the Genius Grant. Barry was awarded the grant for "(i)nspiring creative engagement through original graphic works and a teaching practice centered on the role of image making in communication."[1] The emphasis on pedagogy and the transmission of creativity is a central and unique aspect of Barry's comics work.

Barry's 2019 cohort included the writers Valeria Luiselli and Ocean Vuong and the land artists Mel Chin and Walter Hood. The MacArthur Fellowship is only one more award in a series of distinguished prizes bestowed on Barry in recent years, within and beyond the field of comics field. Her most recent awards include the Eisner Hall of Fame in 2016, the Milton Caniff Lifetime Achievement Award in 2017, the National Cartoonists Society's Cartoonist of the Year award in 2019, an honorary doctorate from the University of Philadelphia in 2015, and the Stone Award for Literary Achievement from Oregon State University in 2021.[2] This range of prizes shows how Barry's picture-making and teaching practice transcend fields to touch on what lies at the heart of all literary and artistic creation, just like her books and comics unsettle fixed forms and formats.

As Professor of Interdisciplinary Creativity at the University of Wisconsin-Madison, Barry teaches university students from diverse programs, from the humanities to the sciences, while also giving regular classes to young children, and even combining the two, pairing PhD students with three- and four-year olds. While teaching is often a given for creative professions, few are the artists and writers who blend teaching guides and creative work. Some of the best-known, recent manuals include

---

[1] "Lynda Barry," *MacArthur Foundation*, accessed December 2, 2024, https://www.macfound.org/fellows/class-of-2019/lynda-barry#searchresults.
[2] For a full list, see Barry's page on the Steven Barclay Agency's website: https://www.barclayagency.com/speakers/lynda-barry.

Lynda Barry

Ivan Brunetti's *Cartooning: Philosophy and Practice,* Scott McCloud's numerous books including *Understanding Comics* and *Making Comics,* and Matt Madden's *99 Styles,* an adaptation of French writer, Raymond Queneau's experimental *Exercises de style* (1947), which explored different writing styes. These guides, like the numerous how-to-draw books since the early twentieth century—consider Clare A. Briggs' *How to Draw Cartoons,* described as Lynda Barry's soulmate in a *Making Comics* review[3]—often remain within the constraints of a manual and focus on teaching budding artist-readers the tips and tricks of the trade. Although didactic codes of the manual are already stretched in McCloud's and Maddens' books, both of which do not offer drawing exercises but theorize comics through comics, Barry's manuals adopt a broader lens to examine the nature and source of creativity itself. Her comics are not only about comics, but about transposing lives in comics, breaking away from the expectations of humor, on one hand, and questioning the possibilities of the form on the other.

In this context of comics manuals, Barry's graphic narratives such as *Syllabus, Picture This, What It Is,* and *Making Comics* carve a unique and fascinating niche. First, very much like Nick Sousanis' *Unflattening,* Barry's manuals theorize not only the medium of comics but drawing and storytelling at large. Second, they differ from other comics teaching guides by unabashedly replacing the confident narrator and avatar of guides by a multiplicity of selves, both present and past, incorporating autobiographical episodes and giving voice and form to anxieties, especially, but not only, those connected to creative work. Barry's books encourage their readers to become makers, not to attain traditional standards of talent, but to make for the sake of making, for expressing and even understanding the self. This making has less to do with talent than with bodily expression and simply using one's hands. As Barry points out in an interview:

> One of the things you'll hear people say, when they tell me they wish they could draw, is, "I see it in my head, but I can't get it onto the page." And then I have to remind them that what they're seeing in their head is not a drawing. Drawing is something that has to come

---

[3] Jay Rath, "Comic Genius: Lynda Barry's New Book is a How-to Book and Much More," *isthmus,* February 27, 2020, accessed September 18, 2024, https://isthmus.com/arts/books/making-comics-book-lynda-barry/.

out of your body. And that horror they have is the same horror they might have if a bodily fluid was suddenly released, like suddenly they got a bloody nose or started drooling. It's that same shame about this thing that's out of their control that seems to be coming from them.[4]

As we will see throughout this guide, the act of drawing, with writing itself being a form of drawing, is central to Barry's works. Barry's teachings emphasize how drawing is a bodily act, an affective response. It is both spontaneous, fueled by the numerous exercises proposed by Barry, and associative, as is the case with the collages in *Picture This* and *What It Is*.

The sometimes loaded and indiscriminate designations of (comics) artist, writer, cartoonist, and illustrator overlap in Barry's case since she experiments with free drawings, copying children's and student's drawings, and incorporating textured collages while also being well-versed in syndicated comic strip production. This guide uses the term comics artist to emphasize the artistic weight of comics work.[5] It is nevertheless important to nuance this concept in the light of the differences and prejudices that exist concerning high art and popular art and how labor-intensive arts and crafts are rarely given the same kind of recognition and respect as legitimized forms of art. Bart Beaty provides an excellent discussion of these tensions in *Comics Versus Art*.[6] Beaty, among other scholars,[7] points out how the legitimization of comics focuses on a very specific kind of comic, the more literary and artistic graphic novel at the expense of the vast majority of comics production. Similarly, claims concerning the potential of comics and the very evaluation of comics is skewed in favor of a framework established for the high arts at the detriment of popular ones.

In "Lost and Found," the final story of Barry's *One Hundred Demons*, her most researched graphic memoir to date, Barry elaborates on the embedded

---

[4]Etelka Lehoczky, "Cartoonist Lynda Barry: 'Drawing Has To Come Out of your Body,'" *npr.org*, November 17, 2019, accessed September 23, 2024, https://www.npr.org/2019/11/27/782921983/cartoonist-lynda-barry-drawing-has-to-come-out-of-your-body.
[5]Simon Grennan proposes the more neutral term of drafter, for instance, and Eszter Szép uses the term drawer. Simon Grennan, *Thinking about Drawing: An Introduction to Themes and Concepts* (Bloomsbury, 2022) and Eszter Szép, *Comics and the Body: Drawing, Reading and Vulnerability* (Ohio State University Press, 2020).
[6]Bart Beaty, *Comics Versus Art* (University of Toronto Press, 2012).
[7]See, for instance, Marc Singer, *Breaking the Frames: Populism and Prestige in Comics Studies* (University of Texas Press, 2019) and Christopher Pizzino, *Arresting Development: Comics at the Boundaries of Literature* (University of Texas Press, 2016).

Lynda Barry

Figure 0.1 From *One Hundred Demons*, 215. Copyright Lynda Barry. Used with permission from Drawn & Quarterly.

hierarchies of cultural forms and how they are enforced from a very early stage in life. Lynda, Barry's autobiographical avatar,[8] who dreamt of becoming a writer, had limited access to books and read the *Reader's Digest*, newspaper classified ads and an advice column, "Hints from Heloise." When she tried to enroll in a creative writing course in high school, she was deemed not "'advanced' enough." Barry recalls, how unlike other writers, who often start writing at a very young age, she only began writing as a teenager, essentially in her diary. This situation only worsened once Lynda entered college (Figure 0.1). This page juxtaposes the college student Lynda who "loved the wrong kind of writing" with the present-day Lynda.[9] The final panel offers the concluding, punchline of the strip: "My trouble ended when I started making comic-strips. It's not something a person has to be very 'advanced' to do. At least not in the minds of literary types."[10]

---

[8]Following the conventions of life writing scholarship, Barry's 'autobifictional' representations of herself are referred to as Lynda, while Barry, the writer and artist, is referred to by her last name. For more on comics life writing see Andrew J. Kunka's *Autobiographical Comics* (Bloomsbury, 2018). Life writing scholar Arnaud Schmitt connects the term 'avatar' to autofiction in his article, "Avatars as the raison d'être of Autofiction," *Life Writing* 19, no. 1 (2022): 15–26.

[9]Lynda Barry, *One Hundred Demons* (Drawn & Quarterly, 2017), 215.

[10]Barry, *One Hundred Demons*, 215.

Introduction

The tone of the writers Lynda converses with in the final panel is condescending and reflects the cultural status of comics and cartoonists. The collaboration they propose—"We write it and you draw it! How <u>fun</u>!"—confirms a power relationship in which the writer takes most of the creative credit by giving instructions to the artist on what to draw. These hierarchies persist in the many *auteurist* studies of comics, which focus on the writer instead of the artists they work with.[11] Unsurprisingly, the first cartooning genre the writers suggest when they learn Lynda is a cartoonist is political, followed by humor. This reflects the overlaps between caricature, cartooning and comics and how comics are mostly associated with political caricature and humorous strips. Even more telling is Lynda's only partially affirmative response to the question about whether she is a humorous cartoonist. As we will see in the next chapter, Barry adopts a very specific kind of ambivalent humor and it is hardly a given feature of her comics, even in her early, syndicated comic strips.

Barry's body of comics work ranges from serialized strips, illustrated novels to hardcover graphic novels and memoirs. These comics do not remain confined to the printed page. They incorporate the exercises and assignments she uses in her courses. Some works have been accompanied by gallery exhibitions, a space that Barry was familiar with from the earliest days of her practice, with exhibitions accompanying or even preceding her books, *Naked Ladies, Naked Ladies, Naked Ladies* and *The Good Times Are Killing Me*. Existing between two worlds that were more distinct in the 1980s than they are now, Barry, as we will see in Chapter 2, had to make a choice between the art world and syndicated strips.[12]

While nowadays Barry's most-read comics are her graphic novels, the vast scope of her comics and illustration work offer the ideal opportunity for understanding comics in all their diversity and for tracing the connections between comics and other visual and literary forms. For this, the guide is indebted to a rich body of scholarship that has deftly unpacked the significance and potential of Barry's comics. Susan Kirtley's award-winning *Lynda Barry: Girlhood through the Looking Glass* stands out through its approach to Barry's comics oeuvre in its entirety and from

---

[11]See, for instance, Isabelle Licari-Guillaume, "Ambiguous Authorities: Vertigo and the Auteur Figure," *Authorship* no. 2 (2017), https://doi.org/10.21825/aj.v6i2.7700.
[12]Hillary Chute, *Graphic Women: Life Narrative and Contemporary Comics* (Columbia University Press, 2010), 98.

the lens of girlhood. Kirtley's recent chapter on Barry's early comics from the 1970s and 1980s collected in *Girls and Boys* (1981), examines the punk and participatory aesthetics of her comics.[13] The pioneering works of Susan Kirtley and Hillary L. Chute on Barry's life writing and representations of girlhood are complemented by Hannah Miodrag's fascinating reading of Barry's use of childish idiom.[14] *Contagious Imagination: The Work and Art of Lynda Barry*, edited by Jane Tolmie,[15] combines perspectives on teaching and practice-based research opened by Barry's comics alongside Barry's distinct ways of incorporating autobiography in comics. Keeping with the focus on autobiography and memoir in comics scholarship, critical interest has often focused on the exclusively autobiographical, *One Hundred Demons* and *What It Is*, which can be seen as its companion, scrapbook variant.[16] Most recently, Eszter Szép's embodied reading of Barry's lines and creativity prompts has further enriched the toolbox for approaching Barry's work while emphasizing the extent to which Barry offers us the possibility, time and again, to deepen our understanding of comics.[17]

Building on the extensive scholarship on Barry's comics, this guide casts its net further by digging deeper into concepts such as trace and archive, emotions and relationality, to chart the rich scope of reflection offered by Barry's comics. It closely reads the comics to unpack the roles of affect and emotion, variations in technique and theme, layers of materiality (often rooted in collages recuperating what is deemed as waste), and their archival

---

[13]Susan Kirtley, *Typical Girls: The Rhetoric of Womanhood in Comic Strips* (Ohio State University Press, 2021), 106–35.
[14]Hannah Miodrag, *Comics and Language: Reimagining Critical Discourse on the Form* (University Press of Mississippi, 2013), 41–58.
[15]Jane Tolmie, ed., *Contagious Imagination: The Work and Art of Lynda Barry* (University Press of Mississippi, 2022).
[16]See, for instance: Chute, *Graphic Women*, 95–134; Nancy Pedri, "Traumatic Layering of Self: Scrapbooking Personal Photographs in *One Hundred Demons*," *Polysèmes* 19 (2018), https://journals.openedition.org/polysemes/3460; Melinda L. de Jésus, "Liminality and Mestiza Consciousness in Lynda Barry's *One Hundred Demons*," in *Multicultural Comics: From Zap to Blue Beetle*, ed. Frederik L. Aldama (University of Texas Press, 2010), 73–94; Özge Samanci, "Lynda Barry's Humor: At the Juncture of Private and Public, Invitation and Dissemination, Childish and Professional," *International Journal of Comic Art* 8, no. 2 (2006): 181–99. Olga Michael, "Graphic Autofiction and the Visualization of Trauma in Lynda Barry and Phoebe Gloeckner's Graphic Memoirs," in *Autofiction in English*, ed. Hywel Dix (Palgrave, 2018), 105–24. Kieron Brown, "Play and Playfulness in Lynda Barry's *What It Is*," *Eludamos: Journal for Computer Game Culture* 12, no. 1 (2021): 127–48, https://doi.org/10.7557/23.6366.
[17]Szép, *Comics and the Body*, 53–78.

Introduction

import. Turning to selected works ranging from Barry's earliest comics to her more recent graphic novels and memoirs, this guide explores Barry's image theories and comics pedagogy to elaborate on the participatory nature of comics-making and to unpack the many "uses" of art in a context that increasingly restricts art appreciation and making to a select few. Showing how Barry's manuals rely on a reconsideration of notions of good and bad drawing, rendering comics-making into an accessible art form, the guide elaborates on the politics of such position-taking. This guide accords special attention to the theme of childhood, the importance of children's drawings, and the relevance of childlike drawing styles.

Note on Book Structure

Chapter 1 sketches the historical and biographical context of Barry's work, focusing on the centrality of children and growing up in comics and the many formats she has worked with over the decades, from newspaper strips to visual novels, children's novels, and graphic novels. The chapter foregrounds the distinctive humor and emotionality of Barry's comics.

The guide then elaborates on key texts (Chapter 2), focusing on Barry's illustrated diaries, comic strips, life writing and comics manuals. It traces the diversity of themes and styles in Barry's early comics, the traumas of young girls and social commentary in the illustrated diaries, *The Good Times Are Killing Me*[18] and *Cruddy*.[19] The final section turns to the diverse forms of comics pedagogy and their intertwining with autobiographical elements in Barry's graphic narratives, ranging from memoirs like *One Hundred Demons* to manuals like *Making Comics*.[20]

Chapter 3 broaches critical themes and questions such as how Barry's comics give shape to different kinds of invisibles, the role she accords to the "aliveness" and animation of images, the multilayered significance of her collages and the specific brand of life writing she develops beginning with the autobifictional *One Hundred Demons* and including the scrapbooked pages of *Everything: Comics from Around 1978-1981*.[21]

---

[18] Lynda Barry, *Everything: Comics From Around 1978-1981* (Drawn & Quarterly, 2011).
[19] Lynda Barry, *The Good Times Are Killing Me* (Drawn & Quarterly, 2017).
[20] Lynda Barry, *Cruddy: An Illustrated Novel* (Simon & Schuster, 2000).
[21] Lynda Barry, *Making Comics* (Drawn & Quarterly, 2019).

Lynda Barry

The guide's final chapter, Chapter 4, turns to the social and cultural impact of Barry's comics by focusing on intersectional representations of class, race, and girlhood. It then turns to the influences behind Barry's comics pedagogy and the key tenets of her exercises. The final section elaborates on how Barry expands the limits of comics through breaking away from the comics form, interactive collages and encouragements to collaborate.

CHAPTER 1
HISTORICAL AND BIOGRAPHICAL CONTEXTS

This chapter introduces Barry's childhood and comics career. It identifies the central currents running through her comics and examined further in the later chapters: storytelling, making images and words come alive, similar to Walter Benjamin's "moving script," which Jared Gardner connects to the overlap between handwriting and drawing in comics;[1] transposing the bittersweetness of (semi-)autobiographical lives; transitioning across genres and book forms; adopting a holistic, non-judgmental approach to art of allowing pictures and stories to emerge; and, ultimately, sharing and promoting the language of comics. While Barry's comics are introduced in more detail in the second chapter, this chapter turns to selected examples from *Ernie Pook's Comeek* strips (1979–2008), *One Hundred Demons* (2002), *What It Is* (2008), *Picture This: The Near-Sighted Monkey Book* (2010), *Everything: Comics from Around 1978-1981* (2011), and *Syllabus* (2014) to explore how the above themes are given form.

The first section, "Growing Up," focuses on a recurring concern in Barry's comics, including her *Ernie Pook's Comeek* strips, which ran from 1979 until 2008, and her long-form graphic novels. In Barry's comics, growing up, like life, is captured in all its messiness, where the non-linear and the processual acquire precedence over the sequential. There are also many ways in which both Barry and her comics characters resist growing up, the most obvious of which is her comics style: colorful and seemingly simple, Barry's style revels in the childlike, just like her stories are often told through children's perspectives.

The second section, "Books, Comics, Graphic (Life) Narratives," connects Barry's inspirations, art education, and practice to the changing comics making and publishing contexts. Barry's career spans the most

---

[1] Jarded Gardner, "Storylines," *SubStance* 40, no. 1 (2011): 53–69, 54–7.

transformative decades of comics history and this section highlights key transformations, beginning with the rise of underground comics, including women comics authors' reclamation of space often denied to them, and extending to the rise of the graphic novel and possibilities for new formats, stories, and readerships. While interacting with, and responding to, tendencies in comics publishing, Barry carves a very distinctive path, exemplifying what comics can be and, even more importantly, how anyone with a paper and a pencil can explore the potentialities of comics.

As we will see throughout this critical guide, Barry's comics offer the perfect key to understanding both comics history and comics theory, how comics have changed and transformed over time, how comics work and how the form's potential overlaps with the broader realm of what art historian W. J. T. Mitchell has called the imagetext, fusing visual and verbal realms, and enhancing the graphic script imagined by Benjamin. In coining the term imagetext, Mitchell's aim is more theoretical than speculative and seeks to highlight the mixed nature of most channels of expression. As he explains in an interview: "Meaning is relational all the way down and the imagetext is just one way of making that fact visible."[2] This relationality can be extended from word and image to sound, especially in comics, when words are often sound. Barry's comics, with their emphasis on handwork, including simply writing the letters of the alphabet, and because of their unabashed wordiness, are perfect case studies for exploring and understanding the imagetext.

Susan Kirtley opens her monograph, *Lynda Barry: Girlhood through the Looking Glass* by drawing a connection between Barry's description of herself as an "image wrangler" and Mitchell's understanding of the image as something that goes beyond the materiality of a picture to encompass abstract and even spiritual understandings of the image.[3] This is evident in Barry's philosophical reflections in *What It Is* (2008). Barry's image wrangling takes numerous forms. It encompasses engaging with the archives—ranging from the personal and collective to the little known and anonymous—meditative coloring-in, repetitive

---

[2]Christine Wiesenthal, Brad Bucknell, and W. J. T. Mitchell, "Essays into the Imagetext: An Interview with W. J. T. Mitchell," *Mosaic: An Interdisciplinary Critical Journal* 33, no. 2 (2000): 1–23, 17.
[3]Kirtley, *Lynda Barry*, ix. Kirtley takes this definition from Mitchell's *Iconology: Image, Text, Ideology* (University of Chicago Press, 1986), 31.

Historical and Biographical Contexts

drawing (of spirals and lines, for instance) and spontaneous, or even automatic, drawing exercises. Like Kirtley, Eszter Szép also connects Mitchell's image theory to Barry's approaches to images by emphasizing how activities such as copying—fervently encouraged in Barry's comics manuals—imbue images with a sociability (Mitchell uses social life[4]) of their own.[5] As Szép emphasizes, Barry's keen interest in the *aliveness* of images and accessing the throbbing heart of images, and not necessarily the pictures that result from them, forms the core of Barry's creative practice.[6] This aliveness is also reflected in the images themselves, which are often animated and sometimes directly address the reader with brief, surprising phrases—"Hello!" or "ICU2"—especially in *What It Is, Syllabus* and *Picture This*. For Chute, such "images signal that they are both looked at and themselves looking,"[7] that "they are seeing us, addressing us; they are undead."[8] Aliveness offers possibilities of looking back and remembering; the act of visualizing becomes "its own form of reexperiencing."[9] As we will see in Chapters 3 and 4, Barry's fascination with the aliveness of images also captures the self-reflexive nature of her comics, which embody comics and image theory while encouraging readers to make images and tell stories.[10]

Growing Up

Lynda Barry was born in Wisconsin to a mother of Filipino and Irish origin and to a father with Norwegian-Irish ancestry. When Barry was still young, her family moved across the country to Seattle, where Barry spent most of her childhood, raised by her mother and her grandmother in a working-class, mixed-race neighborhood. The racial dynamics and

---

[4] W. J. T. Mitchell, *What Do Pictures Want: The Lives and Loves of Images* (University of Chicago Press, 2005), 93.
[5] Szép, *Comics and the Body*, 61.
[6] Szép, *Comics and the Body*, 60.
[7] Chute, *Graphic Women*, 127.
[8] Chute, *Graphic Women*, 128.
[9] Chute, *Graphic Women*, 128.
[10] See Jeanette Roan, "'What is an Image?' Art History, Visual Culture Studies, Comics Studies," in *Seeing Comics through Art History*, ed. Maggie Gray and Ian Horton (Palgrave, 2022), 247–68.

Lynda Barry

Figure 1.1 Table of Contents from *One Hundred Demons*. Copyright Lynda Barry. Used with permission from Drawn & Quarterly.

struggles of working-class homes and neighborhoods are thematized in her comics around childhood, including her syndicated *Ernie Pook's Comeek*, her "autobifictional" works and her illustrated novels.

Life writing is a key genre marking the emergence of the graphic novel, which is introduced in the second section here and examined in more detail in the next two chapters, since most of Barry's comics engage with some form of life writing, often making it impossible to disentangle potentially autobiographical features from other aspects of her work. She problematizes this element by introducing the concept of "autobifictionalography."

The tongue-in-cheek autobifictional label appears under the second table of contents, or list of demons, for *One Hundred Demons* (Figure 1.1). The collaged page includes a torn scrap of green paper with "autobifictionalography" neatly handwritten in red ink, pasted under the table of contents and contrasting with its black, typed words. Further to the left and almost cut off by the bottom edge of the page, another handwritten scrap of yellow paper asks whether the stories are true or false. Both boxes, "true" (in italics) and "FALSE" (in capital letters, which lend it more weight), are ticked. Positioned at a slight diagonal, partially under a panel from the *Ernie Pook's Comeek* archive, this scrap could function as a caption but also maintains a certain distance from the drawing. The despondent girl in the panel, with freckles and cat-eye-shaped glasses could be a portrait of a young Lynda Barry, although, as we will see later, Barry's young avatars never appear with glasses. This girl is Arna, cousin to the teenage Maybonne and her younger sister Marlys, who eventually became the main characters of *Ernie Pook's Comeek*. The title itself, which started as *Girls and Boys* before becoming *True Comeek*, was eventually durably renamed *Ernie Pook's Comeek*, after a pet phrase used by one of Barry's brothers to designate everything he saw.[11]

Reprints of *Ernie Pook's Comeek* by Drawn & Quarterly introduce the comics as inspired from Barry's childhood. Similarly, as suggested by "autobifictionalography," Barry maintains a degree of uncertainty concerning the fictionalization of stories that seem autobiographical. While the complexity of this autobiographical pact—which destabilizes truth claims without completely undoing them—will be discussed in detail in the third chapter, contextual elements that overlap with Barry's own childhood, evoked in her interviews and in her graphic narratives, are discernible in these early comics.[12] The working-class context and unloving, even traumatizing parenting, are especially recurrent.

Even though Arna is not Barry, we already find in this panel, and the collaged elements surrounding it, the sensitivity with which childhood is portrayed. Time and again, Barry introduces us to children who reject the clichéd gazes associated with childhood that are often soaked in nostalgia and paint an idealized period of joy and innocence. Arna is neither happy nor idealized in this panel—everything about her is either disproportionate or just not beautiful, like the dots on her limbs. She seems sad, contemplative, tapping her right foot nervously, and perhaps even staying out of sight. Perpendicular to her body, and roughly half her size, is a cheerful ad for Moo Maid Milk with a smiling cow and flowers. Milk is a central, heavily connoted ingredient of childhood. The seemingly frivolous ad is therefore not as innocent as it seems on first sight. It highlights how something is not right with Arna and enhances the bittersweet mood of the image. Such sensitive, emotionally complex, and honest portrayals of childhood, both Barry's own and fictionalized or imagined ones, are a hallmark of her comics.

---

[11]Kirtley, *Lynda Barry*, 39.
[12]See also Kirtley, *Lynda Barry*, 15–47.

A larger version of the panel appears in *Picture This*, in a different context.[13] Here, the Arna panel appears next to a text on "Who Is In Charge?," which elaborates on the unpredictability of the ink brush, how it entails getting used to and accepting that the brush also has a life of its own. In the strip at the bottom of the page, Barry, in the guise of the multi-eyed sea monster (sometimes also called the Sea-Ma), with a cigarette in one hand and a glass of wine in the other, explains how the brush opened new possibilities for image-making and rekindled Barry's love for drawing, which had been stamped out after years of weekly comic strip drawing.[14] The multi-eyed sea monster, just like the magic cephalopod, are creatures we encounter time and again in Barry's graphic narratives.[15] The former's most memorable, and most discussed, appearance is in *One Hundred Demons*, where it stands in for the prototypical demon in the frontmatter and even announces the "Introduction!"[16] Not only does the demon bear a smiling head of the Near-Sighted Monkey on its body, it also ventriloquizes Lynda's messages and hopes in the third person, cementing a close connection with Lynda. The sea monster, in all its fluidity and daring, personifies creativity and willfulness to face one's demons,[17] which in Lynda's case include her unloving mother.

Arna also acts as the reference figure in the opening pages of *Picture This*, guiding the reader through the constituents of a book that challenges genres and forms, as we will see below, in the second section. While the book's front cover carries a portrait of Arna, placed opposite Marlys' picture, in the elaborate margins surrounding the main image of a *Learning How to Art with the Near-Sighted Monkey* book held between two freckled hands, the back cover shows Arna alone, dozing on a sofa with the same *Near-Sighted Monkey* book in her hands. Here, she is the protagonist of the

---

[13]Lynda Barry and Kevin Kawula (water colors), *Picture This: The Near-Sighted Monkey Book* (Drawn & Quarterly, 2010), 204.
[14]Barry, *Picture This*, 204.
[15]On the centrality of the magic cephalopod and the sea demon in Barry's comics manuals, see Allan Pero, "In the Orbit of the Cephalopod: *What It Is* and Artistic Education," in *Contagious Imagination: The Work and Art of Lynda Barry*, ed. Jane Tolmie (University Press of Mississippi, 2022), 99–111. For the role of these creatures and art in working through trauma, as well as the ambiguity of the Sea-Ma, see Olga Michael, "Excavating Childhood: Fairy Tales, Monsters and Abuse Survival in Lynda Barry's *What It Is*," *a/b: Auto/Biography Studies* 32, no. 3 (2017): 541–66.
[16]Barry, *One Hundred Demons*, 6
[17]Szép, *Comics and the Body*, 59.

scene, occupying almost half of the cover. Her mirror image is a playfully drawn, crowned elephant ghost surrounded by meditative swirls, alluding to the imaginative and even mystical possibilities of engaging with and making art. A small, typewritten piece of advice—"Remember to forget to remember"—at the top of the image serves as an unassuming title.

It is through Arna's eyes that we encounter *Picture This* in a mise-en-abyme in the book. Arna's questions about *Picture This* echo those of many potential readers:[18] "Was it a book for kids or for grown-ups? The monkey drank beer, played cards and bought lottery tickets, was that a good influence?"[19] It is also Arna who reminds readers of the joy of simply moving one's hands and scribbling freely, an act that is interrupted by Marlys, who calls it babyish.[20] Marlys soon changes her mind, in a characteristic Marlys way, after seeing a television reportage on scribbled artworks by "hairy beatniks" fetching high prices: "This is the answer to everything, man!" Marlys exclaims, "Let's be artists, man!" (Figure 1.2).[21] This exuberant main sequence is underpinned by a frieze-like strip in which Barry asks questions that will come back in her comics. In a long strip without panels showing a young Lynda drawing at the age of three and unable to draw at the age of thirteen, Barry adds:

What is it about the hand? The hand and the motion we call handwriting?
What makes us start drawing?
What makes us stop?[22]

These questions establish parallels with handwriting and drawing that are central to Barry's graphic narratives, just like the core question of creative desire and motivation. The hand itself acquires a prominent place in her manuals, as do exercises which emphasize hand movements over the outcomes of those movements. In the frieze on the opposite page, an older Lynda wonders: "Can I draw or not? From the beginning of my time as a cartoonist people have said I can't draw or that my drawing is bad."[23]

---

[18]Barry, *Picture This*, 12–15.
[19]Barry, *Picture This*, 15.
[20]Barry, *Picture This*, 41–2.
[21]Barry, *Picture This*, 43.
[22]Barry, *Picture This*, 40.
[23]Barry, *Picture This*, 41.

Lynda Barry

Figure 1.2 From *Picture This*, 43. Copyright Lynda Barry. Used with permission from Drawn & Quarterly.

And when Marlys decides to become an artist (Figure 1.2), the frieze shows an anxious Lynda asking "What does not being able to draw mean? (. . .) Why do I draw anyway?" while the happy, smoking Near-Sighted Monkey poses next to a true or false statement: "the near-sighted monkey can't draw either".[24]

These pages from *Picture This* illustrate the overlap between Barry's child characters and her own experiences, in particular how the anxiety of being creative, which began in her childhood, persists into her adulthood. She connects this to a shared anxiety and points out how the fear of drawing stamps out the joyful act of unfettered scribbling. Each page carries one panel from the Arna and Marlys story, bordered by a frieze at the bottom, the size and positioning of which relegates it to secondary reading, available to the reader who seeks more and is willing to revisit and connect the two

---

[24]Barry, *Picture This*, 43.

narratives. Going back to reread and re-connect in this way implies we "weave" the narrative.[25] Offering a counterpoint to Thierry Groensteen's concept of braiding,[26] through which comics artists connect individual components of a comic to construct a meaningful and plastic network, Barbara Postema introduces the concept of weaving to describe how readers move back and forth to create meaning in a comic. The weaving reader will notice how scribbles appear in the early pages of *Picture This* as a colorful maze for a Mr. Trunk who "must find the line that leads to don't" with the "Don't" packet of imaginary cigarettes lying at the other end.[27] Quick irregular scribbles represent the smoke coming out of Maybonne's and the Near-Sighted Monkey's cigarettes. Most importantly, scribbles surround the frames for the Arna and Marlys story about drawing. One panel zooms in on Arna's drawing hand and the looping lines emerging on her paper.[28] Smaller, more compulsive scribbles can be seen in the frame surrounding the panel as the young Lynda scribbles in the frieze. These scribbles also adorn the panel frames, becoming increasingly regular and ornamental, with the loops colored in.

Margins are traditionally a space for impromptu doodles and comments on the contents of the main body of the page. The regular use of framing for structure and texture in Barry's comics generates considerable marginal space which Barry actively fills in. In almost compulsively filling in the margins, letting frame, margins, and central content bleed into each other, Barry questions the marginalization of all that happens outside the main frame, eventually allowing the margins and the scribbles to take over the center of the page at the end of this first encounter with Arne and Marlys in *Picture This*.[29] In *What It Is*, Barry recalls how drawing "was a form of transportation. I did it because it helped me to stay. By giving me somewhere else to go."[30] She adds: "Maybe this is why we draw shapes in the margins during meetings or on the backs of envelopes when we're waiting on the phone. Drawing can help us stand to be there. That, alone, is

---

[25] See Barbara Postema, *Narrative Structure in Comics: Making Sense of Fragments* (RIT Press, 2013), 112–13.
[26] Thierry Groensteen, *The System of Comics*, trans. Bart Beaty and Nick Nguyen (University Press of Mississippi, 2007), 144–58.
[27] Barry, *Picture This*, 13.
[28] Barry, *Picture This*, 40.
[29] Barry, *Picture This*, 45.
[30] Lynda Barry, *What It Is* (Drawn & Quarterly, 2008), 105.

something."³¹ The margin drawings therefore bear witness to a compulsive, existential need to draw, offering the possibility to be transported beyond the mundane to relish the joy of making, of moving one's hands. In most of her comics, Barry seems to return to drawn margins, conceptual margins as well as archival margins (by incorporating what is often relegated to waste), to flesh out her image-making philosophy. This philosophy relies on a reciprocal movement of emotions and affect from the creator to the reader-viewer. The centrality of emotions will be elaborated a little further below through Barry's discussion of "feeling-change" in *Everything* (2011), an anthology of her earliest works.

In medieval illuminated manuscripts, margins served as constrained spaces of commentary on the text via illustration and provided room for creativity, giving birth to the famous drolleries or grotesques adorning the books. Margins offer room for marginalia, or notes scribbled in by readers. In all of these cases the margin comes across as an interactive space where artists and readers engage with (or ignore) the text in the main body of the page. By filling in this space with additional drawings, decoration, collaged elements, and comments, Barry uses marginal spaces as moments of self-reflection or simply pictorial excess and pleasure. These margins also prefigure the reader interaction encouraged by her books which, as we will see in Chapter 4, is a central concern since many of Barry's comics encourage the reader to write, draw and create themselves.

When Arna and Marlys get busy drawing in *Picture This*, the reader is given step-by-step instructions on how to join the exercise.³² The final panel of the section carries the title, "Practice a Wandering Line."³³ It is colored in, framed and surrounded by other scribbles (and even a small, doodled creature called Van Dyke, with arms akimbo, who comments on the happenings on the page). The scribbles become the protagonists of this section in *Picture This*, reclaiming an act often confined to childhood. Allowing lines to wander, to scribble without a clear aim is both a manual and visual exercise. It is also a necessary one to reactivate hands unaccustomed to drawing and to get used to the different possibilities of pens and brushes. The centrality of hands is already suggested in the image above where we can see both of Marly's hands, partially colored with a gray wash, as she announces the start

---

[31] Barry, *What It Is*, 105.
[32] Barry, *Picture This*, 44.
[33] Barry, *Picture This*, 45.

of her artistic career together with Arna. Hands were also present on both sides of the imaginary art book at the center of the cover of *Picture This*. Later in *Picture This*, the reader learns how to draw Marlys and Arna, in a larger frieze strip, extending across a double page. The less exuberant and more pensive Arna, we are told, is harder to draw than Marlys.[34]

What It Is advocates for writing with the hand and the different sensory and motoric processes it activates, in comparison to typing: "There is a state of the mind which is not accessible by thinking. It seems to require a participation with something"—that "something" is hand motion.[35] Barry continues:

> Handwriting
> is an image
> left by a living
> being in motion
> it cannot be duplicated
> in time or space.[36]

In highlighting the visuality of written text, Barry shares an understanding of writing that is comparable to Mitchell's imagetext. Similarly, Barry's description of handwriting as a trace or an image of a moving being evokes Marion's concept of graphiation, while placing the emphasis not so much on the author or artist but on the movement of their hands.[37]

The Belgian comics and film scholar, Philippe Marion proposes the notion of graphiation to emphasize the nuances of this presence: the lines we see on the page are not direct imprints of the artist firstly because they are mediated by the reproduction technologies involved; secondly, and more importantly, they are the outcome of constant negotiation between different kinds of styles—including those that are expected for a particular kind of story—and the artist's own skills and artistic intentions. The artist

---

[34]Barry, *Picture This*, 176–9.
[35]Barry, *What It Is*, 106.
[36]Barry, *What It Is*, 108
[37]See Philippe Marion, *Traces en cases: travail graphique, figuration narrative et participation du lecteur: la bande dessinée*, PhD dissertation (Université catholique de Louvain, 1993); see also Jan Baetens, "Revealing Traces: A New Theory of Graphic Enunciation," in *The Language of Comics: Word and Image*, ed. Robin Varnum and Christina T. Gibbons (University Press of Mississippi, 2001), 145–55.

is both present in and hidden behind the line. Each line or stroke is a trace of the artist's hand, recording their presence to different degrees on the transparency scale proposed by Eszter Szép.[38] This scale ranges from the indexical assumptions attached to the drawn line to the sociological and skill-based conditioning and relative anonymization of the line and its narrative capacities, which have been extensively theorized by Simon Grennan.[39]

In addition to emphasizing how the graphic memoir combines changing temporalities, affecting both narration and reading, life writing scholars, Sidonie Smith and Julia Watson identify several "overlapping layers of self-representation":

> the invisible hand of the author-artist that draws the image; the narrating architect of the story whose voice runs above the frame, sometimes in boxes; the narrated "I" as autobiographical avatar who is both imaged and voiced; the characters, including the narrated "I," speaking in dialogue bubbles; the audience, including the addressee within the comic, as well as flesh-and-blood readers; and, often, the artist's hand depicted within one or more frames as a metalevel aesthetic autograph.[40]

As we will see throughout this guide, Barry incorporates all sorts of hands in her works, leaving imprints that can be openly hers or distinct from her personal experiences. This ambiguity, combined with the hybrid nature of her graphic narratives offers the possibility of approaching her works from different perspectives, as manuals on one hand, and "autobifictional," on the other.

While *Picture This* does not share many moments from Barry's own childhood,[41] *One Hundred Demons* and *What It Is,* functioning as graphic memoirs, offer us some insights. Even before the title page of *What It Is* and right opposite the magic cephalopod which dedicates the book to Barry's

---

[38]Szép, *Comics and the Body,* 42.
[39]See Simon Grennan, *A Theory of Narrative Drawing* (Palgrave, 2017).
[40]Sidonie Smith and Julia Watson, *Reading Autobiography Now: An Updated Guide for Interpreting Life Narratives* (University of Minnesota Press, 2024), 252.
[41]There is one exception when Lynda recalls how she enjoyed transforming portraits of people in magazines by making holes or using erasers and how her mother inexplicably yelled at her for it (Barry, *Picture This,* 53).

college art teacher, Marilyn Frasca, we see a full-page portrait of a young Lynda in profile. On the backcover of the book, the magic cephalopod is introduced as "The Pathfinder":

> When looked upon.
> Activated by any
> Activity related
> To the image-world.
> Guides pens, pencils
> and other mark-
> makers through
> exercises. Follow
> the Magic Cephalopod.[42]

In its sister volume, *Picture This*, it is the Near-Sighted Monkey who appears in numerous full-page portraits, which are generally brightly colored and captioned. This contrasts with the dark markers and ink lines obscuring most of the young Lynda's face and body in the full-page portrait in *What It Is*. The scalloped edge on the top and the band with a bird on the bottom place the girl on a kind of stage. The stage motif reappears a few pages later when Barry recalls a childhood "staring game" which involved being as still as possible and waiting "for other things in the room to forget about me and begin to move."[43] These "things" were mostly pictures, all the pictures the family had, which were taped to the walls of the trailer in which they lived. It is no coincidence that Barry devotes the opening pages of *What It Is*—under the title of which we can read "the formless thing that gives things form"—to this childhood game.

Kieron Brown connects Barry's description of childhood play to the pediatrician and psychoanalyst D. W. Winnicott's concept of a "third area," a space established through the interaction between internal and external realities.[44] Brown argues that Barry's works, like *What It Is*, display a kind of playfulness that is both a "willful subversion of convention/interpretative frames" and a means of conveying authenticity through the seemingly spontaneous collages and allusive connections established throughout the

---

[42] Barry, *What It Is*, backcover.
[43] Barry, *What It Is*, 10.
[44] Brown, "Play and Playfulness," 129.

book.[45] As is the case with Eszter Szép's suggestion of Barry's "authentic line," which is also built on the communicative and relational nature of Barry's manuals such as *Syllabus* and *What It Is*, the notion of authenticity needs to be nuanced and perhaps even reconsidered. Immediacy seems to be a more appropriate alternative to capture the ways in which Barry's collages establish connections across pages, books and reader-viewers, since it seems impossible to distinguish between authentic and inauthentic lines as we will see in the discussion of Marion's concept of graphiation in Chapter 3.

Szép elaborates on another aspect of Barry's and other artists' works, vulnerability, which she connects to the gesture of drawing. "Comics," Szép writes, "are created via this unpredictable gesture of engaging with an active line."[46] And it is precisely "the dangerous spontaneity of drawing the line and (. . .) in considering the line as a free-moving active agent" that reflects a certain vulnerability.[47] Following Szép, Barry's vulnerability is not only present through the memories and moments of despair that she shares but runs throughout her work, in the very lines she draws and adjusts over the course of her career. Barry's comics manuals also unfold as spaces of shared creative vulnerability, identifying its sources and tinkering with it.

What It Is is a deep exploration of the image, the idea preceding the picture, its sources and its lives. This drive brings *What It Is* close to W. J. T. Mitchell's *What do Pictures Want?* Mitchell examines the potential desires of images, building on an anthropological understanding of images which approaches images as objects and forms that are animated by us and animate us. Pointing out the similarities between Michell's and Barry's understandings of the image, Szép writes: "The image is a structure of personal experience, not simply a picture" and adds that "Barry uses the word 'image' to describe the experience of aliveness felt in drawing lines."[48]

Seeking, establishing, and understanding our relationships to different kinds of images and using drawing and comics as animating tools lie at the heart of Barry's comics and art education practice. Barry's pages are alive, throbbing with life, through the images, the text, and all the visual matter interspersed between them. In contrast to her black-and-white comic strips,

---

[45]Brown, "Play and Playfulness," 141.
[46]Szép, *Comics and the Body*, 74.
[47]Szép, *Comics and the Body*, 76.
[48]Szép, *Comics and the Body*, 59.

Barry's full-color graphic narratives often reflect a horror of the blank page, the *horror vacui* or fear of the void, that is often connected to outsider art. The art historian Roger Cardinal borrows the term from the psychiatrist, Walter Morgenthaler who used it to describe Adolf Wölfli's intense paintings where "he left not a single empty space, if necessary adding disjointed sentences in the gaps in the picture."[49] Such an approach radically contrasts with carefully planned compositions and offers more room for intuition and chance to come into play. The space of the page and the materiality of the tools and techniques determine the final appearance of the page. The automatic or free drawing essence of some of Barry's exercises are among the key elements that distinguish her manuals from most how-to-draw and comics-making manuals published from the nineteenth century onwards. Many of Barry's graphic narratives are also manuals for creating art outside of established traditions and expectations, for creating art for art's sake, where the process of breathing life into lines and collages and generating images is as—if not more—important than the visible outcome.

To return to Barry's portrait of her younger self where darkness is created by numerous quick lines covering the yellow exercise book paper: most of the heaviness of the image comes through the intense and uneven coloring and the vague source of light—an empty room—allowing us to decipher Lynda's eyes and resigned expression. This is a portrait of a child who is simultaneously young and old, with experiences that are not often associated with childhood. The next page, which is behind Barry's portrait is dominated, surprisingly enough, by Lincoln's silhouette. It is accompanied by a threatening small rhyme, which sounds, and looks, like a child's game since it is written in uneven writing: "Chase me, I will catch ye. I will catch ye."[50] Lincoln subtly haunts the pages since postage stamps with his silhouette reappear on the two pages that follow, but the stamps are gradually pushed to the bottom of the page.

Barry's portrait of herself as a child can be compared to the double-page spread portrait in gray washes of a young and troubled Alison Bechdel among the loose papers at the end of *Are You My Mother? A Comic Drama* (2012).[51] In contrast to the young Lynda, the young Alison faces us without looking at us. Her despairing face is split by the book's gutter, even though

---

[49]Roger Cardinal, *Outsider Art* (Studio Vista, 1972), 59.
[50]Barry, *What It Is*, 3.
[51]Alison Bechdel, *Are You My Mother: A Comic Drama* (Mariner Books, 2012).

the portrait extends across the traditionally white space of the gutter. In book binding terms, this gutter has a more materially unifying function than a comics gutter. Although Alison's face is marked by gray shadows, she remains visible, and readable, while Lynda's portrait is largely obscured. Instead of being tightly contained within a frame and a dark interior like Lynda, Alison is painted with an open landscape looming behind her and her portrait continues beyond the pages and the confines of the book. Containment, within frames, and through blocks of words, is a hallmark of Barry's representations of herself and the characters she draws, especially in her early graphic narratives (*One Hundred Demons, Picture This, What It Is*); only imaginary creatures, like the multi-eyed sea monster occasionally break away from such drawn confines.

What It Is also intersperses additional photographs of Barry, which are explored in further detail in Chapter 3. The rest of this section will introduce the main aspects of Barry's childhood that can be gathered from a selection of short stories from *One Hundred Demons*. The demon-short story form, extending across eighteen panels, is noteworthy since it strikes a balance between the four-panel strips and the long-form graphic narrative. Episodes from *One Hundred Demons* were initially published online on *Salon.com*. They incorporated both the liberty of being in full color on a webpage and the constraint of limited length imposed by the online format, which has to remain scrollable. These episodes can be read as short, slice of life stories.

Short stories have not always had a good reputation. Modern man, Walter Benjamin wrote,

> has succeeded in abbreviating even storytelling. We have witnessed the evolution of the "short story," which has removed itself from oral tradition and no longer permits that slow piling one on top of the other of thin, transparent layers which constitutes the most appropriate picture of the way in which the perfect narrative is revealed through the layers of a variety of retellings.[52]

While Barry's demon-chapters in *One Hundred Demons* are perhaps the closest to the short story in comics form, most of her graphic narratives

---

[52] Walter Benjamin, "The Storyteller: Reflections on the Work of Nikolai Leskov," in *The Storyteller Essays,* ed. and intro. Samuel Titan, trans. Tess Lewis (NYRB, 2019), 52.

interweave episodic moments, like *Picture This* and *What It Is*. They also indulge in some kind of layering. These layers range from the color washes in *One Hundred Demons* to the rich collages in *Picture This* and *What It Is*. These are also stories that call for and reward multiple readings, since Barry's stories and comics form an interconnected network. We already saw this with the appearance of the *Ernie Pook's Comeek* characters, Marlys and Arna, in *Picture This*. The re-readings also flesh out the overlap between fact and fiction, universal and individual childhoods: the brief episodes from different lived and imagined lives flesh out the different characters' stories and feed into each other.

Just like childhood, Lynda's fraught relationship with an unempathetic mother and her closeness to her Filipino grandmother, who lived with them briefly, are equally recurrent themes. Lynda's fascination for the "Aswang" demon and her mother's aversion to it is presented as a piece of transmitted and shared cultural knowledge that strengthened Lynda's bond with her grandmother.[53] The young Lynda gleans snippets of information from her grandmother about the vampiric monster who shapeshifts from dog during the day to a beautiful woman at night, detaching herself from the lower half of her body to fly and suck blood. As with other demon-stories in *One Hundred Demons*, the aswang is not the actual demon. Instead, the short story is about dysfunctional mother-daughter relationships and loving granddaughter-grandmother relationships, which are reiterated across generations, with Lynda's mother being the actual monster. While Lynda's grandmother tempers her daughter's cruelty, she delves out comparable cruelty to her daughter, Lynda's mother.

Perpetually angry and smoking, with the reflection of her glasses hiding her eyes, Barry draws her mother with grotesquely exaggerated features. In *What It Is*, she is likened to the mythological Gorgon, with snake hair and eyes that turn her beholders into stone. A little later, Lynda clarifies that she had encountered the Gorgon in a monster movie and did not know of her role in Greek mythology, just like she did not, as a child, notice the parallels between her mother and Medusa.[54] Lynda eventually learns to look directly at this monster-mother who, as Olga Michael argues, continues in the cephalopod and the Sea-Ma or sea monster, both of whom channel creative

---

[53] Barry, *One Hundred Demons*, 86–97.
[54] Barry, *What It Is*, 65.

acts and exercises while personifying the obstacles to making art.[55] One of Barry's art therapeutic inspirations, Marion Milner, also evoked Medusa's petrifying gaze to personify the "failures of maternal mirroring," which sparks the quest for understanding the self through creative processes in both Milner's and Barry's works.[56]

Like *One Hundred Demons* and *What It Is*, Barry's other comics also overlap with diaries. This was a form of writing and expression that Barry was familiar with from a very young age. Describing herself as a compulsive diary writer in an interview—"like some people chew their nails; I wrote journals"—Barry adds that her nineteen-year-old self was "looking behind me, rather than looking forward or looking straight at the table."[57] Although she usually does not turn to these journals for inspiration, her books frequently explore the past, both hers and fictional children's, in situations comparable to hers. One exception to the direct referencing and incorporation of her early journals is the anthology, *Everything: Comics from Around 1978-1981*, which is bookended by pages and excerpts from Barry's high school scrapbooks and notebooks from the early 1970s.

In *One Hundred Demons*, we frequently see the Lynda from the present and the Lynda from the past writing and drawing. This is thematized in "Lost and Found," named after the newspaper columns Lynda read after school in the absence of books in her house. We see teenage Lynda writing about unrequited love in her journal, her nine-year-old self sending tips to her favorite advice column and, finally, her adult self writing the opening of an advice column, "*Gals*, ever *felt* so intimidated by the *idea* of writing *that* you've never even given it a try? Think writing *is* only *for* "writers"? Sure *is* common!"[58] This panel, introducing a problem shared by both author and reader concerning creativity, foreshadows the manual-like tone of Barry's later books such as *What It Is, Picture This* and *Syllabus*.

These unusual readings and writings, which are generally considered devoid of creative and literary value, continue to haunt Lynda's confidence

---

[55]Michael, "Excavating Childhood," 559–60.
[56]Emilia Haltan-Hernandez, "Milner in the Comic Frame: Lynda Barry and Alison Bechdel's Autobiographical Cures," in *The Marion Milner Method: Psychoanalysis, Autobiography and Creativity* (Routledge, 2023), 150–73, 156.
[57]Thom Powers and Lynda Barry, "The Lynda Barry Interview – Part 2," *The Comics Journal*, January 2, 1989, accessed September 23, 2023, https://www.tcj.com/the-lynda-barry-interview/2/.
[58]Barry, *One Hundred Demons*, 216.

as a writer, especially in contrast to other literary writers who recall childhood readings of children's classics such as Kenneth Graham's *The Wind in the Willows* and C. S. Lewis' *The Lion, the Witch and the Wardrobe*. Lynda remembers Grimms' and Anderson's fairytales and *Heidi*—the three books available in her childhood home—and the *Reader's Digest* "I am Joe's Body" columns in which personified organs introduced the workings of the human body. "Lost and Found" is not only about the columns or other elements that are lost during the transition from childhood to adulthood, especially the "(a)bility to make up stories. Happiness depends on it";[59] the story also shows how Lynda's limited access to books and the cultural capital that comes with them excludes her,[60] from a very young age, from the possibility of developing a career in writing. She is not allowed to join an advanced class on creative writing in high school and the pattern continues in college when she realizes she "loved the wrong kind of writing and (. . .) never could break a story down to find the symbolic meaning."[61] Comics turn out to be the solution since "(i)t's not something a person has to be very 'advanced' to do. At least not in the minds of literary types."[62] This contrast between higher and lower arts and the different expectations attached to them rhythm most of Barry's comics, especially her graphic narratives.

Notebooks themselves have now become an iconic feature of Barry's work, becoming a pillar for her comics-making activities: *One Hundred Demons* is bookended by lined yellow pages in which Lynda addresses the reader directly; *What It Is* relies almost exclusively on notebook paper which also appears intermittently in *Picture This*; while *Syllabus* and *Making Comics* fully adopt the exercise book form, from the cover and binding to the pages. In many ways, the latter two books test the limits of comics. By espousing the forms of the diary and the notebook, they skirt the basic constituents of comics—panels, word balloons, even recognizable characters, because Barry shapeshifts, adopting different, playful avatars, the most recurrent one being the Near-Sighted Monkey, with *Picture This* labelled as "The Near-Sighted Monkey Book." Although its sequel, *What It*

---

[59] Barry, *One Hundred Demons*, 216.
[60] On the relevance of cultural capital for social mobility see Pierre Bourdieu, *Forms of Capital*, trans. Peter Collier (Polity, 2021).
[61] Barry, *One Hundred Demons*, 215.
[62] Barry, *One Hundred Demons*, 215.

Is, does not carry the same label, it also features two monkeys on its cover, one of which floats toward the title in a genie-like posture. The monkey posing as an artist or the artist posing as a monkey in *Picture This* becomes a meditating monkey in *What It Is*.

These avatars thrive on a clear distance from the real by resorting to the impossible form of the anthropomorphic animal. The monkey-artist standing in for Barry in *Picture This* allows for numerous playful liberties such as drawing scribbles, copying, cutting, and coloring in, all of which are often considered childish activities. Barry's avatars, which multiply in *Syllabus*, are an effective and highly comicitous means of fictionalizing. At the same time, they are also a means of connecting with readers, replacing the status of author-artist with a friendly, drawn guide combining scenes from everyday life and sharing tips on drawing practice.[63]

Colin Beineke introduced the term "comicity" to identify comics-like elements that can be transferred to other forms and media. While most of Barry's books are sold as graphic novels, they test the boundaries of comics and, as a result, bring to light elements that can be transposed to other arts while remaining comics-like: her changing avatars are one such example, as are her animated bodies and fantastic creatures and her quest for breathing life into the line. The sequential nature of her collages likewise highlights the comicitous potential of collages.

Barry uses collages to recreate an image-verse that is in itself a space of encounters since it reflects her experiences and collections while merging fragments of collective memories with material that is thrown away; much of this waste belongs to childhood and has to be grown out of but this waste also encompasses the banal. Collage is also a means of filling gaps, in memories, and in archives. None of these are drawings from Barry's own childhood, which were never preserved since neither her mother nor most of her schoolteachers considered her work "good enough." Lynda's mother declares her drawings a waste of paper at several moments, including during a flashback in the "Dogs" episode in *One Hundred Demons*: the young Lynda is shown drawing a dog picture for one of her favorite teachers in school, who was exceptionally understanding and even allowed Lynda to draw during recess or after school, offering precious space and time for creation,

---

[63] See Colin Beineke, "On Comicity," *Inks: The Journal of the Comics Studies Society* 1, no. 2 (2017): 226–53.

which are central to Barry's stories and teaching practice.[64] In contrast to the school teacher, Lynda's mother calls her an idiot and chastises her for wasting stationery.[65] Wasting reappears in *What It Is,* when Lynda's mother does not see why Lynda wastes paper drawing ugly faces.[66] A little later, Barry recalls how she responded to an ad at the back of a magazine offering to evaluate the drawing skills of adult readers and to determine whether they had "hidden artistic talent."[67] Terrified of her mother, Lynda secretly applied and received a free booklet and pencil to continue the test. Her fear of not being good enough seeped into her drawing attempts: "I drew and erased with a sick feeling. There was no hidden talent. (. . .) I'd erased so hard and drew so hard it looked horrible."[68] When the drawing school sent a follow-up letter, Lynda's fear only grew for being discovered as "a liar and a thief and a waster of paper."[69] Here, drawing anxiety and lacking visible "talent" is closely intertwined with lying and stealing, highlighting the intensity of the fear of indulging in acts only permitted to the talented. At the beginning of this episode, Barry recalls how she worried about not writing or drawing well enough, often erasing until the paper tore.[70] This moment coincides with the drawing and writing contests at school for which Lynda was rarely singled out.[71] Such episodes show how deeply rooted Barry's art-making anxieties are, while also questioning notions surrounding artistic talent.

Since her own practice was regarded with suspicion in her home and art-making became a secret activity, Barry has no drawings from her childhood. She does however actively collect drawings by other children which she interweaves in her books, including her brothers' drawings, those made by her students and even, in *What It Is,* anonymous drawings from a school teacher's archive. Barry's brothers' and godson's drawings can be found in *Everything: Comics from Around 1978-1981* next to a childhood picture of hers and the memory of "scribbling, the feeling of it being so alive and unpredictable and also surprising."[72] Juxtaposing scrapbook pages

---

[64]See Haltan-Hernandez, "Milner in the Comic Frame," 159.
[65]Barry, *One Hundred Demons,* 177.
[66]Barry, *What It Is,* 63.
[67]Barry, *What It Is,* 76.
[68]Barry, *What Is Is,* 78.
[69]Barry, *What It Is,* 78.
[70]Barry, *What It Is,* 75.
[71]Barry, *What It Is,* 80.
[72]Barry, *Everything,* 4.

from her high school years in the early 1970s with more recent reflections, *Everything* reconstructs Barry's drawing practices and influences, both visual (underground comics, advertisements, popular imagery) and from children's books (school readers, Dr. Seuss). The personal and collective archives interwoven in *Everything* and elsewhere convey Barry's love for books, fascination with all kinds of images, and interest in childhood culture and non-normative childhoods, all of which inform her diverse body of comics work.

This diversity unfolds through the materials collaged and the mixed techniques employed by Barry, including drawing, collage work and painting. Barry's switch to painting and the ink brush radically transformed her line work: the scratchy, punk style of the earliest *Ernie Pook's Comeek* was replaced by more rounded forms and fluid, meandering lines.[73] This change occurred for a very practical reason around 1984/1985, when Barry switched to brush work because her hands hurt after years of drawing with pens.[74] Not only do brushes create a very different kind of line in comparison to pencils and pens, they also have an impact on the kind of story being told.[75] The anthology *Everything in the World* (1986) is consequently "transitional" in Barry's words, while the collection that followed, *The Fun House* (1987) is fully realized in brush. Kirtley identifies one of the changes in subject as "chronicling the trials of adolescence" and traces the generally positive critical reception this shift attracted.[76] The stylistic and thematic shifts were perceived as symbiotic, offering an honest, powerful portrayal of the process of growing up with all its dramatic ups and downs.

The brush technique is central to *One Hundred Demons*, offering an example of Barry's preferred form of art education, which allows for intuitive, free drawing. While this is carefully explained at both ends of the book, we see Lynda practicing ink drawing throughout *One Hundred Demons*. In "Cicadas," for instance, she tries to paint a portrait of her friend Bob, whom she met when she was fourteen, and who became the first person she knew to commit suicide.[77] We see the present-day Lynda with an ink brush poised over a sheet of paper striving to remember what Bob

---

[73] See Kirtley, *Typical Girls*, 112–26.
[74] Powers and Barry, "Lynda Barry Interview – Part 2."
[75] Kirtley, *Lynda Barry*, 39.
[76] Kirtley, *Lynda Barry*, 40.
[77] Barry, *One Hundred Demons*, 158–69.

looked like but not getting beyond his ghost-like silhouette. Declined in different shades throughout the episode, Bob remains an elusive phantom with empty eyes. At the very end of "Cicadas," we see Lynda with the finished ghostly portrait of Bob in shades of pale orange and gray. Although the page has been filled in, the portrait at the end of story is the silhouette we have been encountering throughout "Cicadas." In this final panel, the silhouette is accompanied by two nectarines that Lynda recovered from a room she had offered to clear up after the suicide of a young boy: "They were so real. Perishables."[78]

This closing panel captures the fragility of life while imbuing it with a sense of cyclicality through the reference to the cicadas' seventeen-year gestation period. Recalling Hillary Chute's observation that "Barry does not display trauma so much as work in the edges of events, unsettling readers by leaving us to imagine the incidents whose aftereffects she plumbs," Yaël Schlick identifies a pattern in Barry's approach to narrativizing traumatic memories: "elements are introduced and orchestrated without their meaning being encoded. The multiple dimensions of the experiences she relates—sensory, psychological, imagistic, intellectual, physical, and linguistic—are bound together but never flattened out."[79] Like many other moments in *One Hundred Demons*, "Cicadas," is also rhythmed by a soundtrack, that of the cicadas, a natural sound, instead of a song playing on the gramophone or radio. Music plays a particularly central role in Barry's comics, including her illustrated novel, *The Good Times Are Killing Me*, which is discussed in Chapter 2.

Barry's short story, "Menopositive," for the anthology *Menopause*, reveals another kind of cyclicality, building on the complicity between the very old and the very young reflected in her close relationship to her grandmother. The story is drawn on lined notebook paper, with quick, scratchy lines and washes in warm colors. Barry begins with her childhood memories of neighborhood myths around hysterectomy and eavesdropping on her mother, grandmother, and other women's conversations around "the change." Barry proposes a different kind of understanding of menopause, as a "change-back," "some kind of shift of focus, that capacity I had to just

---

[78] Barry, *One Hundred Demons*, 167.
[79] Yaël Schlick, "What is an Experience? Selves and Texts in the Comics Autobiographies of Alison Bechdel and Lynda Barry," in *Drawing from Life: Memory and Subjectivity in Comic Art*, ed. Jane Tolmie (University Press of Mississippi, 2013), 26–43, 37.

be somewhere when I was a kid."[80] She shows herself drawing the story in a café observing two teenage girls on their phones and imagines a near future when she is an old lady with her friends being eavesdropped on by a drawing girl. Once again, the child—the universal child, as well as the child that Barry was and children that she encounters or will encounter—takes the center stage, to reflect on both childness, or the state of being a child,[81] and adulthood.

Having drawn out the key elements of Barry's childhood and how it intertwines with the many child characters across her comics, the second section of this chapter delves further into the changing comics contexts that sparked Barry's interest in comics and the publishing and art contexts she engages with.

Books, Comics, Graphic (Life) Narratives

Writing about the rise of the graphic memoir, Jared Gardner begins his article, "Autography's Biography, 1972-2007" with an observation by Alison Bechdel about how cartooning "almost demands people to write autobiographies."[82] Gardner elaborates on these "autobiographical demands of comics":

> It is the graphic memoir that best allows for this simultaneous claim of autobiography and fiction, and for the simultaneous demand on the reader for both distance and identification. If fiction is an ideal form for identification and affective attachment, and autobiography is an ideal form for auratic distance and contemplation (including the transformative silences of testimony), autography is the narrative form that allows both to share the frame.[83]

---

[80]Lynda Barry, "Menopositive," in *Menopause: A Comic Treatment*, ed. M. K. Czerwiec (Pennsylvania State University Press, 2020), 11–16, 16.
[81]Peter Hollindale proposes the term "childness" to counter the negative connotations of "childishness." See Peter Hollindale, *Signs of Childness in Children's Books* (Thimble Press, 1997).
[82]Bechdel quoted in Jared Gardner, "Autobiography's Biography (1973–2007)," *Biography* 31, no. 1 (2008): 1–26, 1.
[83]Gardner, "Autobiography," 22

Historical and Biographical Contexts

Emphasizing how comics both attract and complicate autobiography, Gillian Whitlock coined the term autography "to draw attention to the specific conjunctions of visual and verbal text (...) and also to the subject positions that narrators negotiate in and through comics."[84] Comics rely on the imperative to show and in doing so, the medium challenges traditional notions of representation, truth and ethics. Barry was growing up during this autographic turn, which was symptomatic of a broader transformation of comics that opened the medium to adults and to a variety of adult voices.

Barry discovered the underground comics by, among others, Roger Crumb, at a very young age. Later, she participated in two issues of *Wimmen's Comix* and became a syndicated comics author for alternative weeklies all over the United States. Although finding a publication venue for Barry's books was initially often a challenge, especially for her comics, Barry is now a best-selling, widely acclaimed author of both fictional and autobifictional comics. In addition to Barry's skill in painting childhoods with moving honesty, and carving a niche with her stories of painful childhoods and youth, part of her success story in comics publishing is also connected to the changing perception of comics and the rise of the graphic novel.[85] This not only includes the rise of the memoir as the key graphic novel genre but also a certain market viability accorded to more unusual, "literary" and "artistic" books. As we will see, Barry's books often transcend standard publication formats to form book-objects in their own right.

This section situates Barry's graphic novels and memoirs published by the Montreal-based Drawn & Quarterly, alongside collections of her early comic strips, as both connected to, and distinctive from, other experimental and autobiographical comics through their blending of genres and teasing of forms: while autobiographical tendencies, including the use of a personal style, stem from underground comics impulses and the establishment of the graphic memoir,[86] Barry's meta-reflexive and self-conscious books form hybrid, distinctive book-objects exploring the very limits of comics.

---

[84] Gillian Whitlock, "Autographics: The Seeing 'I' of Comics," *Modern Fiction Studies* 52, no. 4 (2006): 965–79, 966. Whitlock was inspired by life writing scholar Leigh Gilmore's concept of autobiographics. See Leigh Gilmore, *Autobiographics: A Feminist Theory of Women's Autobiography* (Cornell University Press, 1994).

[85] For more on the graphic novel, see Jan Baetens and Hugo Frey, *The Graphic Novel: An Introduction* (Cambridge University Press, 2014).

[86] See Gardner, "Autobiography"; Charles Hatfield, *Alternative Comics: An Emerging Literature* (University Press of Mississippi, 2005).

This section also situates Barry's development of certain trademark elements of her style—child characters, collage, emotionality, teaching manuals, transcending forms and genres—by tracing her early art education and highlighting the different forms and materialities of her early comics, which range from alternative newspaper comics and their collected editions, illustrated stories, scrapbook pages and other forms of collage. The serialized comics in alternative weeklies were crucial to the comics language established by Barry since they offered space for comics that clashed with mainstream assumptions, themes and styles.[87]

The front matter of *Everything* includes a Campbell Soup Jar imitation by Barry from 1972, transforming the soup into a "condensed tomato monster" (Figure 1.3). A dragon with a fiery blue tongue and a tiny tomato on its head emerges from the can, a pastiche of Andy Warhol's iconic Campbell Soup Cans from 1962. The teenage Barry adds a certain transparency to the can and colorful watercolor dots to the background. A note on the top left of the drawing mentions in neat, block letters: "From my drawing book from 1972." Another note below the drawing adds: "I drew this in the 9th grade and felt incredible afterward." The drawing itself is cut out and pasted on three layers of paper, including a decorative paper that forms the background for the page. These layers, and the water-colored spots reinforce the importance of the drawing. Crucially, the importance of this drawing is connected to the emotions it generated, of feeling good and satisfied by creating something and the memory of that feeling.

In addition to copyright and printing information in typed letters, Barry also adds a yearbook photograph from the same year as the drawing. A handwritten emphatic note in letters partially colored in red adds:

PLEASE NOTE

This volume of 'Everything' isn't *for everybody*. There is *bad drawing* and <u>mature content</u>! THIS BOOK *is not for kids* unless they have found it and are *sneak-reading it* because you didn't HIDE IT well enough FROM KIDS.[88]

This page neatly encapsulates the complex negotiations unfolding throughout Barry's comics. First, there is the dominance of child characters

---

[87] See Kirtley, *Typical Girls*, 115.
[88] Barry, *Everything*, 2.

Historical and Biographical Contexts

Figure 1.3 Front matter from *Everything*. Copyright Lynda Barry. Used with permission from Drawn & Quarterly.

in material that is not for children, often juxtaposed to perceptions and prejudices attached to the medium of comics, which is still frequently considered part of children's culture. Second, there is the aspect of life writing and re-writing through unpacking archives, which is especially prominent in *Everything*, a volume that collects Barry's earliest published comics from 1978 and 1981 and augments them with diverse material—drawings, photographs, scrapbooked images—from her high school notebooks. Complementing the biographical details offered by Barry's other books, *Everything* offers direct insight into Barry's artistic interactions with comics and other visual cultures, especially advertisements—by Jean-Michel Folon, Peter Max, Pushpin Studios—through her copies of the images and the texts accompanying them.[89]

At the time when Barry was growing up, in the 1960s and 1970s, the comics scene was rapidly changing and diversifying through a rise in

---

[89] Barry, *Everything*, 11.

underground and alternative publications. The underground comix Barry read as a child led her to the realization that "you could draw *anything* in a comic strip. Even very messed up things found in the park in the dark. A completely new set of things I'd never dealt with before."[90] Artists such as M. K. Brown, Gahan Wilson and Ed Subitzky, all of whom were published in the *National Lampoon*, taught Barry to "<u>watch</u> the people around me and <u>listen</u> to how they talk and to <u>write down WHAT THEY SAY.</u>"[91] In addition to the possibility of transmitting a specific orality, Barry's interest in comics was sparked by the possibility of transposing life, its tumults and traumas, alongside the quotidian, to comics, telling emotionally complex stories that were simultaneously funny, awkward and painful, generating a "feeling-change":

> This seems to be the trick with comics: bitterness and sweetness need something else; some third thing. And its hard to say what that third thing is, but it's something like what music is to lyrics. It's the thing that brings the feeling-change.[92]

Part of the feeling-change is connected to the fact that many of Barry's protagonists are children, distinct from the resistant children recurring in comic strips, who are resistant and unyielding to the extent that children's literature scholar Marah Gubar calls Little Orphan Annie a Teflon child, surviving and bouncing back from the worst of hardships with only her iris-less eyes suggesting any possible trauma.[93] As can be seen from *One Hundred Demons*, these traumatic experiences range from smaller, familiar ones that are part of growing pains to devastating moments such as the sexual assault alluded to in "Resilience."[94] In her feminist conceptualization of trauma, Maria P. P. Root identifies three kinds of trauma: direct trauma, indirect trauma and insidious trauma. Direct trauma "includes being the target of trauma as well as being forced to commit atrocities" whereas indirect trauma refers to "being traumatized by the trauma sustained by another, with whom one identifies in a significant way" and "witnessing

---

[90] Barry *Everything*, 10.
[91] Barry *Everything*, 13.
[92] Barry, *Everything*, 13.
[93] Marah Gubar, "The Teflon Kid," *Public Books*, January 5, 2015, accessed September 24, 2024, https://www.publicbooks.org/the-teflon-kid-how-annie-enables-apathy-about-inequality/.
[94] Barry, *One Hundred Demons*, 62–72.

trauma."[95] Root connects insidious trauma to the "social status of an individual being devalued because a characteristic intrinsic to their identity is different from what is valued by those in power, for example, gender, color, sexual orientation, physical ability."[96] Many of the children, and adults, in Barry's books, including her avatars, reflect these different kinds of trauma. The roots of trauma emerge from Barry's own experiences, as a mixed-race child growing up in an unloving household and navigating a working-class neighborhood marked by the social and racial tensions prevalent in the United States, and from her mother's experience of growing up in the war-torn Philippines.[97]

Barry suggests that child characters are easier to write about because of their heavily constrained lives:

> People often ask me why my protagonists are so often children or teenagers. I can make a top-of-the-mind answer for that, which is that children or teenagers are protagonists who can't drive away by themselves out of a situation. It's just easier to write about.[98]

Pointing out how child characters can offer "penetrating insights into society's structures" on one hand, and how children's art offers a more liberated, even raw mode of expression on the other, Miriam Harris delineates the two interconnected roles accorded to children and childhood in Barry's comics: these comics unfold along the fault lines between the social rules governing childhood and the prejudices associated with childlike, seemingly unskilled art.[99] Further, as Hannah Miodrag explains, the children in Barry's comics also use an "off-kilter deployment of language," comparable to George

---

[95] Maria P. P. Root, "Reconstructing the Impact of Trauma on Personality," in *Personality and Psychopathology: Feminist Appraisals*, ed. Laura S. Brown and Mary Ballou (Guildford Press, 1992), 239.
[96] Root, "Reconstructing," 229–65, 240.
[97] Barry, *One Hundred Demons*, 187.
[98] Lynda Barry in an interview with David Marchese, "A Genius Cartoonist Believes Child's Play is Anything But Frivolous," *New York Times (Online)*, September 5, 2022, accessed September 18, 2024, https://www.proquest.com/blogs-podcasts-websites/genius-cartoonist-believes-child-splay-is/docview/2712026996/se-2?accountid=11077.
[99] Miriam Harris, "Cartoonists as Matchmakers: The Vibrant Relationship of Text and Image in the Work of Lynda Barry," in *Elective Affinities: Testing Word and Image Relationships,* ed. Catriona MacLeod, Véronique Plesch, and Charlotte Schoell-Glass (Rodopi, 2009), 129–46, 131.

Herriman's *Krazy Kat* while being "peculiarly expressive of children's acquisition of language."[100] The child is therefore present in all aspects of Barry's comics, visually and linguistically. And while comics are often considered part of children's culture, and even exclusively for children, Barry's comics are unique in their blending of child characters, childish language and childlike drawing to offer stories and food for thought for adults. The focus on material for adults can be connected to the fact that Barry has always made comics for adults, and that children, despite their dominance in her work, were absent even from her early comics, including *Spinal Comics*, which involved women being propositioned by men who resembled cacti. The commissioned *Modern Romance* strip for *Esquire* magazine, which ran from 1984 to 1989, just like her strips for *Wimmen's Comix*, also focused on adult characters. As we will see in Chapter 2, children only become dominant characters in Barry's fourth comics collection, *The Fun House*, published by Harper Perennial in 1987.

In *Wimmen's Comix* no. 8 (1983), Barry offers a full-page strip on "Seven Deep Psychological Problems."[101] She adds a playful by-line, "As isolated by Dr. Sigmund Barry," which is typical for these early comics and continues in her shapeshifting in her recent comics manuals. Each panel illustrates a different, compulsive issue, ranging from biting and removing lint to obsessions with ham or small animals. While these issues are eccentric to the point of being unrealistic, some of them are troublingly close to actual psychological issues, as in the case of the first panel concerning eating or "Fear of Food Touching on the Plate," which evokes eating disorders. In the next issue, *Wimmen's Comix* no. 9 (1984), Barry returns with another one-page strip, this time in a horizontal, landscape format instead of a vertical portrait one. "Coping with Stress for Under One Dollar" imitates the lexicon of an advice column (Figure 1.4),[102] with anti-stress tips ranging from imagining oneself or one's boss underwater to prank phone calls. It concludes with the suggestion to feed birds in the park in order to find a listening ear.

These comics are drawn in a style characterizing most of Barry's early comics: scratchy lines and a dominance of faces and bodies represented in

---

[100] Miodrag, *Comics and Language*, 45.
[101] Lynda Barry, "Seven Deep Psychological Problems," in *The Complete Wimmen's Comix*, ed. Trina Robbins (Fantagraphics, 2016), 295.
[102] Lynda Barry, "Coping With Stress," in *The Complete Wimmen's Comix*, 363.

Historical and Biographical Contexts

Figure 1.4 "Coping with Stress for Under One Dollar," *Wimmen's Comix* no. 9 (1984), 363. Copyright Lynda Barry. Used with permission from Drawn & Quarterly.

full or three-quarter profile that are both flattened-out and dynamic. The humor of these comics is different from conventional gag strips through the uncomfortable crumbs of truth and reality that seep through. They perfectly complement the diverse cartoonists' voices collected in *Wimmen's Comix*. Showing how Barry's humor "embraces subjects of the public sphere," Özge Samanci argues that Barry's humor is distinctively feminine, even though it often seems non-gendered, because it tries to avoid underscoring a female perspective and triggering the mechanism of othering connected to works by women and the emphasis on women's concerns.[103] Through focusing on Barry's deliberately simplistic and even childlike drawing style, Samanci emphasizes how "Barry blurs the *professional aesthetic* of mainstream comics, avoids being androgynous with her equipment choices, and converts and plays with the established conventions of gaze."[104] These devices include the use of collage and children's perspectives which will be explored in detail later

---

[103] Samanci, "Lynda Barry's Humor," 182.
[104] Samanci, "Lynda Barry's Humor," 185. Emphasis in the original.

in this guide. "Barry's playful and poetic use of the gaze," Samanci concludes, "blurs the strong bond between gaze and masculinity."[105] It also conveys a depth and relationality that is a distinctive feature of Barry's works.

Barry's comics have been on a consistent quest to convey emotional complexity, moving readers while (often) offering the opportunity to laugh. It is therefore not surprising that Charles Burns considers Lynda Barry's weekly strips and Matt Groening's *Life in Hell* comics as the best examples of the form: despite the constraints of short form and seriality, these comics succeed in bringing something new each time and touching the reader.[106] Barry went to the same high school, and college, as Charles Burns. While Burns already had the status of a skilled artist at high school, Barry encountered unenthusiastic teachers, who did not consider her sufficiently talented in art or writing as we saw above.

David Carrier and Joachim Pissaro propose the term "wild art," or art that exists outside of the art system and its institutions, rejected by the art world, low on maintenance and able to grow in a variety of contexts. The school trajectory they trace and criticize for the vast majority of children parallels Barry's description of her own trajectory, which was also built on exclusion instead of inclusion: "we start with the kindergarten system of universal encouragement of creativity in all children and we end in twelfth grade with a small minority of students still exposed to the arts."[107] Carrier and Pissaro argue for a new kind of engagement with art forms that goes beyond institutional gatekeeping and preconceived notions of aesthetics to acquire a more relational form, bringing together different kinds of subjects, viewers, and art objects.[108] Barry's comics, especially those that overlap with manuals, perform precisely this kind of work, encouraging readers, regardless of skills and ability, to engage with and make their own art. Such art will often remain at the margins but it nevertheless has personal—and even collective—significance by virtue of being the result of a creative exercise that is technically open to anyone who is willing to draw.

---

[105]Samanci, "Lynda Barry's Humor," 189.
[106]Xavier Guibert and Charles Burns, "The Interior Worlds of Charles Burns," *du9*, January 2016, accessed September 24, 2024, https://www.du9.org/en/entretien/the-inner-worlds-of-charles-burns/.
[107]David Carrier and Joachim Pissaro, *The Margins of Aesthetics: Wild Art Explained* (Pennsylvania State University Press, 2019), 5.
[108]Carrier and Pissaro, *Aesthetics of the Margins*, 180–95. See also Rita Felski's *Hooked: Art and Attachment* (University of Chicago Press, 2020).

Barry's own art education followed a non-conventional path: she enrolled in Evergreen State College in Olympia, Washington in 1974. Evergreen allowed students to explore and establish a personalized, interdisciplinary curriculum.[109] After modelling for a painting class taught by Marilyn Frasca, who had just begun teaching at the college, Barry ended up signing up for it. Frasca's untraditional, non-judgmental and holistic approach to art had a lasting effect on Barry's work and is especially palpable in her teaching manuals. Frasca began her artistic training during the 1950s at the Cooper Union during the heyday of abstract expressionism before moving for a degree to San Francisco. The importance of textures and the spiritual properties of both representational and non-representational painting in Frasca's work reverberates through Barry's comics.

For Barry, one of Frasca's most important teachings was that an artwork cannot be separated from those viewing it.[110] Frasca rarely taught or commented on technique, focusing instead on what the artwork conveyed for the maker and viewer. She also encouraged her students to keep diaries, which Barry began doing "in a serious way" in 1975.[111] Frasca's approach to treating "writing, reading, and creating art as complimentary practices" reverberates throughout Barry's hybrid oeuvre, and especially in her graphic novels.[112] Further, Frasca's "images" course was an intensive one, requiring students to submit ten completed pieces a week,[113] comparable to the intense rhythm Barry had to maintain when she became a syndicated cartoonist.

While *What It Is* is dedicated to Frasca, as we saw above, Frasca, together with comics artist Ivan Brunetti, and writer Dan Chaon are acknowledged as "critical friends and influences" who shared syllabi and ideas with Barry in *Syllabus*.[114] Hailing from very different backgrounds, all three share a "deep curiosity about images and how they move between people."[115] More than comics as we know them—with sequential images and consistent drawing styles—it is the act of making images that is Barry's central concern, as we

---

[109]Kirtley, *Lynda Barry*, 20.
[110]Leah Misemer, "Teaching the Unthinkable Image with Lynda Barry," in *With Great Power Comics Great Pedagogy: Teaching, Learning and Comics,* ed. Susan E. Kirtley, Antero Garcia, and Peter E. Carlson (University Press of Mississippi, 2020), 168–85, 168–9.
[111]Lynda Barry, *Syllabus: Notes from an Accidental Professor* (Drawn & Quarterly, 2014), 4.
[112]Kirtley, *Lynda Barry*, 20.
[113]Kirtley, *Lynda Barry,* 20.
[114]Barry, *Syllabus*, 7.
[115]Barry, *Syllabus*, 7.

will see in greater detail in Chapter Four. Further, her manuals combine teaching based on a range of practical exercises to overcome blocks and share open questions interrogating the sources of creativity, questions which can only be answered when the reader agrees to explore the questions herself by making images. As Barry explains in *Syllabus*:

> This practice can result in what I've come to consider a wonderful side effect: a visual or written image we can call a "work of art", although a work of art is not what I'm after when I'm practicing this activity. What am I after? I'm after what Marilyn Frasca called "being present and seeing what's there."[116]

Barry is after teaching something more than simply making comics. As we will see in her comics manuals, the final outcome is initially even less important than the process of making images following prompts for automatic drawing or more traditional comics constraints based on characters and panels.

In addition to attending Frasca's classes, Barry also befriended Matt Groening, who edited the college newspaper and who is now famous as the creator of the *Life in Hell* comics and the *Simpsons*. Groening famously published the first *Ernie Pook's Comeek* strips in Evergreen's *Cooper Point Journal* and also shared it with John Keister, who published it in the University of Washington's student paper. Keister would later establish a successful career as music critic, journalist, and comedian. Barry recalls how she

> kept submitting crazier and crazier things—outraged letters to the editor about things that happened to me when I was little that had nothing to do with Evergreen, or comics that were really strange, comics about little girls who could do things like remove their arms and legs at will. No matter what I submitted, he printed it.[117]

The above quote highlights the extent to which the comics were freely drawn, originally without the intention to be published.

---

[116] Barry, *Syllabus*, 4
[117] "Lynda Barry: Comics Deserve To Be Taken Seriously," *Faces of* Evergreen, May 1, 2012, accessed December 4, 2024, https://www.evergreen.edu/faces-evergreen/lynda-barry.

After college, Barry's comics were published in the *Seattle Sun* and within a year, in 1979, she was on the payroll of another alternative paper, *The Chicago Reader*. The *Girls and Boys* (later *Ernie Pook's Comeek*) strips were collected and printed by the Seattle-based publisher, Real Comet Press in 1981.[118] The press had been freshly founded by artist and activist, Cathy Hillenbrand and named after her Comet Tavern which also functioned as a meeting space for upcoming avant-garde artists. The press published Art Chantry's concert posters and Ruth Hayes' flipbooks, with Barry's comic books being a prominent feature of its catalogue.[119] When Fantagraphics organized a retrospective of the press in 2012, it re-issued Bary's "Poodle with a Mohawk" poster (which appears as a panel on the back cover of *Big Ideas*, Figure 1.5) to announce the event.[120] The poster is hilarious, showing a scruffy, angry punk poodle with a spiked collar, twisting clichés associated with poodles and mocking film posters.

Terming the poster "iconic," the Fantagraphics announcement also recalls how Barry's collaboration with the press began with her winning the matchbox cover design competition for the Comet Tavern in 1980. In addition to printing Barry's earliest comics collections, Real Comet Press also published *Naked Ladies, Naked Ladies, Naked Ladies* (1984), Barry's playful coloring book for adults, which imitates and subverts the Playboy playing cards by letting readers color in the diverse women appearing on the cards while, in the text on the bottom of the page, a young narrator shares thoughts on looking at "dirty" pictures and growing up.[121] This book appeared almost thirty years before the trend of adult coloring books—a trend that started with adults buying elaborate, older children's coloring books[122]—and offers a naughtier, more complex version of those books. In 1988, Real Comet Press published another, completely different book by

---

[118] Kirtley, *Lynda Barry*, 23.
[119] Justin Seattle, "31 years later, celebrating the 'seminal' alternative press spawned by the Comet Tavern," *Capitol Hill Seattle Blog. Community News for all the Hill*. 4 March 2012. Accessed 2 December 2024. https://www.capitolhillseattle.com/2012/03/31-years-later-celebrating-the-seminal-alternative-press-spawned-by-the-comet-tavern/
[120] "Celebrate Seminal Seattle Publisher Real Comet Press on March 10!," *Fantagraphics Blog*, February 28, 2012, accessed December 4, 2024, https://blog.fantagraphics.com/celebrate-seminal-seattle-publisher-real-comet-press-on-march-10/.
[121] For more on *Naked Ladies, Naked Ladies, Naked Ladies*, see Chute, *Graphic Women*, 97–108; Kirtley, *Lynda Barry*, 33–9.
[122] See Michelle Ann Abate, *No Kids Allowed: Children's Literature for Adults* (Johns Hopkins University Press, 2020), 1–3.

Figure 1.5 "Poodle with a Mohawk," excerpt from back cover of *Big Ideas*. Copyright Lynda Barry. Used with permission from Drawn & Quarterly.

Barry, which once again transcended genres: *The Good Times Are Killing Me*, an illustrated novel. Both the novel and the play it was transformed into were widely acclaimed and propelled Barry to national fame, even though she had to make numerous financial sacrifices to retain the rights to the book.[123]

Barry continued working for diverse alternative papers—and even *Esquire*, which she regretted[124]—for the next three decades. *Ernie Pook's Comeek* was syndicated to seventy alternative papers in its heyday. But the late 1970s boom in alternative papers with space for comics could not last forever. In 1997, *The Village Voice* stopped running Barry's comics, and those by Groening and Jules Feiffer to devote more space to sports.[125]

---

[123]Kirtley, *Lynda Barry*, 42.
[124]Kirtley, *Lynda Barry*, 31–3.
[125]Kirtley, *Lynda Barry*, 44.

Kirtley points out how this was only the first in a series of papers dropping Barry's comics (and comics altogether) and even closing down.[126] At the same time, Harper Perennial, which had already published four comics collections by Barry, backed out of publishing *The Freddie Stories*. The volume was printed in 1999 by Sasquatch, a publisher of "visual" books, run by Gary Luke, a former high school classmate of Barry's, who was a fan of her work.[127] Sasquatch also reissued *The Good Times Are Killing Me* in 1998. Her second, much darker illustrated novel, *Cruddy* was published by Simon & Shuster a year later, in 1999.

Although Sasquatch published *One Hundred Demons* in 2002, it rejected the proposal for *What It Is*, which was eventually issued by Drawn & Quarterly. Established in 1989 by the Canadian illustrator, Chris Oliveros, the Montreal-based D&Q is now renowned for its prizewinning comics and graphic novels and publishes most of Barry's work.[128] *What It Is* came out in 2008, the same year *Ernie Pook's Comeek* ended, and Oliveros is thanked in the acknowledgments at the end of the book. A much-quoted section in *What It Is* was first published in the famous comics issue of *McSweeney's Quarterly Concern*, edited by Chris Ware.[129] In *McSweeney's*, "Two Questions" is published in black and white, in a smaller, landscape format, with two pages printed side by side. The comic is a reflexive meditation on Barry's artistic and creative anxieties which occupy a central place in her manuals. As the following chapters will show, such an expression of anxiety is also a means of weaving connections with the reader who might be considering becoming a maker. Once again, Barry turns to childhood recollections and practices of drawing to point out how we are quickly schooled into making "good" drawings and how the internalization of collective judgment—the two questions, "is this good?" and "does this suck?"—drains out the joy from drawing. The comic also refers to the critique levelled against Barry's art as lacking skill

---

[126] Kirtley, *Lynda Barry*, 44.
[127] Kirtley, *Lynda Barry*, 45.
[128] For D&Q's impact on expanding the notion of the graphic novel and sharing work that risked being confined to a niche audience to a much broader readership, see Bart Beaty, "Chris Oliveros, Drawn and Quarterly, and the Expanded Definition of the Graphic Novel," in *The Cambridge History of the Graphic Novel*, ed. Jan Baetens Hugo Frey and Stephan E. Tabachnik (Cambridge University Press, 2018), 426–42.
[129] Lynda Barry, "Two Questions," *McSweeney's Quarterly Concern*, no. 13 (2004): 60–5.

or even being "faux-naïve."[130] In addressing these critiques through her books on making comics, Barry makes the weight of self-doubt tangible and highlights both its persistence and the importance of overcoming it.[131] The possibilities of overcoming such obstacles to creativity are examined in greater detail in the next two chapters.

This quick overview of the ups and downs of Barry's publishing experiences also reflect changes across the board of comics publishing: the boom in alternative comics offered an important venue for new, unusual strips that broke away from commercial genres and formulae; their gradual folding also meant that alternative comics had limited access to weekly newsstand publications and that they were increasingly limited to the comic book and graphic novel forms, which in turn offered a new space and marketing dynamic through being sold in specialized and regular bookstores.[132] In his chapter, "Some Classics," for *The Cambridge Companion to the Graphic Novel*, Bart Beaty discusses Barry's relatively tardy "discovery" by academics, despite her long career as a syndicated cartoonist and the publication of her books such as *The Good Times are Killing Me* by HarperCollins, a major international publisher.[133] It was the online publication of the autobiographical *One Hundred Demons* that attracted sustained, scholarly interest. Beaty adds that

> (t)he institutional rediscovery of Barry by Drawn & Quarterly has not only facilitated new work by the artist (. . .) and the reissuing of her earlier work in new formats (. . .) but authorized a series of scholarly interventions into the meaning of her work. The symbiosis between publisher and scholars in the recuperation of Barry's reputation and the construction of "today's contemporary canon" seems quite evident.[134]

---

[130] Barry, *Making Comics*, 14.
[131] Barry, *Making Comics*, 14.
[132] A move in the legitimization of comics that is also forced, often somewhat awkwardly, on artists whose careers pre-date the graphic novel boom. See Beaty, *Comics Versus Art*, 76–91, where he gives the examples of the recent reception of Carl Barks, Jack Kirby and Fletcher Hanks.
[133] Bart Beaty, "Some Classics," in *The Cambridge Companion to the Graphic Novel*, ed. Stephen E. Tabachnik (Cambridge University Press, 2017), 175–91, 177–81.
[134] Beaty, "Some Classics," 178.

The close connections between publisher valorization and reprinting of ephemeral material and academic valorization is crucial. But Beaty is rightfully critical of the direct transposition of value systems and methodologies from other fields, such as autobiography from literary studies, or the primordial role of the "aesthetics of difficulty" and the uncovering of hidden meanings: "Barry's appeal to comics scholars (. . .) resides in her convoluted use of mixed media and mixed genre that require, or, at the very least, enable critical interventions."[135] Although a comics studies critical guide focusing on Barry, and therefore reinforcing the *auteurist* status imposed on her, risks reproducing the same fallacy of valuation and interpretation, this guide also seeks to situate her works in a broader perspective, showing how Barry's comics interact with a range of publication and art worlds and, most importantly, how they help us rethink the possibilities of comics.

While Barry has made a significant contribution to the changing status and perception of comics, exemplifying how "comics can also be understood as art; comics can be 'artists' books," her works resist the binaries surrounding notions of high and low art.[136] In her seminal *The Century of Artists' Books*, Johanna Drucker reminds us of "the tradition of the sketchbook or notebook as the basis of the artist's book."[137] She emphasizes the spontaneity of sketches and the intimacy they have the potential to generate. Drucker highlights how the book form can impose a certain structure or even sequentiality to the sketches, which otherwise function with associative connections. Notably, these connections are highly fluid, fragile and subjective since sketches are unplanned and often reflect, in their arrangement, the moment of drawing and the time accorded to it. Expanding on the sketchbook-as-artist's book, Drucker offers two examples that incorporate the grid as a structuring motif: Arthur Werkner's (Turi) *3500 Meisterzeichnungen* (1975) and Jan Voss' *Brief Marks* (1979).[138] In *3500 Meisterzeichnungen*, Werkner connects the grid to a temporal constraint, carefully timing the drawing within each square of the grid. The book format, Drucker argues, bestows on the drawings a certain intensity, "an aggressive presence" even, due to the close, thick lines.

---

[135] Beaty, "Some Classics," 180.
[136] Chute, *Graphic Women*, 97.
[137] Johanna Drucker, *The Century of Artists' Books* (Granary Books, 2004), 206.
[138] Drucker, *Artists' Books*, 206–7.

Such an intensity would have been diluted had the sketches been presented separately.

In his book on comics materialities, Aaron Kashtan closely reads Barry's comics manuals, *Picture This*, *What It Is* and *Syllabus* to suggest that Barry is a proponent of "biblionecrophilia," a term coined by journalist Ben Ehrenreich to refer to the fetishization of books as objects in the face of the ubiquity of digital books.[139] Kashtan likens *Syllabus* to medieval commonplace books since both "serve as externalized records of (. . .) minds."[140] Commonplace books brought together diverse materials to form personalized mnemonic aids. Barry actively collages material, and even the composition notebooks that make up *Syllabus* and *Making Comics* often contain pages originally drawn on legal pads. Recalling how *Syllabus* resuscitated his own childhood memories of using similar composition notebooks, Kashtan notes that such books probably go as far back as the 1870s and have also been remediated to digital forms, confirming a lasting attachment to the composition notebook's specific materiality.[141] As we will see in more detail in the next chapter, Barry's teaching philosophy emphasizes the handmade, relying heavily on the movement of hands and the traces it leaves, instead of the digital. On the third page of *Syllabus*, for instance, Barry adds in small type: "The chronology is rough and mixed up in places but all kept by hand (. . .)"[142] She was nevertheless quick to use new tools such as tumblr for her courses and published her comics online. She remains active on Instagram and periodically sells her art via Etsy, often for charities and humanitarian causes.

Testing different formats, Barry's graphic narratives reflect the changing perception of comics and an increasing flexibility with the very form of comics: while *One Hundred Demons* maintains the panel structure that is a trademark of Barry's early comics—two large panels per page in an elongated, horizontal format—her more recent comics opt for an all-over aesthetic and more book-like forms, ranging from the composition notebook to much larger formats (280 x 220 cm for *What It Is*, *Picture This* and *The Greatest of Marlys*).

---

[139] Aaron Kashtan, *Between Pen and Pixel* (Ohio State University Press, 2018), 55–6.
[140] Kashtan, *Pen and Pixel*, 71.
[141] Kashtan, *Pen and Pixel*, 73.
[142] Barry, *Syllabus*, 3.

Barry's books also blur high and low arts: while lessons, in life, and in comics, appear in varying shades of humor in her earliest comics, her latest books shift the focus almost exclusively to making comics, irrespective of perceived talent. Through teaching the language of comics—drawing and telling stories—and encouraging students and readers to draw regardless of their skills and perceived talents, Barry both unpacks and expands the possibilities of comics, beginning with the animating potential of lines as we saw above.

Similar to the Near-Sighted Monkey artist-avatar who rejects all notions of artistic genius and ego, while making fun of it, popular imagery from comics, children's and consumer cultures dominate the collage work of Barry's imposing graphic novels, which are comparable to artists' books since they transform the book form to an art object. Barry's collages also share commonalities with modernist and postmodern artists' fascination with, and critique of, popular culture, ranging from the Surrealists to the Situationists: the former encouraged automatic drawing practices and games to tap into the unconscious and a supreme reality removed from the material world;[143] the latter were inspired, and troubled, by the centrality of the image and its intervention in the construction of new, social realities and an alienating society of consumption described by Guy Debord in his *Society of the Spectacle*. Regularly appropriating and repurposing elements from image culture, the situationists sought to critique capitalist society and highlight the damage wrecked by an increasingly all-encompassing consumer society.[144]

Barry's comics regularly engage with and repurpose the idioms of popular culture and advertisement for humoristic ends. We already saw this with the self-help language used in Barry's comic for *Wimmen's Comix* no. 9. The fourth chapter of Barry's illustrated novel *Cruddy* reproduces the advertising rhetoric we saw above to introduce the diary's "sponsor," Vicky Talluso, the diary writer, Roberta's closest friend: "And now a word from our sponsor. You should know about Vicky Talluso. In fact, if you are tired of your life, if you want your life to turn instantly amazing, you should KNOW Vicky Talluso."[145] Roberta's friend becomes a life-changing event

---

[143]For more on Surrealism and comics, see, Gavin Parkinson's excellent critical anthology, *Surrealism, Science Fiction and Comics* (Liverpool University Press, 2015).
[144]Guy Debord, *Society of the Spectacle*, trans. Ken Knabb (AK Press, 2005).
[145]Lynda Barry, *Cruddy: An Illustrated Novel* (Simon & Schuster, 2000), 15.

Figure 1.6 Winter Issue cover, *Picture This*, 9. Copyright Lynda Barry. Used with permission from Drawn & Quarterly.

but this is not without irony as the paragraph concludes, maintaining the promising, exaggerated tone of commercials: "Things happen around Vicky Talluso. Incredible Things. Meeting incredible people. Having revelations. Running from the cops."[146]

The playful imitation of do-it-yourself art manuals on the covers of *Picture This* and *What It Is* also reworks advertisement and self-help rhetoric. Of course, such reworkings are not always intended for critical purposes. *Picture This,* for instance, imitates the children's magazine and is presented as "(a) magazine for imaginary creatures and the people who see them," unfolding in four "issues" to match the four seasons, beginning with winter (Figure 1.6).[147] The handwritten text, "Winter," confirms that the first instalment of the magazine is a holiday special. The festive cover

---

[146] Barry, *Cruddy*, 15.
[147] Barry, *Picture This*, 9. See also Kirtley, *Lynda Barry,* 185.

is enhanced by the cut-out snowflake forms, a small ribbon and glittering dots surrounding the portrait of the Near-Sighted Monkey. A collaged set of dates situates the magazine simultaneously in January 1928, February 1950, and March 1959, rendering it timeless, which is highly appropriate for a magazine for imaginary creatures and readers with vivid imaginations.

In imitating the outdated model of the children's magazine, a central component of children's culture in the nineteenth century, Barry establishes affinities with older forms of print to reclaim a space for materials adults have supposedly grown out of. The reworking of the children's magazine into a graphic novel that is not for children also playfully reverses a historical trajectory through which comics became part of children's culture, notably in the children's corner sections and supplements of illustrated papers at the dawn of the twentieth century.[148]

Engaging with diverse forms and changing styles, one of the constants of Barry's comics and other art is her incorporation of lived, popular, and material cultures, especially their rhetorical and visual strategies. Another recurrent feature is the unearthing of the forgotten and the rejected—the layered, collage works are openly archival, functioning as personalized, and personalizable, rogue archives.[149] Barry's comic strips, which rely exclusively on drawing, likewise rework diverse existing archives from both comics and popular culture. While this chapter introduced key historical and biographical elements for understanding Barry's works and connected them to themes that are fleshed out throughout her comics, the next chapter takes a closer look at Barry's illustrated books and comics. It offers a chronological overview of her oeuvre and the diverse publication contexts in which her works can be situated.

---

[148]See, for instance, Roger Sabin, *Adult Comics: An Introduction* (Routledge, 1993), 22.
[149]Abigail De Kosnik, *Rogue Archives: Digital Cultural Memory and Fandom* (MIT Press, 2016).

CHAPTER 2
KEY TEXTS

Key Texts introduces Barry's works thematically and in chronological order, beginning with her earliest comics strips and stories before expanding on her partially autobiographical work. It ends with the comics manuals that now dominate her publications. This chapter focuses on the changing styles employed by Barry, the different forms of humor and emotions conveyed through the comics, and the recurrent themes of childhood and creativity. For this, the chapter elaborates on notions of ugly drawings and messiness, and possibilities of affective readings through focusing on how the joys and anxieties connected to drawing are conveyed through comics.

The first section begins with *Ernie Pook's Comeek*, Barry's syndicated strip which ran for almost three decades and was published in almost seventy alternative newspapers. Series such as *Two Sisters*, which preceded *Ernie Pook's Comeek* and *Girls and Boys*, are also discussed to trace the themes and styles of Barry's early, serialized comics that remain prominent in her later comics, as we saw in the previous chapter: moving away from the cliché of humor attached to comics by showing "trouble"; childhood and growing up; and making comics.

The second section introduces the illustrated novels, *Cruddy* and *The Good Times Are Killing Me,* highlighting how they combine young adult fiction with a form of illustrated diary-keeping centered on girlhood. This builds on Barry's varied approaches to bookish materialities introduced in the first chapter. The second section then turns to the autobifictional *One Hundred Demons* which combines recollected and fictionalized events from Barry's life, especially her childhood, with a Zen Buddhist automatist drawing exercise. These stories are examined from the prism of the specific hybrid genre established by Barry, combining a wordy comics form with collage, autobiographical stories based on her childhood and young adult experiences and reflections on the artist's anxieties. As we saw previously, the demon-story "Lost and Found," which is about classified advertisements and the unwanted transition from childhood to adolescence, exemplifies Barry's concerns with childhood and the pains of growing up. The second section considers the way in which these works write girlhood in its different phases in light of existing scholarship focusing on the material, bodily, and affective narration of girls' experiences.[1]

The third and final section shows how Barry's later works such as *Syllabus, What It Is, Picture This,* and *Making Comics,* reinforce her expressionistic and messy stylistic concerns, while simultaneously teaching visual narrative and ways to harness drawing anxieties. In *Making Comics,* Barry sums up her teaching ambition as follows: to share "the power of comics as a way of seeing and being in the world and transmitting our experience of it."[2] These experiences are often entangled and interconnected, challenging the presumed simplicity of comics by imbuing the pages, the content of the drawings, and the narratives with ambiguity. It can also be seen as a strategy to counter the objections of simplicity and childishness that have been levied against comics, working in the opposite direction of what Christopher Pizzino calls autoclasm or the "self-breaking" tendency of comics that is a reaction to, and a reaffirmation of, its low cultural status.[3]

Early Comic Strips and Stories

Children abound in Lynda Barry's comics as do awkward, sad, and even traumatic moments. While the incorporation of children's drawings is examined in greater detail in Chapter 4, this section introduces the many child characters in her comics and shows how they voice concerns and inherit traits from the older, adult characters dominating her early comics. Barry's child characters are unapologetically honest and endearing. Reflecting Barry's own coming of age during the rise of underground comics, her characters embrace unabashedly "ugly" and expressive forms. They likewise do not shy away from sharing—and even oversharing—darker aspects of childhood, subverting assumptions that stories with children as main characters, and especially comics with children as main characters, are intended for children. This is reinforced by the emphatic statement in

---

[1] See for instance, Kirtley, *Lynda Barry*; Rachel R. Miller, "Keep Out, or Else: Diary as Body in *The Diary of a Teenage Girl* and *Cruddy*," in *Comics Memory: Archives and Styles,* ed. Maaheen Ahmed and Benoît Crucifix (Palgrave, 2018), 101–19; Michael, "Graphic Autofiction."
[2] Barry, *Making Comics,* 14.
[3] Christopher Pizzino, *Arresting Development: Comics at the Boundaries of Literature* (University of Texas Press, 2016), 48–9.

the front matter of *Everything* introduced in the preceding chapter: "THIS BOOK *is not for kids*."[4]

Ernie Pook's Comeek ran for nearly three decades in alternative weeklies, beginning with quirky insights into adult and feminine worlds before establishing a universe of unidealized childhood. It introduced the now famous Marlys, her siblings, and cousins, who eventually overshadowed Ernie, an earlier protagonist of the comic strips. While Drawn & Quarterly has recently published compilations and re-editions of *Ernie Pook's Comeek*,[5] the strips also reappear in Barry's other books, as is already evident from Marlys's and Arna's portraits on the cover of *Picture This*. The first *Ernie Pook's Comeek* collection was published under one of its earliest titles, *Girls and Boys,* by Real Comet Press in 1981.[6] It was followed by a second collection, *Big Ideas,* in 1983.[7] These early collections are often a medley of strips, combining a diversity of styles and topics as we will see below. Susan Kirtley describes these early works as "comics experiments," in which Barry tests expressive possibilities ranging from themes and character designs to line and brushwork.[8]

More recently, *Girls and Boys* was recollected in *Everything* and augmented with a collaged band of diverse "scrap" material at the bottom: wrapping paper, notebook and exercise book excerpts, striped, lined, and printed paper and even illustrations.[9] In this new format, the comics, which are often only four-panels long, are all collected on one page. The page acquires new layers of temporalities and new connections through the different strips added at the bottom, which both compensate for the difference in format while recalling the newspaper context of syndicated comics, which bring together different comic series and additional material such as advertisements and diverse columns on the same page. The comic below transposes the horizontally formatted, sequential strip to a single page in portrait format (Figure 2.1). Drawn in Barry's early, expressionistic style, it captures the extreme violence of two young boys, with a bigger one beating up a smaller one. The dialogue confirms a cycle of violence with the

---

[4]Barry, *Everything*, 2
[5]Including *The Freddie Stores* (2012), *The Greatest of Marlys* (2016), *My Perfect Life* (2022), *Come Over Come Over* (2022) and *It's So Magic* (2022).
[6]Kirtley, *Lynda Barry*, 22.
[7]Kirtley, *Lynda Barry*, 24.
[8]Kirtley, *Typical Girls*, 110.
[9]Barry, *Everything*, 115–77.

Figure 2.1 Violent boys from *Girls and Boys* in *Everything*, 127. Copyright Lynda Barry. Used with permission from Drawn & Quarterly.

perpetrating boy informing a disembodied voice from beyond the panels that he had been "<u>creamed</u>" by his father when the other boy told on him for beating his brother (who had ended up with a concussion). The third panel focuses on his face and especially his eyes, or two pupils within one eye, both of which are seeing red, as confirmed by the text on top of the lines emanating from the eye.

When, in the last panel, the beaten-up boy asks the interfering adult to mind their own business, the children assert a degree of agency, suggesting that adult interference would not only make things worse (as was already the case with the father beating up the bigger boy) but that the fight is also beyond their comprehension and follows its own, child-specific rules. This is precisely the kind of voice and space offered to children—often in comics not for children—that makes Barry's comics stand out.

The collaged strip at the bottom of the page is one of the most colorful ones in the reprinted edition, closely resembling a comic with its combination of small action-packed panels in bright colors. The jungle setting, the muscled man, and his confrontation with a monkey suggest a *Tarzan*-like strip. The predominance of red seems to echo the violence of the main comic but the actual sequence of events pasted on the page do not go further than suggesting violence, contrasting starkly with the exuberant portrayal of bashing in the main comic. The format used for reprinting *Girls and Boys* in *Everything* also recalls the frieze-comic Barry employs in *Picture This*, which productively juxtaposes different perspectives. In terms of bookish materiality, *Everything* is therefore an intriguing object encapsulating the serialized strips within the longer and broader form of the graphic novel and augmenting the original strips with colored pages and rich, contextual, and autobiographical collage pages.

Let's turn to the first Real Comet Press publication of *Girls & Boys*, which reveals the variety of themes broached by Barry's comics. The collection also reflects her early "punk" style, with sharp lines and expressionist figures, just like in the comic above, which preceded her shift to the ink brush. The comics collected in this volume also stand out through the focus on more adult characters; comics with children appear only intermittently. Most of the comics are limited to four panels, but some extend to eight.

Girls and Boys opens with a single panel cartoon showing a boss scolding an angry "Miss Barry": "some of us do *not* find *voo doo* hot dog very funny. *Some* of us feel that it indicates a *serious attitude problem.* Don't you *like* your job miss Barry?"[10] A sausage with multiple pins and a tag, "You're in for it" sits on the table. It is difficult not to draw parallels between this cartoon and Barry's distinctive humor with its dark tones that does not always fit the generic comic strip scheme of relatively fixed cadences and formulae to create effective gags. The efficiency and functioning of such gag formulae have recently been unpacked by Mark Newgarden and Paul Karasik who take Ernie Bushmiller's *Nancy* comics as an exemplary case study.[11]

Some strips in *Girls and Boys* are so dark that they are not at all funny. This is the case with one of the relatively rarer strips with children. In one four-panel strip, a drunk mother collapses shortly after announcing to her daughter that her father is coming home and that she should get ready for bed. The three panels capture the girl's despair on seeing her collapsed mother, worried, as we find out in the last panel, about her mother getting

---

[10] Lynda Barry, *Girls and Boys* (Real Comet Press, 1981), 7.
[11] Paul Karasik and Mark Newgarden, *How to Read Nancy: The Elements of Comics in Three Easy Panels* (Fantagraphics, 2017).

into trouble with her father. The father is only present through his absence, through the noise he makes as he enters the house and the terror he generates in the crying girl, who holds on to her unconscious mother's hand and orders her father to stay away from her mother.[12] Such strips both reflect the feeling-change Barry sees in her comics from the very beginning and foreshadow the trouble which becomes increasingly palpable in her autobiographical works such as *One Hundred Demons*.

What makes Barry's comics stand out is how they challenge the conventions associated with comics, beginning with her syndicated strips. As Hillary Chute reminds us: "While there had been comic strips with disturbing content in the underground, Barry's 'sad' comic strips in commercial newspapers were new."[13] Although such comics were targeted by indignant reader letters, they also succeeded in attracting a different kind of readership, comparable to how George Herriman's unpredictable and poetic *Krazy Kat* was more appreciated by modernist artists and poets such as e. e. cummings than the lay newspaper reader.[14] Roger Gilbert considers *Ernie Pook's Comeek* as one of the three "great oeuvres" in American comics history, the other two being *Krazy Kat* and *Peanuts*.[15] Calling her strips, "four-panel epiphanies," Gilbert emphasizes the role of both format and Barry's playing with it to add depth: "Barry's work derives much of its formal and narrative energies precisely from the sharp constraint of its format" and specific rules.[16] He adds:

> While Barry's mature work doesn't completely disavow this grammar, it complicates and deepens it beyond recognition. Thus while her fourth panel usually offers some kind of strongly closural effect, rarely do we get a punch-line in the narrow sense (. . .) the richness and relative autonomy of the individual panel in turn permits her to achieve subtler effects as she moves from frame to frame.[17]

---

[12]Barry, *Everything*, 26–7.
[13]Chute, *Graphic Women*, 96.
[14]See, for instance, e. e. cummings, "A Foreword to Krazy," in *Arguing Comics: Literary Masters on a Popular Medium,* ed. Jeet Heer and Kent Worcester (University Press of Mississippi, 2004), 30–4.
[15]Roger Gilbert, "Four-Panel Epiphanies: The Art of Lynda Barry," *Northwest Review* 34 (1996): 78–96, 78.
[16]Gilbert, "Four-Panel Epiphanies," 79.
[17]Gilbert, "Four-Panel Epiphanies," 80.

Key Texts

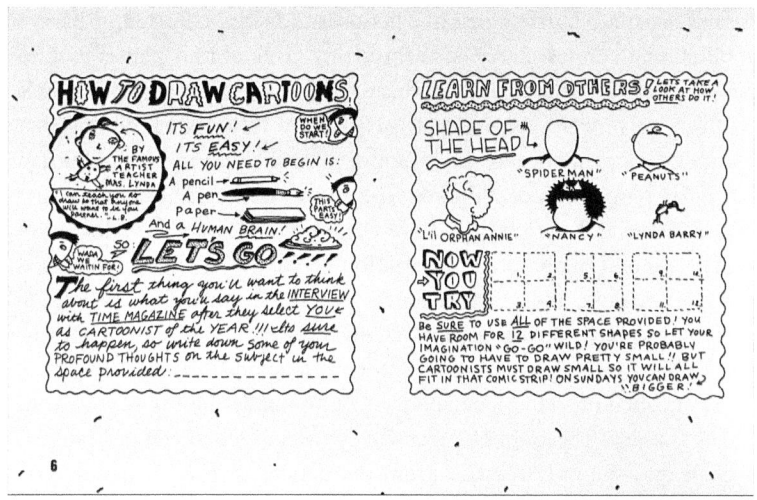

Figure 2.2 "How to Draw Cartoons," from *Girls and Boys*, 6. Copyright Lynda Barry. Used with permission from Drawn & Quarterly.

Although Gilbert's article emphasizes the role of the constraining strip format to generate depth, a comparable layering unfolds in the short comics episodes in *One Hundred Demons* and in the individual pages of the collaged graphic novels, *What It Is* and *Picture This*.

Predicting the direction Barry's later graphic narratives will take, the opening voodoo hotdog cartoon mentioned above is followed by a "How to Draw Cartoons" strip.[18] In four panels with shaggy ends which bestow an almost dreamlike or thoughtful aura to the content, Barry offers a concise comics-making lesson. Next to a cartoon baby, Barry introduces herself as "the famous artist teacher Mrs. Lynda" and promises, "I can teach you to draw so that anyone will want to be your partner" (Figure 2.2).[19] This promise hints toward the self-esteem that is at stake when striving to make "good" art and the fantasies surrounding success, which in Barry's strip also include being interviewed by *Time* magazine. The next panel encourages copying the outlined heads of iconic comics characters, Spiderman, Charlie Brown, Lil' Orphan Annie, Nancy and Barry herself, who appears as a very tiny, abstract form. The lines between being a comic strip character and

---

[18] Barry, *Everything*, 6–7.
[19] Barry, *Everything*, 6.

a comics artist are blurred, just like fiction and fact are blurred in Barry's autobifictional comics. Barry adds three tiny grids of four panels each to practice creating variations of the heads. The panels are tiny but this is something cartoonists have to get used to, she informs us, adding that the Sunday supplements are an exception. Despite all the playful humor, then, Barry's tips are not all jokes. The third panel encourages copying the eyes, nose, and mouth of the five characters, with the "Lynda Barry" character combining an allusive selection of forms: squiggles for eyes, a button for the nose, and a banana for the mouth. She then suggests mixing the components to create original characters. The final panel concerns the storyline, with tips to keep the story simple and original. The story itself is an uncomfortable one about a young dentist falling in love with a young patient. The romantic element is twisted when the girl falls off her chair and the only reaction from the dentist is to look up the girl's skirt. The brief text offers little insight into the girl's feelings and options. After reproducing a four-panel sequence, which is simply numbered, with the final panel designated as the end, Barry adds space for a signature and hands her readers a diploma.

Barry's overly simplified sequence reflects a deeper understanding of how modulable the comics form can be. It does not insist on a beginning or building up toward a climax, but simply an end after three panels, relying on the connections that are automatically generated when panels are juxtaposed in a sequence.

Alluding to another universal concern in its title, the "Nature or Nurture?" strip stars "Lil' Dunkin" the doughnut boy who grew up in a Seattle doughnut factory and is an alternative *enfant sauvage*, brought up at the fringes of human civilization and eagerly studied to understand the role of civilization. Part boy, part doughnut, with burning candles in his hair, which resembles frosting, Dunkin's "habits were quite unlike our own! He was very <u>odd</u>."[20] Dunkin turns out to be the perfect case study for understanding the question baffling scientists "throughout history," "the *awful* question about <u>human nature</u>: does it <u>exist</u>? Are we <u>born</u> with a desire to *get a job* and *eat* twinkies or is this a <u>learned</u> condition?"[21] As with most *enfant sauvage* stories, Barry's comic takes a tragic twist when Dunkin's parents refuse to take him in fearing his ability to fit in society.

---

[20]Barry, *Girls and Boys*, 84–7, 85.
[21]Barry, *Girls and Boys*, 84.

Dunkin becomes listless in the care of social workers and is "left to mold,"[22] until another doctor finds him, insists that he is just like any other child, seeking attention and wanting to avoid employment. Luckily for Dunkin, his new employer at Sears was a former doughnut boy himself and they open to each other after becoming drunk. With this detail, Barry adds a level of reality that is typical for her comics—where children are exposed to adult vices—but rare for family-friendly comic strips.

The strip offers a mock happy end according to which Dunkin changes his name and acquires a Honda Civic, a canary and a small garden. Barry then adds a question below the panel: "Do *you* think this story is *true*??"[23] In addition to selecting "yes" or "no," readers are also given the option to explain why. Barry will, as we saw in the previous chapter, include a similar true or false question on the table of contents page in *One Hundred Demons*. Food itself, and doughnuts in particular, appear frequently in these early comics, often connected to girl and women characters instead of boys, interweaving the critique of consumer society and gendered relationships to eating.

Recalling how she had already collected these early comics in "tiny stapled books," Barry sees them as marking a distinctive change in both style and tone:

> By the end of 1979 (. . .) I wanted to make comics with trouble in them and I wanted to draw in a way that was not sweet because the stories weren't sweet and because something interesting happened when I stopped trying to control my drawing: I got that feeling back from when I was a kid, that feeling of the line being alive again.[24]

Many of the themes appearing in *Girls and Boys* become organizing principles in the second *Ernie Pook's Comeek* compliation, *Big Ideas*, which organizes its comics under the following subsections: "Explanations," "True Stories," "Love," "Nutrition," "Advice," "And More!" The codes of the self-help book are reworked, just like in the drawing manuals characterizing Barry's later work. Like *Girls and Boys,* most of the strips in *Big Ideas* have adult characters and adult themes; the children that will dominate the later

---

[22]Barry, *Girls and Boys,* 85.
[23]Barry, *Girls and Boys,* 87.
[24]Barry, *Everything,* 113.

Lynda Barry

Figure 2.3 "The Creation of the World," from *Big Ideas*, 10. Copyright Lynda Barry. Used with permission from Drawn & Quarterly.

strips still remain relatively marginal. The third collection, *Everything in the World*, continues to focus on adult worlds and it is only in the fourth anthology, *The Fun House*, that children and adolescents take over. As mentioned in the previous chapter, this change coincided with a shift in technique from pen to brush. The drawing techniques and styles are varied and hybrid in the first three collections, ranging from expressive, childlike drawing, to heavily shaded and textured representations and different kinds of cartoon styles. This hybridity accompanies a thematic diversity, showing how Barry was experimenting with different possibilities in comics.

The opening comic strip in *Big Ideas* titled, appropriately enough, "The Creation of the World," alternates between Barry's minimalist cartoon style and almost childlike drawings (Figure 2.3).[25] Promising both "exclusive story and photos," the comic pokes fun at attention-grabbing journalistic rhetoric. The car in the third panel and the chaos of the overabundance of things illustrated in the fifth panel—including house, car, dog, and a rocket ship—are drawn in a more childlike style: "Everything was everyplace," the matter-of-fact narrator informs us. "Everywhere you looked there was at

---

[25]Lynda Barry, *Big Ideas* (Real Comet Press, 1983), 8–10.

least something. Things started to get mixed up then." The italic lettering is done by hand and changes size from panel to panel, according to the amount of text and the size of the captions. In the first two panels of the comic, the text is not even separated by a line from the panels, forming an unusual composite where images and words that are not direct speech coexist.

Two additional strips in the first section, "Explanations," deal with fear and angst. Other comics across the collection explore (failed) relationships and food, both of which are recurring themes in Barry's early comics.

Significantly, the "True Stories" section opens with two stories about children, drawn with extensive crosshatching that adds both depth and darkness to the panels, contrasting significantly with the cartoony, expressionist style Barry uses for most of her comics. "Chuckie and Harry" is drawn by "Big Butt," with an arrow pointing to a naked butt sticking out from the edge of the title caption.[26] The short comic shows a conversation unfolding between two brothers in bed at night, teasing and taunting each other, with the familiarity of siblings and in part with "butt" names. Chuck begs Harry to show him "the pictures" but Harry refuses, insisting that Chuck is too young. In the third panel, their mother's voice intervenes, ordering them to quiet down and sleep. This recalls the numerous *Little Nemo in Slumberland* episodes, where the adult voice and sometimes body intervenes in the final panel, which is also when Nemo wakes up and realizes that the fantastic events of the comic were a dream. In "Chuckie and Harry," however, the adult voice only intervenes in the third panel and we are able to see how ineffective the order is. The boys do not care and even make fun of their mother. The four-panel story does not really have a conclusion, functioning more as a slice of life strip.

In the strip that follows, "Phobia-Phobia," an unnamed boy lists his four fears, with the panel illustrating the schoolteacher, Groucho Marx glasses, the school bully, and a threatening little girl with a baseball bat.[27] While Barry still uses some crosshatching to add volume, each source of fear appears against a white background, emphasizing its power, its ability to exist beyond time and space. The narrator himself appears at the edge of the panel, in a separate, thin caption with his words. The first panel, which has a supplementary heading comprising the written alphabet, is significant if we

---

[26]Barry, *Big Ideas*, 36.
[27]Barry, *Big Ideas*, 38–9.

consider the numerous alphabets we will later encounter in Barry's comics and art instruction manuals and even in the front matter of *One Hundred Demons*, next to the multi-eyed sea monster. The prominence of the written alphabet reflects the centrality of childhood worlds in Barry's later books. The other "true stories," in contrast, deal with relationships, womanhood and even a pet turtle called Gamora.

Everything in the World, which is organized according to different "worlds," of love, growing up, relationships and problems with the body and with the world, echoes *Big Ideas* and *Girls and Boys* in its thematic and stylistic hybridity. Since the comics within the collections are not printed chronologically it is difficult to situate specific styles in specific years. Nevertheless, it is possible to discern a certain change in line and techniques, especially when this collection is compared to *Girls and Boys*: while most of the comics in the latter are made with sharper, often thinner lines, many *Everything in the World* comics rely on more fluid, rounded forms, which will eventually become Barry's trademark style.

It is in *The Fun House* (which was also the title of a comic published in the "Growing Up" section of *Everything in the World*), that childhood and the ink brush take over Barry's comics. This is already evident from the front and back matter of the book, adorned with different kinds of objects associated with childhood or labelled from a child's perspective: a bra is labelled "mystery," a globe is "the world," and we also encounter jello, jawbreakers and a jack-in-the-box ("pop goes the weasel"). In addition, the collection ends with childhood portraits of Barry's brothers, to whom the book is dedicated. This reinforces the centrality of childhood to the comics while anticipating the importance the theme will acquire in Barry's later work. Just like "The Fun House" comic from *Everything in the World*,[28] which is about a child neighbor who was eventually sent away because his mother could not take care of him, the comics in the collected volume, *The Fun House*, are more about childhood anguish than fun. And, like "The Fun House," which imitates the writing mistakes of a child (tense confusion, absent punctuation, spelling mistakes), *The Fun House* also incorporates the narrative voices of different children.

Ernie Pook's Comeek was the first major comics assignment that allowed Barry to work independently as a comics artist.[29] But it was not the very

---

[28] Lynda Barry, *Everything in the World* (Harper Perennial, 1986), 33–4.
[29] Kirtley, *Lynda Barry*, 24

first Barry publication as Susan Kirtley points out by carefully tracing Barry's earliest publications in college newspapers, such as the University of Washington's *Daily* in 1978, alongside the *Two Sisters* weekly comics that were published for a year, from 1978 to 1979, in the now defunct *Seattle Sun*.[30] These were collected in Barry's first self-published and photocopied book, the *Two Sisters* in 1979,[31] accompanied by a portrait of Barry drawn by her brother and reproduced on the very last page of *Everything*. Like some of the *Ernie Pook's Comeek* strips and the vast proportion of Barry's later comics, *Two Sisters* thrusts us into the world of childhood, which is not unusual for the medium if we think of the many popular child characters in comics. Barry, however, portrays childhood in a highly original and unusual manner, reversing expectations and assumptions associated with childhood, and merging an almost dangerous degree of knowingness and the ordinary.[32] While Kirtley connects these observations to *Ernie Pook's Comeek,* they can easily be extended to Barry's representations of childhood in general.

In her concluding page for the *Two Sisters* in *Everything,* which is headed by a single panel introducing Miss Rita and Miss Evette as "Heroin Addicts Back from New York,"[33] Barry already wonders about the "feeling-change":

> When did "my style" become something that was splitting down the middle? That divide between bitter and sweet shifted. Bitter was funnier to me and it began to let me much closer to a certain kind of abyss where that Third Thing dwells.[34]

In an interview from 2011, Barry mentions another kind of third thing that nonetheless follows the same principle of producing images capable of generating feeling and bodily reactions: "crayon, piece of paper, and then this third thing that happens, this image and it makes your body feel a certain way, whether it's scared or excited."[35] Early in her comics work, Barry was already striving to create images and comics capable of generating different

---

[30] See Barry, *Everything,* 61–109.
[31] Kirtley *Lynda Barry,* 22–3.
[32] Kirtley, *Lynda Barry,* 135–47.
[33] Barry, *Everything,* 109.
[34] Barry, *Everything,* 109.
[35] Jesse Thorn and Lynda Barry, "The Sound of Young America: Lynda Barry, Author of *Picture This* and *What It Is*," *Bullseye,* hosted by *Maximum Fun,* January 3, 2011, accessed December

combinations of emotions, many of which were dark and uncomfortable, instead of focusing on humor alone. At the same time, as suggested by her 2011 description of the "third thing," she also seeks an almost visceral and affective connection through the image. Her comics, as a result, become a means of establishing connections.

Just like for other sections reproducing her earlier work in *Everything*, Barry includes a reflective page to introduce *Girls and Boys*. This introduction includes a picture of Barry autographing a copy for a young boy in 1981, followed by a list of elements she was unaware of at that time.[36] The listed elements include her remaining a comics artist and

> that I would *swing* between sweet and bitter drawing and writing styles again and again (. . .) that the question asked: what brings about a "feeling-change" when we read certain kinds of comics?— This question can never be answered with words alone.[37]

For Barry hybridity— especially the combination of words and images, but extending to the transcending of genres and physical formats— is an essential component of her art, and contributes to producing feeling-change. This feeling-change and the "trouble" of her comics that are often bittersweet instead of simply funny can already be seen in the above *Ernie Pook's Comeek* examples. While the comics with adult characters are often more critical, highlighting everyday stupidity and cruelties, including the unfair standards for women and girls, much of the bittersweetness is anchored in the child characters. These characters overturn romanticized and nostalgic assumptions of childhood, reflecting difficult, often poverty-stricken childhoods and children that counter clichés by embracing their disheveled, messy selves and their comic, cheeky, and even wise insights.

Miriam Harris neatly summarizes the tensions articulated through Barry's child characters in *Ernie Pook's Comeek* as follows:

> With these characters as mouthpieces, Barry considers darker themes that have traditionally been the substance of novels, such as

---

4, 2024, https://maximumfun.org/episodes/bullseye-with-jesse-thorn/lynda-barry-author-picture-and-what-it-interview-sound-young-america/.
[36]Barry, *Everything*, 112.
[37]Barry, *Everything*, 114.

the abuse of the disenfranchised and the human capacity for cruelty and violence. There are painful reflections on lost love, betrayal, and disappointment that startle any reader anticipating the frothier fare typically associated with comics. And thrown into the mix are also stretches of sidesplitting funniness, joy, and connectedness.[38]

As we will see in the following section, human cruelty and violence seen through children's eyes is perhaps never so starkly portrayed as in Barry's illustrated novels, both of which adopt the model of a young girl's diary.

Illustrated Diaries

While Barry's first illustrated novel, *The Good Times Are Killing Me,* is about a girl called Edna Arkins and her friend Bonna Willis, Barry draws out the similarities between the two characters and herself and her friend Kay Hatton in the collaged afterword added to the 2017 edition published by Drawn & Quarterly. The very last page of the book, similar to the comics collections discussed above, and added in later editions of *The Good Times Are Killing Me*, is a dedication page, with a portrait in gray washes of Hatton.[39] Barry is careful to trace the blurry contours of her memories:

> *I don't remember being little.* That is to say I never <u>felt</u> little. A part of me stays steady . . . like *the center* point of something *spinning* (. . .) Fifty *years ago* I played on a street very *much like* the street *in this* story, *with* a girl very much like Bonna Willis.[40]

This hints at the non-factual life writing that is at the heart of autobifictionalography introduced by Barry in *One Hundred Demons*. Although the afterword is a relatively recent addition, *The Good Times Are Killing Me* confirms the gradual but growing importance of life writing in Barry's work. In the 1989 *Comics Journal* interview with Thom Powers,

---

[38]Harris, "Cartoonists as Matchmakers," 132.
[39]Barry's 1988 dedications were to her neighbor Ms. Yvonne Taylor, who introduced her to Gospel music, and her elementary school teacher, Mrs. Clara LaSane. Both became the subjects of the essays, "The Guardian Neighbor" (1995) and "The Sanctury of School" (1998), respectively, published in different essay collections. See Kirtley, *Lynda Barry*, 53.
[40]Barry, *Good Times*, n. p.

Barry clarifies that it is not so much the events and characters but the setting of the works that are autobiographical: "The thing that's autobiographical about my work is that I picture it; I see it happening on the streets where I grew up. The characters themselves are fictional."[41]

Barry apparently only took ten days to write *The Good Times Are Killing Me*,[42] which is structured around forty-one short texts introducing the reader to different aspects of Edna's life, much of which is connected to music and to growing up in a neighborhood riddled with class and race conflicts. First published by Real Comet Press in 1988, *The Good Times Are Killing Me* can be considered a work of crossover fiction, before crossover fiction became a global marketing success:[43] adopting a twelve-year-old's perspective and set in a working class, late 1960s neighborhood, the novel speaks to both children and adults as it maps the weight of racism that prevents even ordinary childhood friendships from surviving. Like Hatton, Arkins is Black. The story is set in a rapidly changing Seattle neighborhood with multiple ethnicities and prejudices that are set in stone. In focusing on the children and their school and street politics, the novel regularly points to how children's worlds filter adult assumptions, anxieties, and aspirations.

The Good Times Are Killing Me was not initially intended as a book about racism. Instead, Barry wanted to focus on music at a time when her first marriage was on the rocks.[44] This new focus, away from comics, translated into several portraits of musicians which make up the "music notebook" at the end of the novel. The portraits were exhibited at two galleries, the Linda Ferris Gallery in Seattle in 1986 and, two years later, at the Nine Gallery in Portland. Barry eventually moved completely out of the gallery circuit and onto the pages of newspapers and books, recalling that "I'd get these good reviews, but they'd say stuff like I had to make a decision, was I a painter or a cartoonist?"[45] Ironically enough, as Barry officially moved away from the

---

[41] Powers and Barry, "The Lynda Barry Interview – Part 2."
[42] Kirtley, *Lynda Barry*, 51.
[43] Pointing out that crossover fiction has always existed, for instance, through folk and fairy tales, Sandra L. Beckett in *Crossover Fiction: Global and Historical Perspectives* (Routledge, 2009) dates the popularization of the term to the 2000s, in the wake of J. K. Rowling's *Harry Potter* novels.
[44] Kirtley, *Lynda Barry*, 49.
[45] Chute, *Graphic Women*, 98.

art scene, she moved closer toward "painterly" and artsy comics through adopting the ink brush technique and collage.

In addition to the visual arts, music is omnipresent in her comics and in her teaching practice. Barry had also copied record covers, just like she had copied underground comics artists and other kinds of images. In selecting the musicians she portrayed, Barry focused on those who had died in quick, unexpected ways. As Kirtley points out, both "music and tragedy (. . .) would later interweave throughout *The Good Times Are Killing Me* in all its other incarnations."[46] The novella itself was initially intended as a text introducing and accompanying the exhibition.[47] Much of the music and the portraits of the musicians were about loss, a theme that forms the dominant tone in the novel focalized through two preteen girls.

Already the cover of *The Good Times Are Killing Me* is anchored in the world of music, with a disk turning on a compact turntable. An ex-libris replaces "book" with "record." The title is composed of cut-out letters, bits of foil, and material that looks like Rexene, which is stained near the title. Most of the turntable itself is drawn. The title page inside and additional frontmatter also imitate the texture of wood used to decorate record players, especially since the 1950s.[48] All of these elements surrounding the actual story form what Gérard Genette calls the paratext, with book covers and the immediate elements around a book being peritexts.[49] Barry carefully aligns most of the paratexual elements surrounding her story to music making and listening.

Textures comparable to the cover return, not in the actual novel itself, but in the "music notebook" and, in a different aesthetic, in the afterword at the end of book. The tin foil is most prominent in the music notebook where it is used for the elaborate frames of the portraits and in illustrations of the different music styles. These musical references are subdued on the first cover for *The Good Times Is Killing Me,* which shows two angels, one with a white face and one with a Black one, alluding to the angels adorning the portrait frames in the music notebook. The angels carry records, and records hang in the sky, with the Black angel also holding a boom box. A

---

[46] Kirtley, *Lynda Barry*, 49.
[47] Kirtley, *Lynda Barry,* 51.
[48] See Kate Eichhorn, *Adjusted Margins: Xerography, Art and Activism in the Late Twentieth Century* (MIT Press, 2016), 154.
[49] See Gérard Genette, "Introduction to the Paratext," trans. Marie Maclean, *New Literary History* 22, no. 2 (1991): 261–72.

record replaces a full moon hovering above the house around which the entire image is centered. The cover and its frontmatter is dominated by swirls, the repetitive and meditative gestures that Barry uses as an exercise to activate the hand in her manuals. While the first edition opens with a portrait of Louis Armstrong, whose "What a Wonderful World" was Edna's song, the new edition also includes two framed drawings in gray washes, which shift the focus from the music to children.

The first watercolor drawing opening *The Good Times Are Killing Me* recalls children's drawings and depicts a street scene with several children. The second is less abstract and shows a pensive child, a figure that recurs in Barry's works, as we saw in Chapter 1, with the dark portrait opening *What It Is*. Such children embody interiority. Historian and childhood scholar, Carolyn Steedman identifies the connection between children and interiority as emerging in the eighteenth century onwards, continuing into the twentieth century, culminating in Freudian theorizations of the unconscious and Ellen Key's famous prediction of the twentieth century as the century of the child.[50] "The idea of the child," Steedman writes, "provided the largest number of people living in the recent past of Western societies with the means of thinking about and creating a self: something grasped and understood: a shape, moving in the body... something *inside*: an interiority."[51]

In focusing on child characters that are partially autobiographical, Barry introduces an additional affective charge to her work, especially through her ability to convincingly reproduce child and teenage voices, free of idealized nostalgia and sensitive to the problems of young people. This also leads to the inclusion of images and events that are not associated with childhood, which is already evident in the Madonna-like portrait of the young, tired-looking Edna babysitting her niece, which precedes the first chapter (Figure 2.4). The portrait itself remediates the iconic, religious image of hope and love, intended to be prayed to and to inspire faith, to Edna's lonely world, in which we bear witness to the gradual dismantling of

---

[50]Carolyn Steedman, *Strange Dislocations: Childhood and the Idea of Human Interiority, 1780-1930* (Harvard University Press, 1998), 4; Ellen Key, *The Century of the Child* (G. P. Putnam's Sons, 1909), Project Gutenberg, 2018, https://www.gutenberg.org/cache/epub/57283/pg57283-images.html.

[51]Steedman, *Strange Dislocations*, 20.

Key Texts

Figure 2.4 Edna's portrait with her cousin's baby, from *The Good Times Are Killing Me*, 8. Copyright Lynda Barry. Used with permission from Drawn & Quarterly.

her hopes and aspirations, especially those connected to making music and building friendships through music and across racial barriers.

Edna talks to the reader directly, introducing us to her world, beginning with the changing racial composition of her street. She also introduces us to her music world, imbued with classics such as Armstrong's "What a Wonderful World," and children's songs, such as "I Went to the Animal Fair."[52] We soon find out that the baby Edna is babysitting is biracial, for which her cousin Ellen has been kicked out of her parents' house. The baby is only one of the many instances of racial prejudices and tensions that occur even before Edna sees Bonna and tries to befriend her. The two girls bond over music, creating a new space for themselves in Edna and her younger sister Lucy's basement with the record player their father had surprised them with and which turned out to be a hand-me-down from

---

[52] Barry, *Good Times*, 14–15.

his girlfriend's children. In addition to the red enamel paint to hide the wear and the taped tone arm, the player also has part of the father's hand embossed on it, which Edna likens to "fossils, a million years old."[53] The cut-off hand is an affective memory and a bodily trace, a bitter reminder of a father who has left his family for another one. That this is mediated through a cheap record player that once belonged to his new girlfriend's children adds to the desolation and poignancy of the situation.

Going beyond everyday cruelty and bitterness into unfettered violence, Barry's second novel *Cruddy* is the illustrated diary of Roberta Rohbeson who, as we find out in the opening note, committed suicide at the age of sixteen. Unsettlingly, she shares the same birth date as Barry and even looks like Barry. Comparable to the notebooks Barry asks her students and readers to make in *Syllabus* and *Making Comics*,[54] *Cruddy* opens with a hand print: however, unlike the traced hands that Barry encourages her readers to make as both a warming-up exercise and as a means of personalizing the book, *Cruddy* opens with a blurry x-ray in which the index finger is almost completely cut off. It is only later in the story that we realize that the finger had been chopped off by her father, after an infection resulting from a cut while trying to gut a deer. Both father and daughter share an obsession with knives, which is connected to Roberta's grandfather's profession as a butcher. All of Roberta's grandfather's special knives, which were his discontented son's only inheritance, are given female names, with Little Debbie becoming Roberta's companion and, on many occasions, even savior, during the violent events recounted in the diary.

Like *The Good Times Are Killing Me*, *Cruddy*'s front matter also includes two dark portraits: the first one is a small, elaborately framed silhouette of the androgynous girl with messy hair that Barry uses to represent herself, busily writing above a quote from the seventeenth-century Italian biologist and writer, Francesco Redi whose scientific interest in decay connects with the morbid story;[55] the second one, which takes up an entire page, and is adorned with an equally elaborate frame closes in on two sad girls, Roberta and her younger half-sister, Julie, with closed eyes. The two sisters often fight but they also reconcile their differences in the face of adversity, as when they are abandoned by their mother who leaves them for a week

---

[53] Barry, *Good Times*, 43.
[54] Barry, *Syllabus*, 8; Barry, *Making Comics*, 35.
[55] Kirtley, *Lynda Barry*, 83.

while she takes a vacation with an old doctor she has an affair with (and who Roberta suggests is Julie's father). Roberta's final sentence in the diary dedicates it to Julie but the final words of the book are Julie's handwritten, indignant exclamations, capturing her devastation at being left alone.[56] This ending also destabilizes the reader's own position as an unwanted onlooker and even complicit observer of the string of cruelties described throughout the novel. "The reading experience" of the novel, as Kirtley aptly describes it, "is akin to struggling through a fun-house maze of mirrors; both reader and narrator struggle amidst the illusions."[57] Through metalepsis, which occurs through Roberta's breaking the fourth wall and directly addressing the reader, the reader acquires the alternating and sometimes combined roles of "witness, confidante, friend."[58] Stemming from the narratologist Gérard Genette's highly influential narratological theory,[59] metalepsis is also a familiar comics strategy emphasizing the self-reflexive essence of the medium, which allows for easy transitions between different narrative levels and where attention to the narrator or production context can easily be foregrounded. For Karin Kukkonen, this focus on "producing" instead of "telling" is central to metalepsis in media such as film and comics.[60] In Barry's comics, self-reflection on the stories being told and the techniques of telling stories is recurrent, especially since Barry often incorporates herself into her stories and unpacks the tools she uses to tell her stories.

A third illustration, after the brief first chapter describing Roberta's fear of the glow in the dark Jesus her mother nailed in the room she shared with her sister, reinstalls the writing silhouette in the attic of the house.[61] The dark portraits portend the darkness and tragedy of the story. Roberta, as we learn early in the diary, was also Clyde when she was with her father, who had always wanted a boy and who thought a boy's identity could protect her from sexual predators; this was generally, but not always true, resulting in the murder of a small-town sheriff.

---

[56]Barry, *Cruddy*, 305.
[57]Kirtley, *Lynda Barry*, 81.
[58]Kirtley, *Lynda Barry*, 90.
[59]See Genette, *Narrative Discourse: An Essay in Method*, trans. Jane E. Lewin (Cornell University Press, 1980), 234–5.
[60]Karin Kukkonen, "Metalepsis in Comics," in *Metalepsis in Popular Culture*, ed. Karin Kukkonen and Sonja Klimek (De Gruyter, 2011), 213–31, 222.
[61]Barry, *Cruddy*, 2.

Roberta informs the unspecified reader, addressed as "Dear Anyone Who Finds This," that she had carefully planned her suicide and her diary reaching us is part of her plan and her way of getting her "happily ever after."[62] The dark childhood portrayed in *Cruddy* interweaves several motifs that reappear in Barry's comics, such as the poverty-stricken neighborhood and childhood, unpopularity at school, class differences, friendships, exposure to drugs and alcohol, a cruel mother, who in *Cruddy* is a physically violent mother (in the comics, in contrast, verbal and psychological violence is dominant whereas physical violence is more often suggested as a possibility instead of being shown).[63] Another major difference is the presence of a father figure, who is alcoholic, unpredictable, paranoid, and willing to go to dangerous ends to achieve his aims, which revolve around recovering his imagined inheritance from his family members and acquaintances, all of whom face brutal deaths in the process. *Cruddy* once again confirms Barry's skill at conveying children's and adolescents' perspectives, desires, and fears. She shuns idealization and even happy ends: "*Cruddy* doesn't simply remove the imagined 'ribbons and bows' associated with sweet dreams of girlhood, it slices them to bits and drenches them in blood."[64]

Emphasizing how girls' diaries function as public objects, Rachel Miller argues that such diaries "offer readers a textual body upon which they can perform an autopsy of a public crisis that has evacuated the actual girl's body from the world."[65] Building on the argument of the overlap, even elision, between body and diary, especially in handwritten and drawn diaries, Miller reminds us that Barry used inkbrush to write the first version of *Cruddy*, strengthening the mark-making facet of writing.[66] Miller takes Hillary Chute's understanding of girl's diaries as synecdoches for girl's bodies further,[67] to suggest that diaries like *Cruddy*, which are not really comics, reflect the medium specificity of comics since their focalization through a "fictional protagonist as the primary composer of the text replicates the nature of embodiment that seems to be medium-specific to comics."[68]

---

[62] Barry, *Cruddy*, n. p.
[63] Exceptions include the slap Lynda's mother doles out to the young Lynda in *What It Is* (66).
[64] Kirtley, *Lynda Barry*, 82.
[65] Miller, "Diary as Body," 101.
[66] Miller, "Diary as Body," 105.
[67] Miller, Diary as Body," 108.
[68] Miller, "Diary as Body," 117.

Figure 2.5 Portrait of Roberta and Cookie from *Cruddy*, 12. Copyright Lynda Barry.

Another way in which *Cruddy* is embodied is through the many frontal portraits preceding the chapters in *Cruddy*. Roberta's unsmiling portrait in dark orange tones on the cover stares unflinchingly at the reader, with a suggestion of the partially cracked front teeth, one of the many signs of physical violence on Roberta's body. Another one is the nose broken by her mother by banging a telephone on it when Roberta was desperately calling for her dog Cookie, who had been drowned in a nearby river by her mother. Inside, we first encounter Roberta and the sleeping Julie almost entrapped in an elaborate frame, reflecting the absence of privacy and space in Roberta's home.[69] The second portrait is more devastating as it shows a bald, eleven-year-old Roberta holding Cookie soon after she was found by the police in the wake of the bloody road trip with her father (Figure 2.5).[70]

---

[69] Barry, *Cruddy*, n. p.
[70] Barry, *Cruddy*, 12.

"We looked bad and crusty. The caption called me the Mystery Child and the story underneath told of my shocking condition and amnesia," Roberta tells us.[71] We soon realize that this amnesia was faked so that she did not have to talk about the murders and the hidden suitcases full of money. Just like on the cover, the girl in the portrait looks at us directly, with empty eyes. And once again Roberta's body extends beyond the frame. Such a close-up strengthens the portrait's immediacy and intimacy while highlighting the heavy constraints and lack of exits in Roberta's situation.

The final portrait shows Roberta smoking a cigarette she had taken from the bag of her newly found friend, Vicky Talluso.[72] While still looking directly at the reader, Roberta is further away from her readers than in her other portraits. Her eyes are hollowed out and difficult to decipher, just like the television screen behind her. The darkness around her eyes suggests a distance, as if she is already lost to us, on the verge of becoming a ghost. These portraits of a doomed childhood draw the reader in, confirming that the horrors Roberta has been through have scarred her for life. This final portrait of Roberta also places her somewhere in between a child and an adult who, in her mother's absence, is forced to take care of herself and Julie.

Most of the illustrations in *Cruddy* are portraits, including two of Trina (one full and one with only her severed head), the sock monkey Roberta made while at the Christian Homes, where she had been taken in due to her purported amnesia. She was allowed to keep the intentionally ugly and stiff sock monkey.[73] For five years, Trina stored some of the money Roberta had taken from the suitcases which she would later use to escape the town with Vicky, Vicky's brother Stick who also commits suicide and two rich, almost perpetually drugged boys who had recently escaped from a psychiatric home for adolescents.

Another set of visual elements calling for a different kind of reader engagement are the maps included in the front and back matter of *Cruddy*. Building on Graham Huggan's observation that maps in arts and literature often parody official maps, and the officialness of maps, Nancy Pedri concludes that maps in comics "also challenge readers to adjust their understanding not only of the place that is being mapped, but of

---

[71]Barry, *Cruddy*, 14.
[72]Barry, *Cruddy*, 108.
[73]Barry, *Cruddy*, 141, 229.

the processes that go into mapmaking itself."⁷⁴ The objective, rationalized endeavor of mapping becomes a highly personalized tool to convey specific perspectives and to highlight what the narrator deems as ultimate points of interest. Although Pedri is writing about comics journalist, Guy Delisle's *Pyongyang*, which is a very different kind of diary from *Cruddy*, her observation that the "cartoonist's hand is everywhere" also holds for Barry's illustrated novel to the extent that her hand becomes a stand-in for Roberta's hand,⁷⁵ giving her full control of the narrative, including its visual, world-making aspects. Control is one of the central concerns of *Cruddy*, with Roberta committing suicide to get her happy ending and to make public the story she never told about the violent, death-ridden road trip with her father.

The reliance on maps underscores both the aspect of the road novel that *Cruddy* closely interacts with and the sense of place of Barry's child characters. In the afterword to *The Good Times Are Killing Me,* for instance, Barry writes:

> What is childhood? Where is it located? My street, the street that serves as the setting of this story, is still vivid in my memory and all of us are still kids, all of us still alive and shouting. . .⁷⁶

While most of the other children in Barry's comics are often limited to the typical spaces of home, neighborhood street, and school, Roberta's space, after being dumped into her father's car by her mother, expands to horrific proportions, covering the most destitute and abandoned of areas. This is illustrated by the maps in *Cruddy*, with only one of the four maps referring to Roberta's neighborhood, and the other two tracing the route followed by Roberta and her father through small towns and marked with crosses of the dead bodies they left behind. The final map zooms in on the shifting space of "dreamland," where a rundown motel next to a US Airforce testing site, run by Roberta's father's stepmother, becomes the site where the horrific road trip ends, with Roberta dealing her father a potentially fatal blow to save herself. The three maps, and especially the Dreamland map, also serve as

---

⁷⁴Nancy Pedri, "Re-Visualizing the Map in Guy Delisle's *Pyongyang*," *Arborescences,* no. 4 (2014): 99–114, 112. https://doi.org/10.7202/1027434ar.
⁷⁵Pedri, "Re-Visualizing the Map," 101.
⁷⁶Barry, "Afterword," *Good Times,* n. p.

implicated treasure maps, since finding the money also implies knowledge of the murders that had taken place before the suitcases were found.

As mentioned above, Miller compellingly shows how *Cruddy* adopts comicitous devices, especially embodiment and the alternation between the first-person narration of the diary and the images, to convey a deeply traumatic story with raw immediacy. For Gardner, "it is the discovery of comics' unique ability to represent the impossible demands of trauma, memory, and narration that has made it increasingly a dynamic and even urgent medium for life writing."[77] In the same vein, Marianne Hirsch suggests comics are "biocular texts": "Asking us to read back and forth between images and words, comics reveal the visuality and thus the materiality of words and the discursivity and narrativity of images."[78] This hybridity calls for complex readings and responses. Comics involve readers in ways that are strikingly different from texts, activating multiple registers of interpretation, oscillating between dialogue, narrative voices outside speech balloons and perhaps, most importantly, the visual register through the multiple clues offered by compositions and styles.

Barry's comics had already established an unabashed voice, privileging a distinctive kind of humor which refused to be present on a serial basis and was often replaced by a certain sadness and even critique of the imperfections structuring our everyday experiences. By fully adopting the ink brush, Barry's expressive style traded sharp, pointy lines for rounded ones and focused increasingly on child characters. In addition, the illustrated diaries reveal a desire to elaborate on the personal. Barry's move toward more autobiographical comics seems inevitable, in hindsight, with *One Hundred Demons* introducing a certain instability to the notions of both autobiography and autofictionality which are examined later, in Chapter 3. The multiple connections between girlhood and childhood in Barry's comics are discussed in more detail in Chapter 4. The final section of this chapter turns to the demon-making exercise in *One Hundred Demons* to introduce Barry's comics manuals.

---

[77]Gardner, "Autography's Biography," 6.
[78]Marianne Hirsch, "Editor's Column: Collateral Damage," *PMLA* 119, no. 5 (2004): 1209–15, 1213. Hirsch takes up Peggy Phelan's concept of biocularity used to descibe Samuel Beckett's "reading of images as words, words as images" (1212). Watson and Smith also refer to the specificity of biocularity in graphic memoirs (Smith and Watson, *Reading Autobiography*, 118–19).

Comics-making

While Chapters 3 and 4 interweave explorations of Barry's specific teachings and techniques, this section introduces Barry's comics manuals and their central teaching figures—the multi-eyed sea monster or Sea-Ma, the magic cephalopod and the Near-Sighted Monkey, whom we already encountered briefly— notions of fluid and concentrated creation, and the centrality of techniques that are often looked down upon such as copying, tracing, cutting and coloring.

The relatively small, intimate horizontal format of *One Hundred Demons* shares close affinities with Barry's first comics collections which only allowed for two panels per page. It also echoes the form of the handscroll painted by the sixteenth-century monk, Hakuin Ekaku, reproduced in Stephen Addiss' *The Art of Zen* book as an example of the One Hundred Demons exercise. Similar to *Fun Home*, the front and back matter are adorned with childhood, and girlhood, objects (numerous decorative flowers, Mary Jane shoes, purse, a dancing young Lynda, mascara, lipstick) and the demon-stories in the book, such as the multi-eyed sea monster, louse and of course, several appearances of a monkey. Just like with *Picture This*, Barry's husband Kevin Kawula, who also appears in five stories in the book, is credited with helping with the watercolors and "demon illustration." Somewhat rare for most comic books and graphic novels, a book design team including Barry herself, Amie Z. Gleed, and Tom Greenfelder are also acknowledged. This highlights the extent to which the conceptualization of the book as an object played an important role.

Instead of an ex-libris, *One Hundred Demons* offers a "Your Message Here" box. By replacing a declaration of ownership with a means of communication, Barry unsettles the typical reader relationship with a book by encouraging a form of interaction that entails producing something, beginning with a message and ending, ultimately, with the picturing, and consequent purging, of the reader's own demons. For *The Greatest of Marlys* collection, the ex-libris shows Marlys holding up the lined square, which begins with "My Friend" as Marlys informs the reader: "Excuse me, but, this book belongs to . . ."[79]

Eszter Szép suggests that the "demons are not simple creatures but complex structures of experience (. . .) they are connected to Barry's

---

[79]Lynda Barry, *The Greatest of Marlys* (Drawn & Quarterly, 2016), front matter.

understanding of images."[80] These understandings are entrenched in and influenced by Barry's memories, concretized in *One Hundred Demons* but resurfacing in her comics both preceding and following it: themes such as childhood, dancing and smells acquire specific visual forms that are closely connected to Barry's earlier work. In addition, the very first demon-story, "Head Lice and My Worst Boyfriend," combines Barry's childhood memories of a crush and her relationship with the radio journalist and producer, Ira Glass. This first story can be seen as a transitional work, combining the key themes of Barry's early comics, unbalanced adult relationships often based on misunderstanding, and the childhood struggle to fit in and be popular. A crucial difference, as announced by the autobifictionalography label, is the openly autobiographical nature of these stories, with the precise degree of autobiographical information left to conjecture.

In performing the demons exercise, *One Hundred Demons* resuscitates a string of autobiographical episodes, some of which have already been discussed in Chapter 1. The exercise is a form of free ink painting and the artist is encouraged to follow the strokes of the brush to see which demons emerge forth. As Barry informs us, through ventriloquizing the multi-eyed sea monster, the demons that emerged were unexpected and that "(a)t first they freaked her, but then she started to love watching them come out of her paint brush."[81] This brief warning points toward the obstacles in making something and the necessity to persevere. These opening pages also establish a certain degree of fluidity between the sea monster and Lynda. One page earlier, when Lynda is shown discovering Hakuin Ekaku's ink paintings in Addiss' book, the sea monster holds a different book entitled, *Yourself and Others: The Art of Torment* authored by I. B. A. Demon. The fluid and versatile demon is essentially of Barry's, and our own, making.

Barry began experimenting with sumi brush painting while working on *Cruddy,* both for the portraits and the text. *One Hundred Demons* brings another dimension to Barry's comics that will persist in her later books: for the front matter and the pages separating the chapters, Barry uses a combination of painting and intense collage, mentioning that she "really wanted to use every possible square inch. I wanted it to look like Fruit Loops and sparkle paint!"[82] Her mention of Fruit Loops and sparkle paint

---

[80]Szép, *Comics and the Body,* 74.
[81]Barry, *One Hundred Demons,* 12.
[82]Kirtley, *Lynda Barry,* 152

emphasizes the "girly" dimension of the collages separating and announcing the demons. Just like the portraits in *The Good Times Are Killing Me,* the collages in *One Hundred Demons* introduce an additional, evocative dimension transmitted through the materiality of the pasted objects. Collage becomes a means of mediating different techniques, allowing paintings, which are supposed to be hung on a wall and appreciated individually instead of in a sequence, to productively enter and contribute to the realm of the book. Paintings and isolated images (for Barry also isolates panels in the collages) acquire a degree of movement through the collaged materials and the layered backgrounds.

Chute has likened Barry's collages to the Pattern and Decoration movement which began in the 1970s and which introduced arts and crafts relegated to the domestic space and often made by women to the museum space:[83] Miriam Schapiro made femmages or feminist collages, often consisting exclusively of fabric, Joyce Kozloff made rich, repetitively patterned hanging works, including maps, and Robert Kushner made art inspired by textile patterns. Olga Michael points out how, in contrast to the Pattern and Decoration artists, who sought to introduce crafts to the museum space and the cultural legitimation associated with it, Barry opts for an easily diffused book form, accessible for a broad set of readers who could also be inspired to create their own art.[84] Recalling Ann Cvetkovich's observations on the creative processes of contemporary women artists, Michael considers "the female process of crafting as a significant means of survival in a 'depressive culture,' which rejects women's art as unworthy."[85]

In the same vein, Barry incorporates forgotten or waste material in her collages that often stems from domestic or feminine spaces and print culture. She associates the three-dimensional nature of these collages with "bumpiness," capturing how the reading process is altered, becoming a task of decoding surfaces and depth instead of piecing information linearly and

---

[83]Chute, *Graphic Women*, 110.
[84]Olga Michael, "Scrapbooking Caravaggio's *Medusa*, Reconfiguring Blake: *What It Is, One! Hundred! Demons!* and Lynda Barry's Feminist Intervention in the (Male) Artistic Canon," *ImageText* 9, no. 2 (2017), https://imagetextjournal.com/scrapbooking-caravaggios-medusa-reconfiguring-blake-what-it-is-one-hundred-demons-and-lynda-barrys-feminist-intervention-in-the-male-artistic-canon/.
[85]Michael, "Scrapbooking." Michael quotes from Ann Cvetkovich's *Depression: A Public Feeling* (Duke University Press, 2012).

sequentially.[86] From the many pieces of textiles, drawings and the occasional photograph collaged in *One Hundred Demons,* Barry also includes scraps of her pajamas, which "fram(e . . .) the front and back inside covers of the book. What she wears on her body, the book also wears."[87] The connection between Roberta's body and *Cruddy* that Miller elaborates on, is here transformed into a more playful but also all-encompassing *framing* of the book. The pajamas do not merely decorate the inside covers of the book, they also protect it and confirm the emotional and embodied affordances of the book.

Pointing out how the collages in *One Hundred Demons* were Barry's preferred components of the book, Susan Kirtley reads "the collected artefacts and ephemera along with personal essays in comic form (. . .) as a scrapbook of selfhood."[88] In making this connection, Kirtely emphasizes how scrapbooks blend the realms of the personal and the private. As a domestic activity aimed at preserving memories and consolidating family identities, scrapbooking is closely connected to women's worlds, often made and maintained by women.[89] The themes in *One Hundred Demons,* which include girlhood, Barry's mother and grandmother and her friendships, or attempts to make friends with other girls, perfectly complement the form of the scrapbook.[90] The scrapbooked materials also include girly memorabilia—differing, in this way, from the collage work in *Everything* and even *What It Is* and *Picture This*. Barry's childhood photographs, which are discussed in greater detail in Chapter 3, the drawn flowers, bits of fabric and braids, and generous use of glitter, all thrust us into the world of girlhood or girlness, to take up the title of one of the demon-stories in *One Hundred Demons*. This is enhanced by the predominantly pastel washes used for the backgrounds.

The final, "Outro" section of the book, which opens with a double-page photograph of Barry painting in her pajamas is a typical pitch by Barry, encouraging her reader to take part in the same creative exercises that generated the book: "Paint Your Demon. Come on! Don't you want to try it?? Just turn the page."[91] This final section, handwritten on lined yellow

---

[86] Chute, *Graphic Women,* 110.
[87] Chute, *Graphic Women,* 110.
[88] Kirtley, *Lynda Barry,* 153.
[89] Kirtley, *Lynda Barry,* 174. Kirtley elaborates on Susan Tucker, Katherine Ott, and Patricia Buckler's observations in their seminal critical anthology, *The Scrapbook in American Life* (Temple University Press, 2006).
[90] Kirtley, *Lynda Barry,* 174.
[91] Barry, *One Hundred Demons,* 219.

paper gives careful instructions and practical tips, next to photographs of the necessary tools for painting demons. At the very end, she tells us: "Discovering the paintbrush, inkstone, inkstick and resulting demons has been the most important thing to happen to me in years. TRY IT! You will dig it!"[92] This final disclosure emphasizes the personal importance of the inkbrush painting and demon-making exercise. Ending on this note of honesty and willingness to share a life-changing technique and experience can be considered a typically Lynda Barry trait: strengthening her rapport with the reader, her comics are not about teaching from a know-it-all perspective but rather a friendly sharing of tips and tricks for making art, and most importantly, enjoying making art. Intriguingly enough, Barry's photograph on this page is cut off above her nose and we do not see the rest of her face, including her eyes. But we do see the multi-eyed sea monster who has emerged on the page. This framing once again confirms the close connections between the artist and her monster. Kirtley adds that "Barry disrupts the self-depiction to point the reader back into the fictionalized world, simultaneously inviting the audience to create their own scrapbook of selfhood and shifting the focus from her persona."[93] Barry excels at this management of space and connections with her readers, sharing autobiographical details and comics-making tools but also stepping back to encourage readers to explore their own creativity.

Chapter 1 mentioned "Two Questions," Barry's contribution to the special issue of *McSweeney's Quarterly Concern* devoted to comics. Reprinted in portrait format in *What It Is*, each panel takes up a page and is adorned by an elaborate, colored border, and colored washes.[94] This episode captures the driving force behind Barry's teaching philosophy, which is based on challenging the judgmental voices preventing acts of drawing. After introducing the two questions concerning the quality of the drawing, Barry shifts to a childhood memory:

> When I was little, I noticed that making lines on paper gave me a certain floating feeling. It made me feel like I was both there and not there. The lines made a picture and the picture made a story. I wasn't the only kid it happened to. Every kid I knew could do it.[95]

---

[92]Barry, *One Hundred Demons*, 224.
[93]Kirtley, *Lynda Barry*, 173.
[94]Barry, *What It Is,* 123–32.
[95]Barry, "Two Questions."

Lynda Barry

While "Two Questions" does not provide exercises or other practical tools to create images and stories, it does highlight the close connections between Barry's teaching philosophy and her experiences of drawing as a child and as an adult. This episode gives more than simple drawing instructions: it explains why it is necessary to just draw without evaluating the outcome, to reach the state of the "unthinkable," or "to be able to stand not knowing long enough to let *something* alive take shape!"[96] While simply allowing lines and stories to flow on paper is no easy task, it emphasizes the need to create for the sake of creation and enjoyment, to allow forms and stories to emerge even when they seem poorly drawn. Creation without judgment is a central tenet in Barry's comics manuals. Eszter Szép identifies two important steps in Barry's comics-making exercises: "getting familiar with one's drawn marks" and "unlearning expectations and associations about them."[97] It is also possible to add a third tenet: "JUST SEE," which is written in bold, and taken from a diary entry from 1977 quoting Barry's art teacher, Marilyn Frasca.[98] Appearing on the opening pages of *Syllabus*, these words confirm how simply looking with all one's attention is central to Barry's teaching. Most art skills are based on strong and concentrated observation. Barry suggests a counterpoint, creative concentration, in *What It Is* and *Picture This*, and later in *Syllabus*,[99] to emphasize a form of automatic creation rooted in allowing images to emerge. This approach is summed up on top of a page early in *Making Comics*: "My way of teaching comics is not about developing characters. It's about waiting to see who shows up in certain circumstances."[100] In the two pages devoted to the question "Where do cartoon characters come from?" in *Syllabus*, Barry similarly emphasizes how "I never thought one up. . . . I just draw and—they seem to SHOW UP."[101]

Capturing the multiple genres interwoven in *What It Is*, Susan Kirtley introduces the graphic novel as a "visual Künstlerroman/writing workbook/philosophy text."[102] Yaël Schlick considers it "a primer for self-expression."[103] The intensely visual book begins with Barry's own development as an artist

---

[96]Barry, *What It Is*, 135.
[97]Szép, *Comics and the Body*, 60.
[98]Barry, *Syllabus*, 5.
[99]Barry, *Syllabus*, 3.
[100]Barry, *Making Comics*, 13.
[101]Barry, *Syllabus*, 144–5.
[102]Kirtley, *Lynda Barry*, 179.
[103]Schlick, "Selves and Texts," 34.

which is traced back to her fascination with images as a girl, before encouraging the reader to create through introspection and trying to understand the nature of images, imagination, and memory.[104] The close connection between creativity and personal experiences acquires a central role here. The book's use of collage, which takes over several pages instead of merely separating chapters as was the case in *One Hundred Demons,* fulfills a comparable role of blending private and public dimensions, but also goes further: the collages in *What It Is* "imply a broader story, rather than an individual one, and utilize the remains of childhood, in particular, to build a connection, rather than to shine insight into one individual's experience."[105] Connection is a key concept: Barry uses her art to uncover connections between her past and present but also to connect with her students and readers. These connections are facilitated by the drawn lines, the ink monsters and the messiness of collage. For Schlick the messiness in *What It Is* is both self-reflexive and experiential:

> It is a messiness particularly conducive to the writing of experience, of getting as close as we can to it in autobiographical writing, of bridging the rift between experience and its expression, and of questioning writing's ability to capture experience in the first place.[106]

Although *What It Is* is now presented as the writing counterpart to *Picture This*, the graphic novel was originally conceived as a companion piece to *One Hundred Demons,* to share the process behind writing it and to provide readers with a behind-the-scenes perspective, including how Barry herself turned to art and was trained by Marilyn Frasca.[107] The works Barry shows from these art classes are fascinating in hindsight. They first appear abstracted and pasted, forming three rows of two-panel paintings, while she gives a longwinded explanation to Frasca who, the text confirms, spent a long time looking at the works and made very brief comments.[108] Barry likens this looking to the "staring game" she played as a child in her trailer home, which made pictures come alive. Recalling a childhood activity *and* a state of being, Frasca's quiet teaching practice strengthens the connections between childhood and making art.

---

[104]Kirtley, *Lynda Barry,* 179.
[105]Kirtley, *Lynda Barry,* 181.
[106]Schlick, "Selves and Texts," 35–6.
[107]Brown, "Play and Playfulness," 127.
[108]Barry, *What It Is,* 118.

Lynda Barry

Figure 2.6 Barry's two-panel paintings, *What It Is*, 119. Copyright Lynda Barry. Used with permission from Drawn & Quarterly.

Below and slightly tangential to Lynda's explanation of her work to Frasca, the present-day Barry confides to the reader: "I copied the work of a photographer I had a crush on. He did 2 panel photos. I did 2 panel paintings just like him but I wouldn't admit it." [109] The centrality of the panels and the fact that they are arranged in pairs and always connected renders these early assignments comparable to comics, especially the two panel per page comics characterizing much of Barry's early work. They are also a microcosm or prototype of the form of books such as *What It Is*, *Picture This*, *Syllabus* and *Making This*, where the entire page is often a panel.

The page that follows offers a close-up of the panel paintings (Figure 2.6), which are strikingly realistic and bare, almost verging on the abstract. Devoid of the many lively figures that usually populate Barry's pages, and that appear on the margins of the page, the only movement seems to come

---

[109] Barry, *What It Is*, 118.

Key Texts

Figure 2.7 Portrait of Frasca and a variation on Giotto's *Madonna and Child* from *What It Is*, 117. Copyright Lynda Barry. Used with permission from Drawn & Quarterly.

from the cables and wires connected to the socket. The drawing above the reproduced paintings, in which Lynda the art student is shown holding the paintings, confirms their relatively small, intimate size, resembling the panels of a comic book, or at least the preparatory drawings for a comic, which can be bigger than the reproduction. Barry made a series of similar paintings called *Erotic Space* for the ten paintings per week assignment that was compulsory for Frasca's class. These paintings stand in sharp contrast to the kind of work Barry is now known for. Barry describes the series as "the one place in my work that images stayed out of."[110] In hindsight, however, the *Erotic Space* series seems to be the perfect, preliminary exercise for exploring and understanding the scope and compositional possibilities of regular, framed panels and how to eventually break away from them.

When recalling how Frasca never taught any technique, beyond showing Barry how to use a razorblade to sharpen a pencil, Barry also remembers

---

[110] Barry, *What It Is*, 120.

Figure 2.8 Giotto di Bondone, *Madonna and Child*, 1310/1315, National Gallery of Art in Washington.

her reaction to a poster of a Giotto painting in Frasca's office (Figure 2.7): while Lynda tries to evaluate the painting, Frasca simply draws her attention to the Madonna's teeth. Giotto's *Madonna and Child* from 1310/1315 is one of the rare Madonna paintings in which her teeth are visible (Figure 2.8). While Barry's reproduction introduces a fresh dynamism in the painting, with the Madonna looking directly at us, making it impossible to miss her gap-toothed smile, the Madonna's teeth in the original Giotto are far less obvious. This very human detail in the sober panel painting is highly intriguing not only because of its rarity—the Madonna almost never smiles wide enough to show her teeth—but because of the effect of "aliveness." This aliveness is not only about the painting itself, but also about how Lynda was looking at it: "The difference between trying to decide what I thought (of the painting) and having something actually happen to me while I was looking was my first clue about images."[111] Aliveness is then also connected

---

[111] Barry, *What It Is*, 118. My insertion in parentheses.

to how the painting is experienced, on its own terms, as it were, instead of imposing evaluative criteria of whether the painting is "likeable" or not. This approach echoes Mitchell's understanding of the social lives of the images. The infant Jesus in Barry's drawing makes the sign of benediction, the more common posture for these early medieval paintings, instead of reaching for the white rose in Mary's hand as he does in Giotto's painting. Through these details—the subtle, shy gap-toothed smile, the infant clutching his mother's finger and reaching out for a flower—the Florentine painter added a degree of naturalism and even humanity to the holy figures, breaking away from the tradition of stiff and distanced portrayals.

The gap-toothed smile, a moment of imperfection that adds to the beauty of the painting, also evokes gaps in general which are central to comics and to Barry's work, especially her combination of diverse image-making techniques. Gaps are present in the space between the two-panel paintings Barry made for her painting class. Numerous additional gaps are at work within the comics form, from the gutter to other ellipses contributing to the comics story. Finally, Barry herself seeks to bridge different kinds of gaps with her comics: between autobiography and creative processes, between creator and reader-viewer and between different expressive forms and techniques.

Very early in *Picture This*, the book following *What It Is,* we encounter a cephalopod staring straight at us: "The *Staring Cephalopod* invites you to <u>attend</u>! Please <u>attend</u> to the back of your Mind."[112] The cephalopod in black ink takes up most of the two double dictionary pages it is painted on. It personifies the importance of looking and *attending* to the mind. Attentive looking, both inwards, and outwards, at the world and at works of art are crucial prerequisites for drawing and creating. In an essay in comics form titled "On Copying," artist and researcher Ebony Flowers, one of Barry's former students, mentions that the students in her classes, similar to Barry's and Frasca's, do not discuss the pictures they make. This "helps carry the state between thinking and non-thinking over to looking at a picture. I am trying to teach students the difference between seeing a picture and watching it."[113] This approach grants equal importance to each picture, according a distinctive presence to every image. Like Barry, Flowers also

---

[112] Barry, *Picture This*, 8.
[113] Ebony Flowers, "On Copying," in *With Great Power Comes Great Pedagogy*, ed. Susan Kirtley, Antero Garcia, and Peter E. Carlson (University Press of Mississippi, 2020), 85–91, 91.

teaches students with diverse graphic skills and turns to children's drawings for inspiration, illustrating how every visual form can impart valuable insight into making images.

Both *What It Is* and *Picture This* were not planned like traditional books: instead, Barry began with a question and structured the books around it.[114] For *Picture This*, Barry explains in an e-mail interview with writer Jeff VanderMeer:

> I start with a question—in this case it was "What makes us stop drawing?" and I make pictures while I think about the question and pretty soon the book just sort of starts to gel. (. . .) with *Picture This* I had to have the pages up on a wall where I could see them. And there were a lot of pages so I had to create "walls" to put the pages on in my studio—there isn't enough wall space to do it—and it turns out the 4 x 8 sheets of blue styrofoam used for construction insulation worked perfectly. The sheets are long, lightweight, sturdy and really portable. So I could put about 40 pages on each sheet and drag the sheets all over the studio so I could move the pictures around until they started to interact with each other.

In the same interview, Barry adds that the "biggest challenge was accepting the fact that *Picture This* is a picture book. It was really hard for me to just put in pictures that weren't comics. I was worried about that. I've never been known for my drawing skills. I was worried that people would feel ripped off."[115] *Picture This*, then, takes the experimental and evocative collage work of *What It Is* a step further: it is, as already mentioned in Chapter 1, a picture book for adults. In contrast to *What It Is*, the intensity of the collages and the scope of the questions is reined in and loosely organized as an imaginary quarterly. The book's pages appear in the colors of the relevant season: blue for winter, green for spring, peach pink for summer, and an orange-brown for autumn.

Instead of autobiographical episodes, *Picture This* gives space to recurrent characters from Barry's comic strip world, Arna and her cousin Marlys.

---

[114]Jeff VanderMeer and Lynda Barry, "Amazon's Omnivoracious Interview with Lynda Barry," *Drawn & Quarterly*, November 30, 2010, accessed December 3, 2024, https://drawnandquarterly.com/press/amazons-omnivoracious-interviews-lynda-barry/.
[115]VanderMeer and Barry, "Omnivoracious Interview."

Barry herself adopts the avatar of the Near-Sighted Monkey, a practice that will continue in *Syllabus* where she tries on numerous playful personas. While small autobiographical moments still appear, most of the narration focuses on Arna and Marlys, with the Near-Sighted Monkey offering funny interludes alongside numerous coloring, copying, and cutting exercises. More often than not, the Near-Sighted Monkey faces the reader, looking directly at them, while her own eyes are hidden by the reflection of her glasses. A serially drawn meditating monkey also makes frequent appearances. As Barry explains through a 2011 notebook entry in *Syllabus*: "When I start feeling concerned that all the words I write be <u>very</u> smart and about something worthwhile, I find my urge to write replaced with an urge to draw monkeys."[116] The monkeys are both playful and meditative figures, offering an entry point into the world of drawing by being familiar and easy to draw.

Highly conscious of its unusual status as a picture book for adults, *Picture This*, following the precedent established by *What It Is*, questions the nature of artistic practice and why we stop indulging in it, while offering different prompts for image-making. These prompts themselves are often practices that are looked down upon, such as copying and coloring in, two techniques which occupy a prominent place in all of Barry's comics manuals. Like *One Hundred Demons*, the winter issue of *Picture This* also offers an unreliable table of contents, including the claim, "(i)n this Issue . . . We swim. We see icicles . . . We drink lemonade. We wear warm caps"[117]—suggestions that in themselves combine winter and summer activities and confirm the imaginary nature of the magazine. Barry adds another list, near a quickly drawn face, one of the many scribble heads we encounter later in the issue, illustrating the hesitation in drawing faces. This list includes "Dots, Lines, Blots, Stains (. . .) Beatnik art, Rabbits, Monsters, Smoking (. . .) Chickens, Giving Up."[118] As random as the list may seem, all its components appear in the issue. Smoking is a constant and both the Near-Sighted Monkey and Maybonne take regular puffs. Barry's comics also frequently show children smoking, with Roberta in *Cruddy* smoking regularly from a very early age. As shown in the previous chapter, the cigarette smoke is also a playful visual element. In *Picture This*,

---

[116] Barry, *Syllabus*, 9.
[117] Barry, *Picture This*, 11.
[118] Barry, *Picture This*, 11.

Lynda Barry

Figure 2.9 From *Picture This*, 10. Copyright Lynda Barry. Used with permission from Drawn & Quarterly.

the numerous advertisements for "Don't" cigarettes also offer an occasion to repurpose commercial rhetoric for ironic and humorous ends. True to magazine customs, a full-page advertisement for "Don't" appears behind the front cover and acknowledges the imaginary cigarette brand as the publication's main sponsor (Figure 2.9).

The key figures in this advertisement are a rabbit, a ghost, and an abstract stain figure, all three of which smoke. A collaged note and form promises schools "(a)n attractive colored wall chart entitled 'Why imaginary creatures smoke Don't.'"[119] "The imaginary cigarette with controllable smoke" promises "(i)maginary flavor, imaginary fun."[120] The Don't advertisements, which connect cigarettes to imagining, seem to incarnate the first, crucial obstacle preventing most people from making art after a certain age: we

---

[119]Barry, *Picture This*, 10.
[120]Barry, *Picture This*, 10.

don't draw, don't make because we don't think it is sufficiently good enough. The don't's that prevent us from creating are as omnipresent as cigarette advertisements. These don't's, as we see very early in *Picture This*, also prevent engagement with basic artistic exercises that are deemed too easy and too childish, such as coloring, tracing and copying. Copying, however, remains a crucial basis for all art-making. In the fine arts, it was and is a practice that is encouraged in order to learn directly from the masters.[121] Barry's comics manuals are peopled with animals and monsters that she encourages her students and readers to copy. Her own tracings of her students' drawings are a means of understanding and learning new forms. In *Picture This*, the prejudices associated with these easier and less original artistic practices are voiced by the older Maybonne and her sister Marlys and directed at Arna, the main focalizer or protagonist of *Picture This* who, like the model reader, tries Barry's, or the Near-Sighted Monkey's exercises.

"Coloring books are bad for you (. . .) they wreck your imagination," Maybonne tells Arna at a kitchen table, where we only see Arna's hands coloring in a drawing. Maybonne, smoking Don't's, adds: "It's not creative."[122] Surrounding this panel are examples of colored-in templates of several creatures that are traced from the cardboard cutouts on the opposite page: while one set of stenciled creatures remains uncolored, the other two are partially or fully painted over, showing how coloring bestows the creatures with a new life. These panels push the panel with Maybonne's claims into a corner and contradict her claims.

A few pages later, Barry turns to the color blue, showing how layers of paint can transform the shade and intensity of the colors. She also introduces the factor of time and waiting, since each layer has to dry before a new layer is added and suggests copying a monkey or making another drawing while waiting:

> We wait while drawing and we draw while waiting. When we get stuck we move our brush along. We take it where it likes to go, the certain shapes it likes to make in the margins will help us.[123]

---

[121] The Copyists program at the Metropolitan Museum, established in 1872, followed the footsteps of the Louvre, which established the tradition when it opened in 1793.
[122] Barry, *Picture This*, 19.
[123] Barry, *Picture This*, 22.

Here Barry introduces the principle of automatic drawing that is central to her teaching, encouraging motricity, accustoming the hand to make lines and forms without imposing a set of goals and outcomes. Notably the above words are written within painted lines, the outcome of another meditative exercise based on a repetitive gesture. Inspired by Barry's classes, which include a tandem copying exercise in *Making Comics*,[124] Flowers encourages her students to work in pairs to copy the drawings made by each other while they make it. This "drawing to watch what happens" is distinct from the "drawing to illustrate a premeditated thought or mental image."[125] Flowers opens her comics essay by elaborating on the contrast between copying in academic practice, which counts as plagiarism and is strictly forbidden, and its centrality in learning how to draw.[126] She reminds her class, and us, that copying is important for comics and other drawn forms because it helps us to understand and accept how we draw.

Copying can also help break a drawing block as suggested by the chicken in winter exercise. In *Picture This*, the Van Dyke figure suggests making an "inexpensive and effective" "chicken in winter" as a recipe to counter sadness, a kind of visual chicken soup for the soul.[127] This involves drawing the outline of the chicken on "dark moody paper." Barry provides the outline just in case the reader feels incapable of drawing a chicken. The aim is to glue "wads of sadness" made of cotton wool or tissue paper to the chicken's body (wads that are comparable to balls of bread Barry playfully encourages readers to make in the "Coping with Stress for under One Dollar" comic, see Figure 1.4). As Barry warns us early in the exercise, the resulting chicken will be far from beautiful but it will be an effective guardian chicken. Instead of aesthetic perfection, the goal of this chicken made of different textures is to offer comfort. This echoes the concerns of both picturing the invisible and expanding comics that are broached in Chapters 3 and 4, respectively. While the chicken does not appear as frequently as other figures, such as the monkey and the sea monster, it does reappear next to the Near-Sighted Monkey on a syllabus cover and a little later bears the label of teaching assistant in *Syllabus*.[128]

---

[124]Barry, *Making Comics*, 70–1.
[125]Flowers, "On Copying," 89.
[126]Flowers, "On Copying," 85.
[127]Barry, *Picture This*, 32.
[128]Barry, *Syllabus*, 11.

Like copying, coloring books offer a means of overcoming hesitation to draw and color. Barry recalls a childhood memory when she could not draw any more: "If someone had given me a blank drawing book, I would have been too afraid of ruining it to use it. Blank pages made me nervous, but I could trust a coloring book."[129] The coloring book is hardly a new concern for Barry. As mentioned earlier, she had already made the *Naked Ladies, Naked Ladies, Naked Ladies* coloring book for adults in 1984 which, in a typical Barry-like mélange of genres and conventions, had been preceded by an exhibition at the Linda Farris Gallery in Seattle.[130] The coloring book juxtaposes the experiences of an adolescent girl recalling her encounters with "dirty" pictures of naked ladies. Underneath the playful, sometimes explicit pictures, the adolescent voice shares the secretive rituals of looking at naked women and drawing naked women and phalluses on school walls and in schoolbooks. The girl's fascination for naked women is first fueled by curiosity and finding pleasure in the forbidden and the sensual. But the women eventually become a standard of comparison for the narrator's own and her classmates' changing bodies, and the perspective changes from identification to alienation as the girls become increasingly aware of and dissatisfied with their own bodies. However, Barry's portraits, both in their painted and line drawn forms, are far removed from the Playboy playing cards they ironically rework by showing a variety of women, of different ethnicities and age groups. Chute considers the *Naked Ladies, Naked Ladies, Naked Ladies* coloring book as an invitation to readers to "'fill in' the narrative with their own experience" and that the coloring book itself "implies interactivity and interaction," much in the vein of the narrator's sharing of secrets.[131] This is a central tenet of Barry's comics manuals. While this section introduces and briefly explores the possibilities of interaction ensconced in the exercises, the "Teaching Comics" and "Expanding Comics" sections in Chapter 4 elaborate further on these elements.

Throughout its four issues, *Picture This* offers numerous images to color, copy, trace, and even cut and paste. The summer issue, which focuses on color, includes the Near-Sighted Monkey's own coloring book.[132] This issue also leads the reader step by step into the world of color, beginning

---

[129]Barry, *Picture This*, 102.
[130]Kirtley, *Lynda Barry*, 33–9; Chute, *Graphic Women*, 98–108.
[131]Chute, *Graphic Women*, 105.
[132]Barry, *Picture This*, 181–5.

Figure 2.10 "Sear's Portrait Marlys," from *Picture This*, 145. Copyright Lynda Barry. Used with permission from Drawn & Quarterly.

with an exercise relying on one color alone, and then combining an increasing number of shades. Earlier, in the spring issue, next to the "Sear's Portrait Marlys," with an uncharacteristically demure and poised Marlys, Barry suggests coloring, in the absence of art supplies, with food color combined with water and applied with cotton swabs (Figure 2.10).[133] This is comparable to the outro in *One Hundred Demons* and the reproduction of several paintbrushes across a double spread in *Picture This*, when the Near-Sighted Monkey encourages readers to use the brush instead of the phone, emphasizing the importance of using one's hands.[134] In the "Sear's Portrait Marlys," the necessary tools are taped below the portrait and the entire page is covered with dots made by swabs dabbed in different combinations of food coloring. Technique, tools, tests and the final outcome are all combined

---

[133] Barry, *Picture This*, 145.
[134] Barry, *Picture This*, 172–3.

on the same page, merging the different temporalities of the creative act while also transforming it into an exemplary and instructional image.

The disparagement of color comes up in the "Essay Topic of the Week" for the spring issue of *Picture This*. We return to the same kitchen table scene from the beginning of the book, but this time we see only Marlys and Arna and it's Marlys who exclaims: "You don't got it Arna. That's why you color," while we hear Maybonne declaring again: "Creative people don't color, copy, or trace. That's only for people with no imagination."[135] Toward the end of *Picture This*, in the fall issue, we see Maybonne, Marlys and Arna still around the kitchen table with Maybonne suggesting that instead of coloring they should draw from their imagination.[136] What Barry's manuals strive after is a combination of automatic, unconscious drawing, drawing with constraints, and drawing using the imagination.

Barry offers additional repetitive exercises in the winter issue of *Picture This*, such as making small dots, foreshadowing the colored dots of the "Sear's Portrait Marlys." Such exercises have an almost therapeutic, calming function while serving to activate the hand.[137] A spiral is introduced as a specific kind of line by the heart-broken Mr. Trunk in *Picture This*: "portable, reliable and takes up unbearable time and space and thoughts that torment. IT gives us an active place to rest and be. (. . .) A line curled up in space + time."[138]

As Barry mentions in a panel pasted on one of the lined sheets of *Picture This*, "(t)he worst thing I can do when I'm stuck is to start thinking and stop moving my hands."[139] Many of her exercises are consequently short cuts to help unaccustomed hands take their first steps in drawing. The spring issue even offers a doodle cheat sheet.[140] Another exercise Barry proposes to encourage the drawing and painting hand to move freely and to make is stain figures and faces. This is introduced in a brief episode that is comparable to the autobiographical moment opening *What It Is*, when the young Lynda stares so intently at the few images plastered on the trailer walls that they begin to move. In *Picture This* it is Arna, next to a sleeping Marlys, who watches the ceiling acquire new shades and forms during a

---

[135] Barry, *Picture This*, 100.
[136] Barry, *Picture This*, 194.
[137] Barry, *Picture This*, 34.
[138] Barry, *Picture This*, 69.
[139] Barry, *Picture This*, 120.
[140] Barry, *Picture This*, 128–9.

spell of heavy rain.[141] Across a double-page spread, Barry transforms a few blobs into moving images. These are comparable to the opening exercises of *Picture This* which involve torn and cut-out scraps of paper to make a range of figures and familiar objects like houses and trees.[142]

Unlike the next two comics manuals, *Picture This* does include two instances of more traditional comics drawing exercises in which Barry breaks down Marlys' face in twelve steps and Arna's face in ten steps.[143] *Syllabus* and *Making Comics*, in contrast, adapt Ivan Brunetti's cartooning manual to create generic figures as a starting point for more intuitive character studies. Instead of the large hardcover formats of *What It Is* and *Picture This*, both *Syllabus* and *Making Comics* adopt the smaller, humbler form of the composition book. In addition to bringing in a very specific and even nostalgic materiality, the smaller format of the composition books is both familiar and intimate. It also reflects the centrality of notebooks in Barry's teaching and in her own work as a hybrid entity where diary entries, drawing experiments, assignments, and the scrapbook archiving of materials coexist. In *Syllabus*, a typed diary entry dated February 14, 2011 clarifies (with comp books underlined in red ink): "Using comp books and handwriting and the natural human instinct for storytelling as a means of transferring something from one person to another. Transferring what?"[144] A handwritten text next to the column of typed text seems to offer an answer to the question: "I need *students* to *help* me *figure out* how images move."[145] The notebook, then, also becomes a means of transmitting, playing with and understanding the comics form.

Color and copying continue to play a central role in Barry's comics and art philosophy. This is already evident on the third page in *Syllabus*, where we encounter three towering creatures, two dogs and a monster in the middle, with a monkey-like figure in its stomach, who leans toward the reader. Each of the monster's uneven, floating hands are marked as "Hand," with each letter of the word touching a finger. The image seems to bear a title or at least a caption at the bottom: "Coloring things in by hand as study aid."[146]

---

[141] Barry, *Picture This*, 56.
[142] Barry, *Picture This*, 24–30.
[143] Barry, *Picture This*, 176–9.
[144] Barry, *Syllabus*, 9.
[145] Barry, *Syllabus*, 9.
[146] Barry, *Syllabus*, 3.

Key Texts

Figure 2.11 "The Hand," from *Syllabus*, 8. Copyright Lynda Barry. Used with permission from Drawn & Quarterly.

In addition to emphasizing the importance of making by hand, *Syllabus* also translates concerns around the creation and circulation of images expressed in *What It Is* and *Picture This* into practical exercises adjusted to the rhythm of the semester, moving away from autobiographical moments to focus on creativity. The space and organization of the university classroom and working with students often new to comics-making play a strong role.

A few pages later, a hand traced in ink wash and decorated with glittering studs explains the purpose of the course: "A semester of writing and drawing by hand until we arrive at the *unthinkable* and put it in a book" (Figure 2.11).[147] The emphasis on making by hand is reinforced by the "by HAND" note Barry adds next to a wandering line exercise below the palm. Also visible on the page are familiar components of Barry's books, including the entire alphabet and single-digit numbers and the multi-eyed

---

[147]Barry, *Syllabus*, 8.

sea monster. Making by hand is reinforced by the "pulled lines" that appear on the page forming the background. Most of the pages in *Syllabus* are covered by pulled lines, either in crayon, as is the case here or in pencil and, occasionally, in brush. Similar lines mark the background of many of Barry's other books, including *One Hundred Demons, What It Is, Picture This*. They are, as explained in an Instagram post by Barry from April 12, 2024, not merely decoration but an exercise: "One of the things I hope you have at the end of our time together as a class is knowing your compbook can help you play around and figure things out. We've been 'pulling lines' with brush and ink in class. I use my brush to draw lines in my compbook all the time."

"Pulling" lines is very close to traditional drawing techniques where students are asked to cover pages with lines in different directions to improve line quality and application of diverse drawing and painting tools. This exercise is meditative and improves motricity, similar to the spiral exercises mentioned above. The backgrounds full of pulled lines add a layer of three-dimensionality to the contents of the notebook, which always consist of at least two pages pasted on top of each other with additional collaged material. The composition book combines diary, which Barry's students have to keep, exercise book and even keepsake book, storing memorable objects. The standardized, omnipresent object becomes a highly personalized and further personalizable one.

The syllabus Barry shares with us is for the "Unthinkable Mind" class. The class was originally called "What It Is: Manually Shifting the Image" and began with a brief but elaborately visual, four-page syllabus that is also included in the graphic novel. This contains more practical details instead of actual exercises, with the exception of the fourth and final page of the syllabus.[148] Titled "Classroom Rules," this empty gridded page is intended for jotting down the rules, which are specified later in the book.[149] It has playing card symbols in almost each of the twelve panels with a tiny, final slot for students to invent their own symbol.

Barry's teaching and artistic influences acknowledged in *Syllabus* were already mentioned in Chapter One. Many of these colleagues, including Ivan Brunetti and Dan Chaon, alongside Matt Groening and Ryan Knighton, author and creative writing professor known for his memoir on becoming

---

[148] Barry, *Syllabus*, 7.
[149] Barry, *Syllabus*, 55.

blind, are announced as guest speakers on the penultimate page of the syllabus. The trademark characters introduced by Brunetti in *Cartooning* (based on the intensive fifteen-week course Brunetti taught at Columbia College Chicago), are one of the first exercises in both *Syllabus* and *Making Comics*: Brunetti introduces figures with simple shapes and curved arms and legs to create motion.[150] Barry also adapts a storytelling exercise from Dan Chaon called "Story House" to construct a visual story step by step, starting with a character and building different kinds of scenes around it.[151]

While *Making Comics* also adopts the form of a composition notebook, it is more structured than *Syllabus*, with one exercise following another. It often steps away from the university classroom setting with more generalized exercises, which dominate the content of the book. In contrast to *Syllabus*, the pulled lines on the background pages are often painted. Both books follow a similar structure, beginning with a brief introduction to theory, both of which go back to childhood and foreground the inextricability of drawing and writing. Barry also draws attention to the "aliveness" of children's drawings, which can be difficult to imitate. While both books generously incorporate the drawings of Barry's students, from the very young to university students, the opening pages of *Making Comics* are devoted to exploring the expressivity of children's drawings and how children are fluent in visual language: "This language is what I'm trying to teach in my comics classes. This language moves up through your hand and into your head. Young children are native speakers."[152] The connection with children's drawings will be explored further in Chapter 4.

In contrast to *What It Is* and, to a lesser extent, *Picture This*, both *Syllabus* and *Making Comics* reflect more briefly on the broader nature of images, where drawing comes from, the temporality of drawing, and notions of "bad drawing." These serve as necessary prerequisites to facilitate all kinds of drawing before zooming in on teaching how to make comics, covering basic tools, character design and storytelling techniques. Just like in *Picture This*, coloring plays an important role. *Syllabus* also devotes several pages to the importance of using difficult, unwieldy materials like crayons to color. Crayons are introduced early, in one of the first sessions of the class

---

[150]Barry, *Syllabus*, 17; Barry, *Making Comics*, 39.
[151]Barry, *Making Comics,* 184–8.
[152]Barry, *Making Comics*, 8.

Lynda Barry

exercises reproduced in *Syllabus*.[153] The mix of free drawing exercises and rapid, specific tasks combining collective and individual work are illustrated by drawings by Barry and from her collection of student drawings, which also include drawings rescued from trash. These pasted drawings effectively illustrate the exercises without being proscriptive. They become almost a means of sharing, facilitating exchange, just like Barry's tips and exercises. In Barry's hands, comics, and drawing and writing in general, becomes a collective activity. More than the actual exercises, the books are also means of sharing images and sources of images. *Syllabus*, for instance, ends with a smiling monster with twiggy hands and a fire burning above its head. Barry writes next to it:

> Draw me
> Trace me copy me
> Ink me
> Write
> Me
> A
> Story
> We can
> Both
> Be
> In[154]

In encouraging tracing and copying, Barry offers multiple lives to the monster, making it a collaborative entity opening new creative possibilities despite being based on copying. The fire burning above its head could symbolize the "burning idea" mentioned on the back cover of *Syllabus*, inscribed on the trapezoid body of another creature with multiple legs and fantastic arms and an idea fire above its head. Its geometrical forms and malleable limbs confirm its affiliation to Brunetti's cartoon figures.

Such collaboration, as suggested earlier, is one in which Barry eagerly partakes. Her courses, are likewise about learning together, with Barry sharing exercises and tips that she continues to incorporate into her own practice. A coffee stain space baby, for instance, is accompanied by a note

---

[153] Barry, *Syllabus*, 48.
[154] Barry, *Syllabus*, 200.

on the relevance of these exercises and how Barry uses them herself: "These are exercises I go back to when I'm out of ideas. They open doors and windows I'd forgotten. Improvisational line and shape carry me on."[155] The learning path Barry proposes is no linear, straightforward trajectory, even if it is contained on lined sheets and in a compositional notebook. Instead, the process is far more intuitive and organic, just like her drawing exercises and suggestions.

In addition to its proximity to the stain picture making exercise we encountered in *Picture This*, the "space baby" image "found" in a coffee stain recalls the many staring exercises that reveal and animate images in Barry's earlier books.[156] Such images are in a certain way comparable to ghost images or pentimento, which refers to reworked and hence covered parts of a painting (and also to repent or *pentirisi*, the root of pentimento). Shiamin Kwa uses this concept to unpack the multiple temporalities and tensions between drawing and painting in Jerry Moriarty's painted and drawn memoir, *Whatsa Paintoonist?*, in which he recreates himself as a young girl, who becomes a constant companion in the book as he visits family members.[157] Ghosts, as we will see in Chapter 3, and as we already saw in the case of the Aswang in Chapter 1, play an important in Barry's works. The pentimento or ghost image is also useful for understanding the images that Barry encourages to emerge from stains. Here the act of repainting, or moving the brush serves to make the image visible.

Chapter 3 on Critical Themes and Questions, builds on the elements introduced here and in Chapter 1 to further elaborate on the diverse kinds of ghostly and invisible images interacting in Barry's works. It then examines the role of writing and comics as a hybrid language in Barry's manuals. The chapter unpeels some of the many textures discernible in Barry's graphic novels and the role of individual and collective archiving. The final section of the chapter dives deeper into Barry's form of life writing, already broached at the beginning of this chapter. Like her collages, her autobiographical and autofictional episodes negotiate the personal and fictional, individual and collective, and even universal memories.

---

[155] Barry, *Making Comics*, 94.
[156] Barry, *Making Comics*, 94.
[157] Shiamin Kwa, "Making Magic: Comics and the Ekphrastic Art of Almost There," in *The Routledge Companion to Art and Literature*, ed. Neil Murphy, W. Michelle Wang and Cheryl Julia Lee (Routledge, 2024), 290–306, 296–305.

CHAPTER 3
CRITICAL THEMES AND QUESTIONS

> That very idea that writing and painting and all of these things we call the arts are the same thing, that they come out of something that's lively. I mean even, even if you think of Art Spiegelman's (...) *Maus* (...) You can ask those same questions (...) Are those characters alive? Well, they're not alive in the way we are, but are they dead? Hell no.
>
> Lynda Barry (interview with Hillary Chute)[1]

This chapter opens with one of the most recurrent themes in Barry's graphic novels, beginning with *One Hundred Demons*: accessing and representing the invisible. This ranges from incorporating elements that are difficult to represent in words and images, such as music, dancing or smells to creating multisensory experiences. The chapter also discusses the symbolism of the demons and monsters that play a central role in *One Hundred Demons* and persist in Barry's other works, acquiring both friendly and threatening forms, personifying personal and creative anxieties.

In her quest to find lost images, often through automatic drawing practices, and in tracing the unrepresentable and unthinkable, Barry plays with the very limits of comics. Building on the notions of graphiation and trace, the chapter's first section also turns to concepts around animation (animatedness, animistic media) to delineate the basic components of Barry's approaches to image-making. It then elaborates on the role of writing and the childlike idiom Barry uses for many of her comics. Following a section on textures and Barry's use of collage, the chapter ends with the "autobifictional" form of life writing interwoven in Barry's illustrated novels and comics.

---

[1]Chute and Barry, "Lynda Barry," 60–1.

Lynda Barry

Picturing the Invisible[2]

In her article on shame in graphic memoirs, Sarah Richardson cites Adrienne Rich on the necessity of giving form to the invisible:

> Whatever is unnamed, undepicted in images, whatever is omitted from biography, censored in collections of letters, whatever is misnamed as something else, made difficult-to-come-by, whatever is buried in the memory by the collapse of meaning under an inadequate or lying language—this will become, not merely unspoken, but unspeakable.[3]

While Richardson mentions the role of "childhood shame around class, race and creative ability" in Barry's comics,[4] she focuses on the more confessional graphic memoirs of Art Spiegelman's *Maus* and Alison Bechdel's *Fun Home*. Barry's life writing, as we will see in the final section of this chapter is rarely confessional in the same way and often has a more interrogational tone, seeking to evaluate the impact of the past, to understand it or, simply, to remember.

This section focuses on Barry's recovery of forgotten, lost or invisible images and the importance she accords to them. Before being voiced, the unspeakable and the invisible is found through, for instance, uncovering and recovering the forgotten or the discarded (such as childhood drawings) that takes center stage in her comics. The layers introduced by these images and their archival dimensions are further unpacked in the third and final sections of this chapter on textures and life writing. Picturing the invisible in all its diversity, this section argues, is one of the foremost critical questions raised by Barry's comics.

The invisibles which play such a central role in Barry's comics are closely connected to the concept of trace. Philippe Marion's theory of graphiation or graphic enunciation transposes film scholar, André Gaudreault's concept

---

[2]An earlier version of this section appeared as: Maaheen Ahmed, "Tracing the Invisible: Lynda Barry's Comics," *Mediascapes* 22, no. 2 (2023): 35–51, https://rosa.uniroma1.it/rosa03/mediascapes/article/view/18635/17685.

[3]From Rich's 1976 coming-out speech "It is the Lesbian in us . . ." quoted in Sara Richardson, "'Perseveration on Detail': Shame and Confession in Memoir Comics," in *Cultural Excavation and Formal Expression in the Graphic Novel*, ed. Jonathan C. Evans and Thomas Giddens (Brill, 2013), 149–58, 155.

[4]Richardson, "Preservation on Detail," 150.

of monstration, which emphasizes the act of showing instead of telling.[5] Graphiation is also connected to Jacques Derrida's notion of *trace*, which has a strong connection to absences and the archive. While this section focuses on the absences and the invisibles behind drawn lines, the third section in this chapter elaborates on the archival work carried out by the trace.

The concept of animation and animatedness, based on Sianne Ngai's affect-based aesthetic theory and Shiamin Kwa's discussion of comics as an animistic medium,[6] can help us understand what Barry wants her images to do, beginning with the very search for images and their conjuring. This section shows how Barry deliberately seeks animatedness. Through rescuing drawings and images from trash, she breathes new life into them. *Making Comics* begins with an endorsement of the untutored style, of drawing the way we once drew as children which, for Barry, has a certain "aliveness" to it.[7] Such drawings, according to Barry, are impossible to copy or to "animate." Animation is also connected to her strategy for comics which, as we saw in the previous chapter, is "about waiting to see who shows up in certain circumstances."[8] Finally, animation or breathing life into images also plays a role in the many synesthetic experiences Barry generates through her comics, such as the demon of smells in *One Hundred Demons* and the representations of music and dancing that recur in most of her graphic narratives.

Many of Barry's comics are about seeking images and visualizing the invisible, reflecting her description of herself as an image wrangler.[9] These "invisibles"—themes and concerns that are wrangled with and accorded visual form—encompass: personal demons; the "power" of the image for channeling, communicating, and even healing; the mystery of image-making and creation; the inexpressibility of childhood; the aliveness of children's drawing and untutored drawings in general. The invisible is also connected to Barry's concern of tracing the sources of images, how they

---

[5]André Gaudreault, *From Plato to Lumière: Narration and Monstration in Literature and Cinema,* trans. Timothy Barnard (University of Toronto Press, 1997).
[6]Sianne Ngai, *Ugly Feelings* (Harvard University Press, 2007), 89–125; Shiamin Kwa, "Life Writing in Comics," in *The Cambridge Companion to Comics*, ed. Maaheen Ahmed (Cambridge University Press, 2023), 185–203.
[7]Barry, *Making Comics,* 4.
[8]Barry, *Making Comics,* 13.
[9]Kirtley, *Lynda Barry,* ix.

are transferred, and what they communicate. As we have already seen in the previous chapters, Barry books combine her own and found images, ranging from images in her imagination; images that emerge from automatic drawing exercises; images that she collages; images made by her students that were thrown away; images gifted to her or left over from her classes. All of these images are a means of getting closer to the invisible, of unpacking and surpassing self-judgment and the tension between idea and form.

The invisible in Barry's work is therefore not between the panels, as McCloud suggests in his comics theory, according to which the gutter becomes a space for readerly closure.[10] It is, instead, located in more universal, transmedial issues of the unsaid and the unsayable (as is the case with the demons populating *One Hundred Demons*), the not drawn or the undrawn (drawn and then erased), which stems from the desire of making ideas emerge and giving ideas an appropriate form. That said, Barry's invisibles rely on, and emerge through, the workings of comics as an invisible art, through comics-specific devices such as braiding and its counterpoint, weaving, which underpin the structure of comics and transmit meaning.[11]

As pointed out in the previous chapter, Barry's comics manuals openly challenge and undo notions of "bad" and "good" drawings, as a prerequisite for making comics and art in general. These moments are frequently illustrated through Barry's own drawing anxieties and those of her students. Barry's anxieties often go back to her childhood when, after a certain age and like many children, she was no longer considered sufficiently talented to continue taking writing and art electives.

We see the young Lynda trying in vain to draw "correctly" and despairingly failing at it on several occasions. One of these is the memory, already mentioned in Chapter 1, of trying to complete a test for a correspondence drawing school in *What It Is*. The young Lynda's fear of producing a "bad" drawing and failing was so strong that she did not succeed in copying the pictures and erased "with a sick feeling" to the extent that the paper was ruined.[12] A comparable moment of despairing and impossible drawing can be found in *Picture This,* when she recalls how she stopped drawing faces as a child and asked an older cousin for a drawing of a girl's face that

---

[10]See Scott McCloud, *Understanding Comics: The Invisible Art* (HarperPerennial, 1994).
[11]See Groensteen, *System of Comics*; Postema, *Narrative Structure*.
[12]Barry, *What It Is*, 78.

Critical Themes and Questions

Figure 3.1 Impossible drawing, doodles, stain heads, and the Near-Sighted Monkey with a sandwich from *Picture This,* 61. Copyright Lynda Barry. Used with permission from Drawn & Quarterly.

she could copy (Figure 3.1).[13] The face is broken down into different steps, beginning with the eyes, followed by the nose, the mouth, the chin, the neck and ending with the bust. The young Lynda however, never gets beyond the first step of eyes. The final image shows a distressed Lynda, surrounded by papers speckled with outlined, ghostly eyes without irises or lashes: "I *remember* trying to get the eyes to match *and being* yelled at for wasting paper. And I *remember* realizing I could not draw."[14] Barry connects this block to the act of drawing "in a certain way, with intention."[15] Abandoning intention, an act embodied by the squiggly, meandering lines surrounding the despairing Lynda, leaves room for the invisible to emerge.

---

[13]Barry, *Picture This*, 60–1.
[14]Barry, *Picture This*, 61.
[15]Barry, *Picture This*, 61.

Lynda Barry

Meandering lines frame the boundaries of the different components of the page. In the drawing above, with the Near-Sighted Monkey offering a grilled cheese sandwich to us, similar meandering lines float upwards from the "Don't" imaginary cigarette in her hand. The cigarette is smoked by imaginary creatures and generously advertised throughout *Picture This*. Right next to the monkey portrait are two "stain heads," one in a pale brown wash and one in much darker tones. Stain heads and numerous "scribble heads" can be found on the page opposite this one, contradicting the young Barry's claim that she cannot draw faces anymore. While the scribble heads are drawn in felt pen with minimalist but varied expressions and poses, the stain heads have a different kind of presence which has a fluid, aleatory quality through the shades generated by layers of washes. Such images resemble ghost images or images that appear if one allows them to, which is a central tenet of Barry's teaching. They can also be linked to the issue of wasting paper, mentioned by Barry in the scene above. By illustrating possibilities of recuperating and animating what is deemed as waste, these images are also antidotes to the issue of wasting paper, mentioned by Barry in the scene above. As we saw in the previous chapter, Lynda's mother accused her of wasting paper because she made monstrous drawings, of the Gorgon, for example, as a kind of votive, or protection which backfired for, as Barry realizes in retrospect, her mother was the Gorgon.[16] Just like Barry's recuperation of thrown away drawings and the remedial archival gesture that it implies, Barry's use of stain and scribble heads challenges ideas of waste, wasting paper, and wasteful drawing. Both are born of drawing gestures that can be considered informal, using ordinary, even poor materials and almost automatic movements for the scribble heads and imagining pictures in stains in the case of stain heads. The use of informal gestures and materials complicates Jacques Derrida's conceptualization of the trace, which was central to his post-structural theory. In *Of Grammatology*, Derrida proposes the trace as a precursor to the sign dominating structuralist thought. Derrida elaborates on this concept through dichotomies such as "The Written Being/The Being Written" and "Inside/Outside." In the latter, he writes:

> writing is at the same time more exterior to speech, not being its "image" or its "symbol," and more interior to speech, which is already

---

[16]Barry, *What It Is*, 64–6.

in itself a writing. Even before it is linked to incision, engraving, drawing, or the letter, to a signifier referring in general to a signifier signified by it, the concept of the graphie (unit of a possible graphic system) implies the framework of the instituted trace, as the possibility common to all systems of signification.[17]

As Gayatri Chakravorty Spivak explains in her translator's preface, the French word, *trace* also signifies track and imprint.[18] Spivak elaborates further on the connections between the sign and the trace:

> the sign, phonic as well as graphic, is a structure of difference (. . .) what opens the possibility of thought is not merely the question of being, but also the never-annulled difference from "the completely other." Such is the strange "being" of the sign: half of it always "not there" and the other half always "not that." The structure of the sign is determined by the trace or track of that other which is forever absent.[19]

The understanding that writing itself is graphic and that letters form images is closely connected to the concept of trace. This visuality of writing will be examined in more detail in the next section. The rest of this section will explore the potentialities of considering drawn lines as traces.

In the vein of the Deconstructive thought that Derrida pioneered, the trace encourages us to confront contradictions and invites us to consider the absences inherent in a presence. Building on the Derridean notion of trace, Marion introduced the concept of graphiation in his doctoral thesis.[20] In *The Graphic Novel: An Introduction*, Jan Baetens and Hugo Frey explain graphiation as follows:

> This concept, which can be read as a neologism for "visual enunciation" or "graphic expression," refers to the fact that the hand and the body—as well as the whole personality of an artist—is visible

---

[17]Jacques Derrida, *Of Grammatology*, trans. Gayatri Chakravorty Spivak (Johns Hopkins University Press, 1998), 46.
[18]Derrida, *On Grammatology*, xv.
[19]Derrida, *On Grammatology*, xvii.
[20]Philippe Marion, *Traces en cases: travail graphique, figuration narrative et participation du lecteur. Essai sur la bande dessinée*. PhD dissertation (Université catholique de Louvain, 1993).

in the way he or she gives a visual representation of a certain object, character, setting, or event. It allows for a wide range of possible styles, which can be placed on a sliding scale between two extreme positions: the highly subjective style in which the personal expression of the author takes all priority over the representation itself (what matters at the subjective pole is the personal way something is drawn, not the object of the representation), and the decidedly objective style (in which the object of the representation is the highest priority, at the expense of the personal expression of the author who wants to stay as neutral and invisible as possible).[21]

Graphiation therefore does not refer to the drawing style as such but more to the presence of the author and how the kind of style they adopt reflects this. The style itself can vary from seemingly objective styles, especially in the case of series with standard house styles that the artists conform to, to highly subjective, personalized styles, which characterize Barry's comics. Although we are occasionally provided with glimpses into the many stylistic variations Barry is capable of, as in the case of the realistically drawn art school assignments mentioned in the previous chapter (Figure 2.9), or the variety of styles in *Everything*, it is the expressive, energetic and seemingly childlike style that has come to symbolize her comics. In his seminal "Storylines" article, Jared Gardner emphasizes that acts of graphiation, of drawing lines "give us access to the labored marking of the storyworld we are encountering (and participating in crafting)."[22] He adds: "with every graphic narrative we have an inevitable encounter with the laboring body of the graphiateur and the constrained body of the form itself."[23] Gardner, like Baetens and Marion, is careful to emphasize that there is nothing natural or unmediated about the drawn line. On the contrary, the lines we encounter in the printed comic are heavily mediated, not only through the technological frames imposed by printing processes but also because drawing itself is the complex result of schooling, training, influences, and the imperatives of stories and themes being drawn.[24]

Gardner supplements his observations with selected artists' understanding of their drawn lines. While Mary Fleener and Mark Newgarden liken the line to the performing voice, for Gary Panter it is

---

[21] Baetens and Frey, *Graphic Novel*, 137.
[22] Gardner, "Storylines," 64.
[23] Gardner, "Storylines," 66.
[24] See also Grennan, *A Theory of Narrative Drawing*.

"shaped by the technical (nib, ink), the physiological (hand, breath, chemical responses to the impending depletion of ink or dulling of the pen nib), as well as, of course, the story being told and the character of line called for at a given moment."[25] In his chapter introducing Marion's concepts of mediagenius and graphiation, Baetens also emphasizes the relationality between the artist and the reader implied by the line.[26] Mediagenius "designates the way in which the three notions of style, storytelling and medium are inevitably and necessarily intertwined and mutually dependent."[27] In emphasizing the constraints of drawing and the medium itself, alongside the kinds of connections established with the reader, graphiation and mediagenius offer a holistic lens through which to approach comics.

In light of the above, what has become Barry's trademark style is, on one hand, the result of technical constraints since Barry switched to inkbrush in the late 1980s because drawing made her hands hurt. On the other hand, her style also suits the demands of the narrative, which combines stories in varying shades of autobiography, focuses on childhood and adolescence, reflects on image-making and storytelling to question standard notions of talent and to encourage readers to draw, regardless of perceived skill.

The art in Barry's comics are embodied traces, tailored to the specificity of each book. Her comics reflect only one of many possible Barry styles. In his article on play and playfulness in Barry's comics, Kieron Brown turns to the *Little Women* collage in a diary entry from November 2, 2006 in *What It Is*.[28] Barry had submitted the collage to Penguin for Louisa May Alcott's classic novel, but it was rejected by the publisher for "not being Lynda Barry enough."[29] Building on Kirtley's interpretation of this diary entry as yet another instance which Barry shares "for personal satisfaction,"[30] Brown suggests that the *Little Women* collage

> could not be more "Lynda Barry." In positioning these figures in her second pad, along with various presumably improvised figures and patterns, decorative scraps of paper, as well as the mild incredulity

---

[25] Gardner, "Storylines," 66–7.
[26] Baetens, "Revealing Traces."
[27] Baetens, "Revealing Traces," 146.
[28] Barry, *What It Is*, 200.
[29] Barry cited in Brown, "Play," 140.
[30] Kirtley, *Lynda Barry*, 183.

suggested by the handwritten component, Barry reinforces that this *is* her authentic style, which—as the rest of the book testifies—is inherently linked to an improvisational process.[31]

As already mentioned in Chapter 1, the label of authenticity seems all too easy to attach to Barry's work because it seems spontaneous, unfiltered and honest, even though Barry tempers truth claims. Barry's style ranks high in Szép's transparency scale due to "an immediacy between the drawing agent and the result of the performance of drawing."[31] It "postulates a transparent, almost organic relationship between the line and the drawer."[32] Conventional or more objective styles lie at the other end of Szép's scale. Barry's privileging of spontaneous, automatic drawing and even the use of seemingly messy collage seems to reinforce effects of transparency and immediacy. However, as Barry's description of her artistic process in *Picture This* confirms,[33] her collage work is far from spontaneous. It seems more improvisational than it is, camouflaging the labor of collaging—another form of hidden labor in which personal style is generated through an amalgamation of cutting and pasting acts instead of the drawn line. Both the expressive, seemingly untutored line and Barry's distinctive collages attract associations of authenticity. Such assumptions of authenticity, in turn, confirm the persistence of certain connotations attached to highly recognizable personal styles. And, as we saw with the rejection of the *Little Women* collage, an artist or *graphiateur* is often associated with a particular style, which becomes their trademark and recognizable mode of expression, and to which they are often encouraged to adhere to.

Barry's expressive line also gives voice to another, overlooked aspect of comics which Michael Chaney identifies as "the child in and as the comics."[34] "Regardless of the graphic novel's pretensions, the child or youth remains an emblem of the comics and an archetype of its mediation."[35] It is, consequently, highly telling that Barry focuses on this iconic character type, which persists across diverse comic forms,

---

[31]Brown, "Play," 141. Emphasis in the original.
[32]Szép, *Comics and the Body*, 42.
[33]See VanderMeer and Barry, "Omnivoracious Interview."
[34]Michael A. Chaney, *Reading Lessons in Seeing: Mirrors, Masks and Mazes in the Autobiographical Graphic Novel* (University Press of Mississippi, 2017), 57–119.
[35]Chaney, *Reading Lessons*, 57.

from the humble newspaper strip to the graphic novel. Building on Chute's observations on how autobiographical graphic novels such as Marjane Satrapi's *Persepolis* interweave adult and child perspectives in the same panel,[36] Chaney concludes that the comics child encourages "philosophical reflection on the complicated nature of temporality."[37] Going further, Chaney also highlights the paradox at the heart of the content, perception and policing of comics (most notoriously, in the United States, with the enforcement of the Comics Code): "comics promote adolescence and its rejection; they encompass both the view of (or as) the child and the child's view under verbal erasure. It is this paradox that lies at the heart of the comics' formal preoccupations with the child."[38] This paradox is also evident in the discourses around the "growing up" of comics that automatically translate into cultural legitimation and a move away from childishness.[39] What makes Barry's comics stand out is her embrace of the childish and her rejection of flattening clichés around innocent and happy childhoods. The following observation by Chaney concerning comics children holds especially true for the ways in which Barry incorporates children in her works: "the child also configures lost ways of knowing."[40] The forms of knowing relevant to Barry's works include children's access to imagination and their willingness to draw and tell stories unhindered by perceived drawing and writing abilities. Although, as demonstrated by the two previous chapters, the child is visually almost omnipresent in Barry's comics, the child also wields an invisible or implied presence in Barry's drawing styles, techniques and even her teaching prompts.

In the *Naked Ladies, Naked Ladies, Naked Ladies* coloring book, for instance, the child is visually almost completely absent, with the exception of a young girl posing with fake breasts. The child's presence is fleshed out through the diary-like entries under each drawing and the very form of the coloring book, a kind of book traditionally intended exclusively for children. *One Hundred Demons* similarly relies on very childlike, girly collages for its chapter separators and occasionally includes photographs of

---

[36]Chute, *Graphic Women*, 140–4.
[37]Chaney, *Reading Lessons*, 57.
[38]Chaney, *Reading Lessons*, 59.
[39]See Pizzino, *Arresting Development*, 21–45; and Cruficix, *Drawing*, 15–19.
[40]Chaney, *Reading Lessons,* 91.

Lynda Barry

Figure 3.2 "Head Lice" chapter separator, from *One Hundred Demons*, 15. Copyright Lynda Barry. Used with permission from Drawn & Quarterly.

a smiling Barry to reinforce the implied presence of the child in the use of glitter, bright colors and simple, repetitive drawings.

Many of the different demons populating *One Hundred Demons* are likewise invisibles: nuisances such as head lice, which are tiny and often difficult to spot and which Barry juxtaposes to being in love with the wrong person without realizing it. The smiley louse and the heart-shaped symbol signifying love form a symbolic whole summing up the story. This imbrication is already foreshadowed by the chapter separator (Figure 3.2) and the louse with hearts emanating from it, which appears behind the letter of the comic's opening sentence and reappears twice toward the end of the story. This recurrence contributes to the braiding mechanism identified by Groensteen that allows comics to form networks within and across their pages. The reader-weaver theorized by Postema can find multiple possible connections on each collaged page, linked to the specific story the collage introduces but also to other stories throughout *One Hundred Demons* and even beyond.

Although the louse is drawn in an extremely simple and even childish manner, it becomes an effective carrier and transmitter of feelings, of love and longing (represented by the heart) but also of being looked down upon. The first demon, as the chapter separator announces, actually combines two demons (or two manifestations of the same demon)—lice and Lynda's first boyfriend—both of whom are introduced on an extremely girly, tactile and textured separator, combining scraps of fabric, three thank-you notes on one side, colorful photographs of flowers and, of course, numerous drawings of the smiling louse.

Other invisibles resurrected by Barry include feelings such as hate and abilities like resilience. Sensory elements such as smells and even dancing, which relies on movement that transcends the comics form bound to the space of the page, are also some of the invisibles rendered visible by Barry. Additional demons are connected to childhood memories, including "Lost Worlds," making visible what has been forgotten. The process of visualizing the invisible in stories that look to the past becomes a means of remembering and even understanding. Making these elements visible is in itself not new to comics and encompasses all kinds of forms and genres, ranging from the popular newspaper comic strips to the graphic novels of the past few decades which have made autobiography and memory their chief concern. Newspaper comics quickly developed a highly efficient vocabulary for visually conveying sounds, indicating smells and emotional states, to the extent that these elements are taken for granted, as givens of the multisensorial worlds comics offer us within the confines of the imagetext. In transforming these elements into demons, Barry breathes in a new dimension and life into them and, as a result, draws our attention to the specificities of these sensorial elements and how they become comicitous.[41]

The importance of rendering the invisible visible is evident from the space Barry accords to allowing demons to emerge from ink. As we saw in the previous chapters, the sea monster accompanying Barry's explanation of the One Hundred Demons inkbrush exercise hints at the mystical powers Barry ascribes to her images. This mysticism is not without its tongue-in-cheek and even self-deprecating humor, which can be considered comicitous in its refusal to take itself too seriously. However, such a convergence of humor, conviction in automatic creation and traumatic moments from the past recurs in Barry's comics which often maintain a delicate balance between the humor that comics and cartoony drawing are associated with and using comics to convey deeper, philosophical and emotional truths. The techniques of rendering the invisible visible include the animation of impossible, drawn and painted creatures, further amplified by the visual symbolism attached to them and their braiding across stories. Collages are

---

[41]See Beineke, "On Comicity."

another means of letting the invisible seep through and are discussed in detail further below from the perspectives of their archival and texturing potential. The remaining part of this section focuses on the animating gesture giving form and life to invisibles such as the many demons blossoming from Barry's sumi brush.

Shiamin Kwa describes John Porcellino's self-published poetic and autobiographical *King-Cat Comics and Stories* as generating

> an animistic medium of uncertainty, where what the text "asks" of the reader shifts in register even in sections of the same page. This kind of reading process challenges traditional linear notions of time and the location of identity within a text, thus suggesting a dynamic communal vision for life writing and, perhaps, for viewing life itself.[42]

The animism here comes from the unsaid, the temporal intertwinings, metalepses and other aspects calling for readerly involvement and deciphering. Animism and its close relatives, animation and animatedness, have long roots in the comics form. This is evident from Scott Bukatman's study of the early nineteenth-century strip, *Little Nemo in Slumberland* by pioneering animation and comics artist, Winsor McCay. Bukatman expertly draws connections between the increasing mechanization of society and notions of individuality at the dawn of the twentieth century and the liveliness of emergent forms such as the newspaper comic and the animated film. He builds on Sianne Ngai's conceptualization of animatedness as an ugly feeling. For Ngai, a key feature connecting ugly feelings is that they stem from restricted agency. While animatedness for Ngai is closely connected to racialized representations, which are often compounded with exaggerated emotions, Bukatman suggests that "animatedness is an ugly feeling but also a romantic, and somewhat heroic, condition—if the world judges the overanimated harshly, that is the price to be paid for autonomy and independence."[43] Comics and animated characters, Bukatman claims, are unruly, offering "little utopias of disorder, provisional sites of temporary resistance."[44]

---

[42]Kwa, "Life Writing," 185–6.
[43]Scott Bukatman, *Poetics of Slumberland: Animated Spirits and the Animating Spirit* (University of California Press, 2012), 22.
[44]Bukatman, *Poetics of Slumberland*, 2, 27–76.

Like all comics, which rely on animating drawn lines, Barry's work is animated because the medium itself implies animation. But animatedness is present in more profound ways, as a central feature of Barry's comics. This is connected, in part, to the incorporation of art-making elements, which imbue the comics with a metareferential level embodied, for instance, by the intro and outro sections in *One Hundred Demons*. It is also connected to Barry's preferred brand of art pedagogy, which often works with automatic methods. Animation is also present in her searching for images and characters, often by simply letting them appear. Further, the strong, untutored, and childlike elements in Barry's graphic novels reconfigure notions of animatedness, acquiring contours and nuances that can be read in the light of cultural legitimacy, and alternative understandings of drawing, challenging notions of good and bad drawings.

Barry's animation strategies include the conjuring up and purging of monsters through the One Hundred Demons exercise, leading to a rememorying exercise that becomes even more tangible in the philosophical collages of *What It Is*. Allan Pero rightly observes that "Barry's persistent use of collage in *What It Is* (...) like the presence of the 'magic cephalopod' and the many-eyed 'sea demon,' works to generate the freedom of movement necessary for 'writing the unthinkable.'"[45] He adds that the "(c)ollage becomes a means of managing anxiety through worklessness and play."[46] Barry's comics manuals strive to teach readers how to "find" their own images and generate their own stories; the collages reflect both the kind of creation and the path toward it, stemming from the diverse exercises and questions, including overcoming anxiety.

Barry deliberately seeks animatedness in other departments. In *What It Is*, she incorporates a schoolteacher's archive in her collages. These archives mediate between the personal and the collective. By incorporating Doris Mitchell's papers, Barry prevents the material from being thrown away and forgotten, bestowing a new life and relevance to an archive that is both personal and anonymous. She also recuperates drawings her older students throw away. In *Making Comics*, next to multiple drawings and even lists, Barry writes, "Once, a student asked me why I liked 'messed-up' drawings so much. They don't look messed up to me. There is a realness in them

---

[45] Pero, "Orbit of the Cephalopod," 100.
[46] Pero, "Orbit of the Cephalopod," 103.

that is hard to come by."⁴⁷ Barry, then, also animates and incorporates animatedness through her fascination with her students' drawings, both young and old. The collaged pages in these instances function as animistic media in openly uncertain ways, allowing the reader to read in multiple directions and not only in a linear, sequential manner.

Finally, as confirmed by her most recent comic, *Making Comics*, children's drawings have an animating potential that is unique to them. Barry draws over children's drawings. Such gestures allow her to participate in the drawings.⁴⁸ They are a means of reactivating the affective power and rawness of the drawings and exploring whether her own, more trained hand can reproduce the same energy. As she mentions early in *Making Comics*, drawings by children and people who start drawing after having stopped for years have a certain "aliveness" to them (Figure 3.3). She illustrates the notion of aliveness with her copy of a child's drawing which "is missing something. To me it's just a little less alive than the original."⁴⁹

According to Jeanette Roan, "Barry's language suggests a view of drawing as an animating practice."⁵⁰ Roan adds that Barry's

> efforts at explaining the "aliveness" of an image—like memory, like the ocean, like experiences—offer a view of the image very much at odds with an approach to it as an inert object of analysis and interpretation. But this line of thinking has much in common with developments outlined (. . .) by art historian Keith Moxey in which he traces the emergence of a renewed interest in what he calls the presence of an object or image.⁵¹

The "image magic" at the heart of Barry's books and teaching does exactly what a certain strand of visual studies does, exemplified by art historians such as Hans Belting, Georges Didi-Huberman, James Elkins, W. J. T. Mitchell: it allows for images to exist on their own turf and not as mere illustrations. Barry succeeds in performing image theory through comics. As Roan observes, "(i)n offering images in response, images that are drawn,

---

[47] Barry, *Making Comics*, 50.
[48] Barry, *Making Comics*, 13.
[49] Barry, *Making Comics*, 4.
[50] Roan, "What is an Image?" 258.
[51] Roan, "What is an Image?" 258.

Critical Themes and Questions

Figure 3.3 Unpracticed drawings and a copy by Barry (top right), from *Making Comics*, 4. Copyright Lynda Barry. Used with permission from Drawn & Quarterly.

seen, sent, and received, Barry shows us how images can begin to argue and how scholars can see, and study, the images in comics with new eyes."[52]

On the page above, Barry adds a third image to illustrate a student's fear of noses and feet, which she left out of her drawings. Despite the absence of otherwise crucial elements, the drawing is effective and emotionally loaded. Part of the effect of these drawings is connected to the carefully constructed bookish context in which they are placed, in the lined notebook pages, surrounded by Barry's own pulled lines and decorations and, most importantly, other drawings made by untutored hands. The page opposite Figure 3.3 in *Making Comics* illustrates how Barry approaches writing as a visual element, illustrating the Derridean graphie. Next to a small white sheet with writing by a four-year-old listing her friends' names, Barry observes the "spacing happening in unexpected ways" and concludes that

---

[52]Roan, "What is an Image?" 262.

Figure 3.4 Fire story in the making, from *Making Comics*, 17. Copyright Lynda Barry. Used with permission from Drawn & Quarterly.

"(t)he letters are in real relation to both each other and to the page."[53] We will return to the visual and oral approach to language and how it articulates different kinds and timbers of voices in the next section, after one final example of animation and animatedness in Barry's comics.

Opposite a page peppered with illustrations of fire by 4K children, Barry captures the interactions between the children in one of her classes across three tiers of two panels each (Figure 3.4). This moment is a perfect illustration of collaborative storytelling, with the children drawing, discussing and changing their stories along the way. The comic focuses on the drawing and storytelling girl who reappears in every panel, roughly crayoned in warm tones of red and orange. In addition to echoing the theme of drawing fire introduced on the preceding page, these colors also allude to the fire of creativity we already encountered above the creatures

---

[53] Barry, *Making Comics*, 5.

Critical Themes and Questions

on the final page of *Syllabus* and its inside back flap and back cover.[54] In the final panel, another girl tells her storytelling and drawing classmate that her generous use of blue marker to represent vain attempts to put out the fire is wasteful. She repeats the word twice. This comment recalls moments from Lynda's own childhood when she was accused of wasting paper by her mother. The same admonishment is repeated by the numerous monsters in the "Two Questions" sequence in *What It Is*. In incorporating this careful but insistent remark in her final panel in Figure 3.4, Barry once again raises the issue of hesitation and lack of confidence that is the biggest hurdle to creation.

On the page following this comic, Barry's conclusion to this introductory section of *Making Comics* emphasizes the importance of allowing for animatedness and animism:

> Stories show up on their own when kids draw—the drawing itself propels the story, changing it in a living way. . . . Words and pictures together make something happen that is more than good or bad drawing. You don't have to have any artistic skill to do this. You just need to be brave and sincere.[55]

Perceived skill and talent are irrelevant; allowing stories and images to appear is paramount. We will return to one more aspect of animation, the animation of archives in the third section, which takes a closer look at Barry's approaches to collage. Before broaching collage, however, it is important to unpack the first level of hybridity, the coexistence and confluence of words and images and Barry's distinctive approach to writing and language.

Writing and Language

In a 2019 radio interview promoting *Making Comics,* Barry observes

> Anyone who can write the alphabet and numerals from 0 to 9 can make comics. And I would argue that those things are comics. There's a reason we call the letters of the alphabet characters. And when

---

[54] Barry, *Syllabus*, 200.
[55] Barry, *Making Comics*, 18.

people are learning to write the alphabet, they are actually learning to draw.[56]

Writing and drawing share the common trait of mark-making on surfaces. Notably, Derrida's explanation of trace, initially a linguistic and not a visual concept, also emphasized its visual aspect, "the graphie," the basic unit of a graphic system, "the framework of the instituted trace, as the possibility common to all systems of signification."[57] The visual mark therefore lies at the heart of the trace itself. Barry's comics accord special attention to the role and visuality of writing. Time and again, we encounter the alphabet and numbers written across her pages, testing different techniques and forms. In *One Hundred Demons*, Barry mentions, "I write the ALPHABET every day with a brush."[58] Chute suggests that this "material and intellectual foregrounding of handwriting calls attention to the visual rhythms that permeate comics."[59] As we will see throughout this guide, even as Barry's more recent works break away from the traditional comics form, they remain comicitous, retaining comics-like qualities. In *Syllabus*, Barry considers handwriting "to have something like a voice, something we can recognize as belonging to a specific person."[60]

This second section elaborates on the visual and affective dimensions of writing, which in Barry's case is often handwritten. The only major exception are her collages, which combine different forms of writing, typed or written by diverse, anonymous hands. Writing plays a crucial role in all of Barry's comics, from her earliest comic strips to her most recent graphic narratives. First there is the visual weight and space accorded to writing— a distinctive feature of Barry's comics. Barry's comics balloons and captions are often space-consuming and unsteady, rejecting the convention of even lettering, personalizing the text while contributing to its visual facet, and ultimately collapsing the boundaries between word and image. Her deliberately wordy comics challenge mainstream comics constraints. The recurrence of handwritten alphabets in her comics manuals function both as lettering and drawing exercises while taking inspiration from children's culture.

---

[56]Power and Barry, "Cartoonist Lynda Barry."
[57]Derrida, *Of Grammatology*, 46.
[58]Barry, *One Hundred Demons*, 223.
[59]Chute, *Graphic Women*, 111.
[60]Barry, *Syllabus*, 148.

This section also considers the distinctive childlike idiom created by Barry that "is particularly expressive of children's acquisition of language" while remaining comparable to the timeless idiom of George Herriman's *Krazy Kat*. There is, as Hannah Miodrag masterfully shows, a telling difference between the two idioms: while Herriman's characters distort specific rules, the language in Barry's works tends to "be more free-flowing"; it does not reject specific syntactic rules, but revels in linguistic awkwardness. Part of this awkwardness stems from distorting multisyllabic words, using slang or even non-existent words.[61]

From Barry's earlier works, *Cruddy* offers perhaps one of the most generous examples of oral writing, imitating Roberta's direct speech. This effect was possibly enhanced by Barry's unusual approach to the novel, which involved writing the first draft of the text in inkbrush before typing it on a manual typewriter and then retyping it four times.[62] This laborious process, as pointed out by critic Alice Sebold in her review of *Cruddy*, was reflected in the inherent physicality of the novel.[63] Kirtley observes that "(t)his hyper-kinetic, dynamic process of painting, writing, and typing, and of calling up what Barry told (artist and publisher) Benny Shaboy was a 'living thing,' is reflected in the reckless energy of *Cruddy*."[64]

Writing or painting the words of the text are central to the process of generating an embodied and visceral text.[65] While the published novel is printed in type, *Cruddy*, as mentioned in the previous chapter, maintains two key inscriptions of handwritten text: Roberta's name followed by "1955-1971" under the note introducing the diary, Roberta's writing on the four maps and Julie's angry and terrified responses at the end of the diary:

fuck you roberta!!! I hate you Roberta!!! where are you??[66]

In contrast to Roberta's careful, controlled writing, incarnating the role of the omniscient author of her diary and narrative, Julie's response is emphatic with numerous exclamation and question marks. Writing unevenly, and dismissive of capital letters (for Roberta's name and for the beginning of

---

[61] Miodrag, *Comics and Language*, 45–6.
[62] Kirtley, *Lynda Barry*, 80–1.
[63] Kirtley, *Lynda Barry*, 81.
[64] Kirtley, *Lynda Barry*, 81. My insertion in parentheses.
[65] See also Miller, "Diary as Body."
[66] Barry, *Cruddy*, 301.

each sentence), it is Julie who gets to end the diary, not Roberta; the girl snatches control from her older teenage sister and messes up the final page, creating confusion concerning the author of these words. The possibilities of authorship range from a random book vandal to Julie herself, which confers a sheen of authenticity to a story that often crosses over into the realm of the macabre.[67] Like most of Barry's young characters, Julie and Roberta, do not subscribe to the stereotypes of young people and children; they seem unabashedly real. The direct speech and the handwritten text reinforces this sense of the real.

The previous chapters have already highlighted the importance Barry accords to using hands for making art. Scholars such as Hillary Chute, Jared Gardner, and Eszter Szép have considered the implied presence of the drawing hand as central to the expressive and affective potential of comics. Szép suggests that the aura of the original work of art that Walter Benjamin saw fading away in an era dominated by easy and multiple reproductions should be adapted to reflect the printed essence of comics: "Even printed works establish an embodied connection with the moment and embodied performance of creation with the drawn line."[68] Szép's emphasis on embodiment is a response to Gardner's observations on the relevance of the handwritten text in an era which has all but erased the need for handwriting. In comics, "the act of inscription remains always visible, and the story of its making remains central to the narrative work of the graphic narrative form."[69] In this way, graphic narratives provide a new connection, generating "living immediacy" between the storyteller and the story being told which, for Benjamin, had been disassociated with the rise of print.[70] Handwriting combines the impression of spontaneity and directness with the presence implied by graphiation since the visual form of each letter is unique in contrast to the typed text and the careful even lettering that dominates comics and most of our text-based encounters.

Chute describes Barry's distinctive mode of writing as performing a specific kind of "shifting." Pointing out how "Barry's handwriting changes color (. . .) stylization and size" in graphic novels such as *One Hundred Demons*, Chute concludes that "this shifting is enacted to 'break up' the

---

[67] Kirtley, *Lynda Barry*, 99.
[68] Szép, *Comics and the Body*, 5.
[69] Gardner, "Storylines," 57.
[70] Gardner, "Storylines," 55.

actual visual surface of the text. Barry creates the textural unevenness as a way of slowing down the experience of reading."[71] This slowness connects to the artisanal ethos privileging the handmade that Barry advocates for, exemplified by the heavily collaged pages of works like *What It Is*. But writing is also more intrinsically connected to Barry's creative practice as confirmed by the two-page introductory comic, "Forestory Backward," in the reprinted collected volume, *The Greatest of Marlys*, published in 2016 by D&Q, eight years after *Ernie Pook's Comeek* ended.

In this comic, Barry connects children's storytelling practices and spontaneous creation with her own creation of Marlys. It begins by recalling the first comic introducing the four children, Arna and her brother Arnold and Marlys and her brother Freddie in "The Night We All Got Sick," when all four cousins ended up with upset stomachs.[72] Barry provides us with a behind-the-scenes glimpse into this comic. Her representation of her first encounter with Marlys enacts her principle of allowing characters to emerge by themselves, through the act of drawing, fed by her memories, which are often childhood memories:

> When I make a comic strip, I let these sorts of images lead and combine as I move my pen. I try to let one line lead to the next without plan. The only thing I have to do is stay in motion. That's what I was doing when I first saw Marlys.[73]

Marlys, Barry suggests, was dreamt up, with the many characters populating her world, such as Arna and Freddie, emerging soon after.

"I let (my hand) . . . write the pictures and draw the words," Barry adds, reversing the gestures associated with pictures and words.[74] These observations reappear in *Making Comics*, where she emphasizes how very young children do not make a distinction between drawing and writing and that they are "native speakers" of the language of comics she strives to teach in her classes: "This language moves up through your hand and

---

[71]Chute, *Graphic Women*, 110–11.
[72]For more on the comic and the autobiographical relevance of the comic, see Rachel Trousdale, "Autobiography and the Empathic Imagination in *Ernie Pook's Comeek*," in *Contagious Imagination*.
[73]Barry, *Greatest of Marlys*, 4.
[74]Barry, *Greatest of Marlys*, 4. My insertion in parentheses.

Figure 3.5 Second and final page of "Forestory Backward," from *The Greatest of Marlys*, 5. Copyright Lynda Barry. Used with permission from Drawn & Quarterly.

into your head."[75] In the introduction to *The Greatest of Marlys*, Barry also transposes children's storytelling processes which are constructed in a flow and informed by immediate reactions to the context: "Kids do this all the time when they play with dolls and action figures. They are both watching the scene unfold and responding in real time" (Figure 3.5, see also Figure 3.4). [76] Barry also emphasizes the relationality between herself and the characters she creates: "Marlys conjures me as much as I conjure her. The portal between her world and mine is a pen line made by the living mystery of this hand, this hand that looks like yours."[77] Crucially, this "pen line" is multimodal, drawing text and writing images, and the hand can be anyone's hand.

---

[75]Barry, *Making Comics*, 8.
[76]Barry, *Greatest of Marlys*, 5.
[77]Barry, *Greatest of Marlys*, 5.

Just like with the "Menopositive" comic discussed in Chapter 1, this recent comic also ends with an interaction between an aged, potentially hesitant Barry and a young girl, Marlys, who seems much smaller in the final panel in comparison to her other representations in the graphic novel and elsewhere, where she tends to dominate the panel and the page. The caption above them reflects on a childhood "half-memory" of Barry's, which opened the two-page comic and which acquires a metaleptic twist at the very end, when the addressee is no longer the reader but Barry's grandmother: "We're all living together in a big, run-down house; the parents sleep upstairs, us kids sleep on two double beds with grandma, it was the night we all got sick, grandma, tell us that story <u>again</u>!"[78] It is Marlys who offers the concluding sentence to that memory and orders Barry: "<u>Write</u> it. Then you'll be done. Then let's <u>do</u> something!"[79] Marlys' command emphasizes writing, not drawing, suggesting that the act of writing is essential to completing the story and that drawing and writing are inextricable. Further, since the speech balloon for the final sentence actually points toward the cover of the book for which the comic was made, what Marlys seems to want to do is to read the book they're in and which is about her, together with Barry and perhaps even the reader. Boundaries between reality and fiction are blurred, just like memory and narrative, metafiction and autobiography, past and present overlap across the eight panels. Similar to Barry's comics manuals, the story's main theme is creating comics stories.

As we saw in the previous section, both Chute and Chaney evoke the overlapping temporalities incarnated by the comics child and its juxtaposition to a narrating adult voice. Temporalities blend in Barry's recent comics with transgenerational encounters; the concept of childhood and Barry's specific childhood memories are inextricably intertwined with the diegetic present. This overlap and even blurring between collective and specific childhoods, between fictionalized stories and autobiographical memories is a central principle determining many of Barry's stories.

Some of the comics in *The Freddie Stories,* which focus on Marlys' brother Freddie, exemplify additional, close connections between writing and language.[80] "The Lost Stories," supposedly penned and drawn by Freddie himself, transpose Barry's childish drawing style directly to a

---

[78]Barry, *Greatest of Marlys*, 5.
[79]Barry, *Greatest of Marlys*, 5.
[80]Barry, *Freddie Stories*, 133–77.

child's world and forms of expression. Freddie is frequently bullied and called a fag and even, in one of the many traumatic incidents of bullying directed at Freddie, a girl.[81] The reason for this lies in Freddie's interest in activities such as cooking and empathy for the tiniest of insects, including flies, and even dolls, which his mother forbids him to play with.[82] All of these characteristics counter conventional notions of boyhood and, worse, are relegated to the realm of girlhood. After a brief stint at a juvenile detention center for arson (inadvertent, in Freddie's case), Freddie emerges seeing skulls instead of living beings—a personification of the bully and pyromaniac Jim-Jimmy-Jim's threat that Freddie was a "dead boy."[83] Only the baby of an alcoholic, bitter, single mother, Dennis, does not have a skull head and, in another subversion of gender roles, Freddie becomes the baby's carer.[84] While *The Freddie Stories* are told through Freddie's perspective, it is in "The Lost Stories," and in an earlier four-panel story, "Stuntman!,"[85] that Freddie also takes over the visual dimension, transporting the reader out of the often horrific realities of Freddie's everyday existence to more imaginary realms of ghosts, animals, fish, or other moments from his life, ranging from school lessons to his own birth.

Freddie begins "Stuntman!" by mentioning, in a wordy, very Barry-like caption, which takes up most of the unevenly drawn panel, that his mother had stopped talking to him in February: "'The sins of the father,' was the last thing she said. Dad was a fag. Is, was, I cannot tell you. I do not actually know him. In the future, for a job, I shall be a stuntman."[86] The remaining three panels imagine the fantastic life he will lead, culminating in a book comprising "770 thrilling pages and 900 action drawings."[87] Written in a childlike idiom and enthusiasm and drawn in a simplified, equally childlike style, the story is moving and poetic. The "stickiness" of this touching quality can be traced to Freddie's seemingly complete authorial control. Writing and drawing stories becomes a means of channeling his mother's rejection, his father's absence and the destruction of his favorite doll, while imagining a glamorous outcome. "I got time," is Freddie's mantra in the two

---

[81] Barry, *Freddie Stories*, 59.
[82] Barry, *Freddie Stories*, 6–9; 95.
[83] Barry, *Freddie Stories*, 27.
[84] Barry, *Freddie Stories*, 34–5.
[85] Barry, *Freddie Stories*, 104–5.
[86] Barry, *Freddie Stories*, 104.
[87] Barry, *Freddie Stories*, 105.

Critical Themes and Questions

Figure 3.6 Second and final page of "Enjoying Anteaters," from *The Freddie Stories*, 147. Copyright Lynda Barry. Used with permission from Drawn & Quarterly.

final panels, reinforcing the sense of a child's view of time and possibility despite the bleak circumstances.

Two additional stories animate Freddie's school assignments: a Spanish lesson with the moving title, "Adonde tu estas" and an extra credit report on anteaters,[88] where Freddie commiserates with their condition but is interrupted by a classmate repeatedly calling Freddie a fag. The resulting squabbling eventually attracts the attention of the teacher (Figure 3.6). As with the majority of Freddie's stories, the ending is not in his favor and he is sent to the counselor's office.

"Enjoying Anteaters" draws a direct connection between comics-making and the deviant, young minds historically, and misleadingly, associated with comics, popularized by works such as the German-American psychiatrist Fredric Wertham's *Seduction of the Innocent* (1954). Wertham's book contributed to the comics scare and the implementation of the Comics Code in the United States, which heavily restricted the kinds of stories told in comics form, eliminating gruesome horror genres and drastically reducing violence in favor of more wholesome entertainment.[89]

---

[88] Barry, *Freddie Stories*, 148–9.
[89] See for instance, Amy Nyberg, *Seal of Approval: The History of the Comics Code* (University Press of Mississippi, 1998); and Bart Beaty's nuanced account of Wertham, *Fredric Wertham*

Lynda Barry

"Enjoying Anteaters," was drawn in 1992, at a time when the Comics Code and the seal of approval it affixed on comics covers had become irrelevant. The Code was completely abandoned by 2011. Freddie's comic, however, is seeped with the less commendable features associated with comics readers. With messy, uneven writing and unskilled, ugly drawing, Freddie uses his unfettered imagination to construct the "very lonely and very sad" life of an anteater and how Freddie would fare if "a scientist (evil)" transformed him into one. Freddie's concluding words reflect additional disparaged characteristics associated with comics readers—poorly performing students using inappriopriate language and unable to adhere to the rules. "That is why I like Tony Delarosa." Freddie continues, "If a scientist (evil) turned me part anteater he said he would want to be one too. Does this equal us Fags?? Oh well there goes my extra credit I can't turn this in with the word Fag because . . ."[90]

Although, at this point, the teacher has snatched away the assignment, the small, vertical "to be continued" suggests several levels of continuity and even, to underscore the cyclical and not necessarily linear nature of the events, seriality: Freddie will continue to draw his comics, he will also be regularly bullied as a "fag," achieve less than spectacular grades and unwittingly get into trouble.

The messy drawing and uneven writing evoke the causality that had once been established between comics and delinquency and how the supposed immaturity of a form dominated by formulaic and simplistic storylines also rubbed off on its readership.[91] The comics drawn by Freddie blend his outsider status among his classmates with the marginalized status accorded to comics readers and comics makers. While the incorporation of childish drawing styles is far from new—think of Barnabé Gogo's portraits and history drawings in Cham's *Un génis incompris* (*A Misunderstood Genius,* 1841)—in the wake of the graphic novel, and the legitimation of a certain kind of adult comics it has ushered, Freddie's comics acquire a new significance. Christopher Pizzino draws our attention to how a revenge comic against Wertham penned by author Joe Hill (known for the *Locke & Key* series) "assumes that comics are made out of the damage the medium

---

and the Critique of Mass Culture (University Press of Mississippi, 2005).
[90]Barry, *Freddie Stories*, 147.
[91]See, for instance, Christopher Pizzino, "Doctor versus the Dagger: Comics Reading and Cultural Memory," *PMLA* 130, no. 3 (2015), 631–47.

has suffered—and out of the memories, true or false, of that damage—more than they are made out of aspirations to legitimacy."[92]

"The Lost Stories" and other comics Barry draws through Freddie's persona draw direct parallels between the marginalization of the comics form and marginalized, troubled childhoods such as Freddie's. In these comics ostensibly drawn by children, Barry bestows agency on the immaturity associated with comics and often suppressed by the legitimization of comics, which has permitted the reissuing of the Freddie comics and numerous other Barry comics in long-lasting, hardcover books. The underbelly of childishness that is part of the comics form is rich in expressive potential—something which also lies at the heart of Barry's teaching philosophy as we saw above. Drawings like Freddie's might be labelled as bad, just like his writing does not follow the conventions of even lettering in imitation of print, or even correct syntax. However, just like the four-year-old's writing in *Making Comics* mentioned above, Freddie's writing and drawing are rich in emotional information. And herein lies the distinctive power and potential of the form or medium of comics, exemplified by Barry's comics and manuals.

The remaining part of this section turns to the "using drawing to write" section in Barry's first manual, *Picture This*, printed in the spring issue, the second of the four issues structuring the book according to the rhythms of a quarterly magazine.[93] While the first part of the issue turns to coloring and copying shapes, this section elaborates on the often ignored overlaps between "characters," such as letters of the alphabet and "figures," or outlined creatures.[94] Barry turns to her childhood memories of when she could not read and was just learning to write: "I could pick out certain letters. But they were still pictures to me. And I was drawing them."[95] In the final tier of the page, she adds: "If you were to draw the alphabet instead of writing it what would the difference be? Where would it be?"[96] On the next page Barry explains, through the multi-eyed sea monster, the inextricability of words and images in her work: "When I'm making a comic strip the words and the pictures come to me at the same time."[97] A few pages later,

---

[92] Pizzino, "Doctor versus the Dagger," 642.
[93] Barry, *Picture This*, 118.
[94] Barry, *Picture This*, 118.
[95] Barry, *Picture This*, 119.
[96] Barry, *Picture This*, 119.
[97] Barry, *Picture This*, 120.

Barry animates letters and numbers by bestowing them with eyes, noses, legs and even arms and hands.[98] The letters come alive in these cases, losing their symbolic significance to become mobile creatures. This page offers a deconstruction of what Barry calls "alphabet lines." These are combined with "amoeba lines" which, true to their names, are highly amorphous forms consisting mostly of curved lines. By breaking down each letter according to its visual component and combining them with amoebic lines, Barry offers her readers—and potential comics artists—with a plethora of animating possibilities and a new means of *looking*, echoing the list of words on the contents page of the spring issue of *Picture This*. This list—"Seeing Looking Staring GAZING Watching Glancing Observing"—confirms the centrality of learning how to look in the spring issue.[99]

Barry often repeats the alphabet and single-digit numbers across diverse pages of her graphic novels: on the title page of "The Lost Stories," for instance, where all the letters of the alphabet are colored in.[100] The frontmatter of *One Hundred Demons* displays the neatly-written alphabet on one side of the multi-eyed sea monster, opposite the friendly injunction "Row away from the demon."[101] This image, which imitates a Japanese print, appears on the first page of the graphic narrative, with a typed, false table of contents. The text on this page offers a strong structuring counterpoint to the pictorial elements that incorporate a degree of uncontrollability, be it through the central demon, the uneven coloring that ignores the clear outlines of the figures and the waves, the squiggly lines adorning the frame and even the fingerprint transformed into a smiley face. These sets of alphabets and numbers evoke the world of learning and childhood, when the basic tools of reading, writing, and communication are acquired. They also bear a strong resemblance to the letter and number stencils used in schools. Devoid of all linguistic and mathematic meaning, such sets emphasize the visual dimension of letters and numbers.

To build on the often quoted observation that "drawing is a way of thinking," which is most frequently associated with Chris Ware,[102] and remains a central aspect of all artistic practice, writing too can become a way

---

[98] Barry, *Picture This*, 123.
[99] Barry, *Picture This*, 95.
[100] Barry, *Freddie Stories*, 133.
[101] Barry, *One Hundred Demons*, 1.
[102] See for instance, David M. Ball and Martha Kuhlman, eds., *The Comics of Chris Ware: Drawing Is a Way of Thinking* (University Press of Mississippi, 2010); see also Simon Grennan's

of thinking, whether it is through drawing and transforming the alphabet, or through writing by hand which, as we saw above, Barry encourages and does herself, and portrays herself in the process of doing. The connection between drawing and thought became a central tenet during the Renaissance through the concept of *disegno*, which combines both the act of drawing and the conceptualization that occurs before it or emerges through it. In his famous *Lives of the Artists* (1568), Giorgio Vasari, himself a painter and architect, considered drawing the father of the three arts of painting, sculpture, and architecture.[103] He suggested two means of perfecting *disegno*: copying the great masters and live drawings of the human figure.[104] The former, as we have seen, plays a central role in Barry's manuals. It is accorded considerable space in *Picture This* and is closely connected to tthe emphasis on making by hand. In *Disaster Drawn*, Hillary Chute carefully traces a long history of drawing as a means of documenting and bearing witness. Recalling Spiegelman's observation on how "comics talks with its hands," Chute emphasizes the subjectivity and layering of temporalities ensconced in the hand-drawn line.[105] This corresponds with Chute's earlier work on autobiography, which teases out the specificities and expressive potential of the drawn line and how it generates a certain immediacy and presence, which is comparable to Marion's understanding of graphiation.

In addition to making by hand, Barry also incorporates rich tactile elements in her comics: these range from the different kinds of drawing, coloring, inking, and painting materials she uses and a vast gamut of elements she collages, including print, fabric, glitter, and diverse objects. The next section turns to these intensely three-dimensional collage pages and the archival gestures they imply.[106] Building on the notion of trace, Derrida's concept of *restance* or the part of a life that remains but is also altered, is useful for understanding how the drawings and objects that Barry

---

excellent *Thinking about Drawing* which emphasizes the exploratory and embodied nature of drawing over centuries and across diverse cultures of image-making.

[103]Giorgio Vasari, *The Lives of the Artists*, trans. Julia Conaway Bondanella and Peter Bondanella (Oxford University Press, 1998), 85 (with reference to the sculptor Lorenzo Ghiberti); see also the chapters on Paolo Uccello and Michelangelo.

[104]Vasari, *Lives,* 511.

[105]Hillery L. Chute, *Disaster Drawn: Visual Witness, Comics and Documentary* (Bellknap Press, 2016), 69.

[106]For the close connection between comics and archival gestures such as collecting, selecting and swiping see Benoît Crucifix, *Drawing from the Archives: Comics Memory in the Contemporary Graphic Novel* (Cambridge University Press, 2023).

combines are recontextualized while maintaining links with possible,[107] alternative archives built on what would generally be relegated to waste.

As Neale Barnholden has shown in his book, *From Gum Wrappers to Richie Rich: The Materiality of Cheap Culture*, comics and trash culture are closely intertwined: comics were often considered trash and "trash is important to the culture of comics because, as an absence, it defines the value of the present objects, making them existing copies, rather than just copies."[108] Barry's acts of recycling, of pushing waste to the foreground can therefore also be read in light of the diverse, often ignored materialities of comics that have long been part of the medium's essence, including the prominent role of comics in consumer culture, excessive serial production and reiterations. Such textures of waste layer Barry's collages, acting as alternative, rogue archives as we will see below.

Textures

This section unpacks the material layering that characterizes Barry's graphic novels, focusing on her collages of found objects, personal items, student's drawings and lists, and other elements often rescued from trash. Such collages bring in an archival dimension to Barry's comics, simultaneously exemplifying an archival methodology, an archive-in-the-making, and a curated archive. Questioning notions of the archive and archival policies on one hand, Barry also highlights possibilities of creating with archives and how comics and notebooks function as archives. *Syllabus* and *Making Comics*, both of which adopt the form of a lined notebook, function as archives of Barry's comics courses, combining the instructions and tenets of her classes with the work produced by students. As we saw in the previous chapters, *Everything: Comics from Around 1978-1981* is a carefully curated archive of Barry's earliest works, many never printed and dating back to her high school years and some now out of print, such as the *Two Sisters* comic and early *Ernie Pook's Comeek* strips, including *Girls and Boys*. The smaller, horizontally oriented publications were transposed to the bigger, vertically

---

[107]Jacques Derrida, *Trace et Archive, Image et Art* (INA, 2014), 49. Jacques Derrida, *Limited Inc*, trans. Samuel Weber (Northwestern University Press, 1988), 51–2, 83.
[108]Neale Barnholden, *From Gum Wrappers to Richie Rich: The Materiality of Cheap Comics* (University Press of Mississippi, 2024), 146.

oriented format of *Everything*, which is identical to the *Picture This* and *What It Is* volumes. In the process, Barry adds another layer of recuperated material, as we already saw in Chapter 2 (Figure 2.1).

The different techniques Barry incorporates in her books introduce specific layers and textures. As we saw in the previous chapter, Barry's notebooks are already layered, with smaller sheets pasted on top of a "background" page that imitates—and appropriates, rendering personal and subjective—the mechanically drawn, standardized lines of the notebook with lines in color "pulled" (drawn or painted) by hand. The hand and the handmade are central to Barry's creative and teaching practices. This extends to the gestures of cutting out and pasting both handmade and commercially produced images and objects, gestures that in turn are encouraged by the exercises presented in *Picture This*. Almost all of Barry's comics, which are not collections of her comic strips, contain additional layers of pasted materials and mixed media techniques.

Cultural memory scholar, Aleida Assmann, has emphasized the fine line between the archive and waste and how "waste is as important to the archive as forgetting is to memory."[109] For describing the process of breathing life into waste, Assmann turns to museum scholar, Krzysztof Pomian's concept of the semiophor, "a visible sign of something invisible and ungraspable, like the past or a person's identity."[110] The transition from waste to semiophor involves transforming what was seen fit for the trash can into an object loaded with (new) meaning. Barry's eager cutting and pasting informing the intense, heavily collaged pages of *What It Is* partake in a similar meaning-making activity, according new, multidirectional signification to waste originating from anonymous mass-produced publications and objects to local, community archives. In the case of *What It Is*, Barry incorporates elementary school teacher Doris Mitchell's archive. The Wisconsin-based Mitchell began teaching in the mid-1920s. In her thank-you note to the Mitchells, Barry explains: "Many of the handwritten bits and children's schoolwork are from her vast collection of papers she kept all throughout her life. I am lucky to have access to such treasure while making this book."[111]

---

[109] Aleida Assmann, *Cultural Memory and Western Civilization: Functions, Media, Archives* (Cambridge University Press, 2011), 14.
[110] Assmann, *Cultural Memory*, 14. Assmann references Posnian's *Der Ursprung des Museums. Vom Sammeln* (Berlin, 1986).
[111] Barry, *What It Is*, 210.

Mitchell's archive acquires the status of a treasure for Barry's book because of her interest in childhood expression, drawing, writing and childhood memories. Although *What It Is* interweaves numerous personal moments from Barry's life, it also borrows from, and breathes new life into, Mitchell's collection, which forms a personal archive of school, and by extension, community life. Although the archive would have attracted a limited public on its own, in forming a substantial part of the layers underpinning *What It Is*, the archive, in its new, partially camouflaged form of Barry's collages reaches a wide readership. At the same time, it also shares fragments of collective, shared childhoods from a not-too-distant past.

Rubbish, the increasing mounds of human waste, are a side product of modernity that extend, in the twenty-first century, to encompass human lives and existence beyond the globalized world, as Zygmunt Bauman points out in *Wasted Lives: Modernity and its Outcasts*. The accumulation and treatment of waste, as well as the fine line between waste and archive, or what should be thrown away or treasured, had already been traced by the late Romantic French poet, Charles Baudelaire.[112] The activities of the *chiffonnier*, based on triage, emphasize these wavering, all too easily exchangeable categories:

> Everything that the big city has thrown away, everything it has lost, everything it has scorned, everything it has crushed underfoot he catalogues and collects. He collates the annals of intemperance, the capharnaum of waste. He sorts things out and selects judiciously; he collects, like a miser guarding a treasure, refuse which will assume the shape of useful or gratifying objects between the jaws of the goddess of Industry.[113]

Benjamin famously adopted the chiffonnier's method to his *Arcades Project*, exemplifying how the ragpicker could also be a critic, interweaving fragments to offer a pertinent critique of the modern condition; a form of critique that was effective precisely through its fragmentariness. Barry's collages perform comparative work and encourage the reader to re-read and interweave the visual layers, to collaborate in archival and detective work.

---

[112]See Assmann, *Cultural Memory*, 371.
[113]Cited in Walter Benjamin, "Rag Picking: The Arcades Project," in *Walter Benjamin's Archive: Images, Texts, Signs*, ed. Ursula Marx et al., trans. Esther Leslie (Verso, 2007), 251–65, 251.

Critical Themes and Questions

Figure 3.7 "What Is Where Is Your Imagination" collage, from *What It Is*, 20. Copyright Lynda Barry. Used with permission from Drawn & Quarterly.

Thierry Groensteen's famous concept of *tressage* or braiding, and Barbara Postema's complementary notion of weaving, acquire new dimensions in the collaged richness of *What It Is*: the reader is encouraged to move back and forth and across Barry's other books to fully grasp the potential range of connections opened by each page, including the significance of recurring motifs such as the spirals or beings such as the multi-eyed sea monster and the magic cephalopod. One of the earliest collages in *What It Is* asking the question, "What is Where is Your Imagination?" (Figure. 3.7), effectively captures the multitude of potential connotations Barry interweaves on one single page. The lined sheet of yellow notebook paper, pasted against a light blue sheet bearing the book's page number, recalls the paper of the intro and outro in *One Hundred Demons*, for which *What It Is* is a companion volume.[114] Recalling the ghostly portrait of the young Barry opening

---

[114] Brown, "Play," 127.

the book and discussed in Chapter 1, this page incorporates a reworked photograph: a very young Barry sits in front of a house and looks at the camera but her face is almost completely blotted out. An inked demon poses next to her, with multiple dots and the label "Me." The caption at the bottom of the photo, "The Both of Me," confirms the composite, multifaceted identity presented by Barry: one photographed and reworked, young and human, the other, incomprehensible and ghostly, drawn in ink. A closer look reveals another child behind the inked demon. The claim above the photograph, "existed first in the imagination," further mystifies the situation. The collaged photographed confirms the fluidity of identity and even unsettles the documentary function of the photograph. Another, bigger "Me" appears right next to the photograph, an inked cephalopod with human eyes and a clock replacing a face. Lynda and cephalopod become one, hybrid, fluid entity, just like the sea monster in *One Hundred Demons* who adopts Barry's words.

The cephalopod is already present right opposite the portrait of the young Lynda on the second page of *What It Is*. Reflecting the dedication to Frasca, the creature's face comprises a big printed "Teacher" and two nocturnal animals, an owl and a bat. In the collage above, the cephalpod mirrors the ghostly sheen of the uncanny collages anchored in the world of childhood, which blur the boundaries between Barry's childhood and multiple anonymous childhoods. The carefully written texts in cursive blue ink on scraps of notebook paper could be part of the material Barry has integrated from Mitchell's papers. A cut-out photograph of a kitten, scraps of fabric patterned with the colors and forms associated with childhood—cute, round animals and flowers in pastel colors—collate an entire imaginary surrounding childhood, from consumer culture to school life onto this single page. This page in turn dialogues with the page opposite, with its title question "What is the Past Made of?"[115] Once again cute animals and the lined notebook paper introduce the realm of childhood. Despite the elements of cuteness, this is no idealized, nostalgic realm. Barry offers three answers to the title question and confirms all three possibilities, echoing the true and false answers on the table of contents page of *One Hundred Demons*. The past is made of "things that happened," "things that never happened," and "both."[116] This confirms the refusal to offer categorial

---

[115]Barry, *What It Is*, 19.
[116]Barry, *What It Is*, 19.

answers or a straightforward storyline in *What It Is*. Although *What It Is* breaks away from the comics form, completely ignoring the panels that were so dominant in *One Hundred Demons*, it remains comicitous because of the implicit braiding of different sections and layers on the page that extend to form a network across the book and Barry's oeuvre.

The collage works also foreground what Gardner has identified as the "structural affinities of the comics form with the 'database aesthetic,' that has contributed to the increasing visibility and relevance of the comics form in the twenty-first century."[117] This database aesthetic privileges the fragmented over the linear, edging closer to what the semiotician and comics fan Umberto Eco has called the *opera aperta* or open work of art, without entering into the conceptual and abstract realm, which risks alienating readers.[118] The database aesthetic as theorized by media scholar Lev Manovich is heavily reliant on archives, notably, "multilayered, nonhierarchical, navigable archives."[119] Although Gardner focuses on more traditionally structured comics, instead of the collage, Barry's collages both activate and create nonhierarchical, mobile and layered archives. The layers are material, informed by changing media and techniques. In the self-referential stories the collages are sometimes the glue, merging autobiographical episodes with comics-making exercises and reflections on the very personal sources of creativity. Through these collages Barry enmeshes her identity with her vocation as an artist. This is reinforced by the scrapbook-like *Everything,* which elaborates further on Barry's drawings as a teenager and as a budding comics artist, offering more detail on these early years instead of a longer life narrative, such as the one pieced together in several episodes and interspersed across *What It Is*.

The collaged layers, as we have already seen, bring additional meaning while recuperating waste. Underscoring the importance of waste for cultural memory, Aleida Assmann mentions the relevance of art installations and fantasy in revealing the role of rubbish through "their experimental archiving of whatever the current culture has rejected."[120] As confirmed by the ghosts, monsters, and additional doodles in the image above, and in the

---

[117] Gardner, *Projections*, 149.
[118] For a transposition of Eco's concept of the *opera aperta* to comics from several Western cultural spheres, see Maaheen Ahmed, *Openness of Comics: Generating Meaning Within Flexible Structures* (University Press of Mississippi, 2016).
[119] Gardner, *Projections,* 177. See also Lev Manovich, "Database as Symbolic Form," *Convergence* 5, no. 2 (1999): 80–99.
[120] Assmann, *Cultural Memory*, 14.

preceding section on animation, Barry's collages also rely on the fantastic in their interaction with the debris of print culture and personal and collective memories.

In addition to theorizing cultural memory and its relationship to waste, especially in contemporary art practices, Assmann has also identified seven forms of forgetting, most of which are the inevitable corollary of archival work.[121] Barry's collages with their seemingly chaotic and unorganized sheen, rejecting clear categories and even reading paths, reflect on at least three of Assmann's seven forms: automatic forgetting, preservative forgetting, and selective forgetting. The first category, automatic forgetting refers to the inevitable failings of memory, including biological, material, and technical failings. Preservative forgetting is connected to the functioning of the archive, which in its preservative function excludes material. Selective forgetting builds on individual and collective memory dynamics

> hinged on processes of selection. While storage space can be infinitely extended and supplemented, memory space remains a rare resource. While the external storage space of computers is growing exponentially, our brains will have to go on working on the more or less limited and invariant basis of their biological infrastructure. This accounts for the huge difference between storing and remembering: while storing provides a device against forgetting, remembering is always a co-product of remembering and forgetting. For this reason, all processes of remembering include various shades of forgetting such as neglecting, overlooking, ignoring. In other words: the gaps created by forgetting are an integral part of remembering, providing its contours.[122]

Barry's collages, as we can see in Figure 3.7, foreground the gaps in the constructions of stories and memories, which once again confirms their comicitous essence, even though the form is more closely connected to the world of modernist and avant-garde art than comics.

Barry's collage work also embodies the inverse of the sixth form of constructive forgetting, since remembering or "rememorying," a concept

---

[121] Aleida Assmann, "Forms of Forgetting," *Herengracht 401: Research, Art, Dialogue*, https://h401.org/2014/10/forms-of-forgetting/7584/.
[122] Assmann, "Forms of Forgetting."

developed by Toni Morrison and Barbara Christian, is essential to Barry's creative and storytelling processes, as we will see in greater detail in the next section.[123] Connecting rememorying to comics autobiographies, including *One Hundred Demons*, Jane Tolmie describes the process as "the active and deliberate reconstruction of memory to void fixed categories."[124] The multiple, potential young selves presented by Barry in the above image reflect on how even self-identity and autobiography become questionable. Such images can also function as antidotes to forgetting and the unreliable processes of remembering.

Finally, there is also a material way in which forgetting, and gaps, are signified in *What It Is*: some sheets are sprinkled with holes and while these holes are sometimes relegated to the margins of the page, recalling pre-perforated sheets, ready to be filed in a folder, many of the holes are randomly placed, as in the image above (Figure 3.7). These holes, which allow most of the notebook paper to seep through are drawn by Barry, imitating a punching machine while skewing the outlines to highlight the traces of the human hand. They replace the intericonic spaces between the panels or the gutters, emphasize the materiality of the page while suggesting that all gaps cannot be filled, all waste cannot be recuperated and some elements will slip through the holes and be forgotten.

In *Picture This*, two typed sets of words, "Don't" and "Throw It Away", appear respectively at the top left corner and the bottom right corner of a page from Robert L. Stevenson's *Treasure Island*. The multi-eyed sea monster inked over it and dominating the page, brandishes an ink brush as if to add further weight to the words.[125] Is the injunction to not throw away coming from the sea monster or the two monkey figures or the many birds painted over Stevenson's adventure classic?

Safekeeping, revisiting and incorporating become tenets as central to Barry's comics as the injunctions to copy and cut, draw automatically and create. Her collage works also have close affinities with scrapbooking as we saw in connection to *One Hundred Demons* in Chapter 2, functioning as keepsake books and offering unstable life narratives that will be broached further in the final section of this chapter. The remaining part of this section will explore the potentialities of creating collages out of waste and

---

[123]Tolmie, "Introduction," *Drawing from Life*, xx.
[124]Tolmie, "Introduction," *Drawing from Life*, xx.
[125]Barry, *Picture This*, 94.

its interventions in the realms of both collective memory and notions of authorship. Recalling Ilya Kabakov's museum of waste from the 1980s, which the artist created in response to the crumbling systems of the Soviet Union, Assmann proposes waste as "a metaphor for life itself in its ephemeral state, dominated by the forces of disappearance."[126] By recuperating waste and thematizing it, Barry's collages become a highly apposite means of life writing in all its complexity, just like the issues of "can't remember, can't forget" which appear on the collage page for "Resilience" in *One Hundred Demons* and form a central concern in *What It Is*.[127]

The combination and interlinking of diverse materials and the suggestion of three-dimensionality in the collages generates what Barry calls "bumpiness."[128] This bumpiness is connected to the textures of the page and the elements of surprise and possibilities of signification introduced by each disparate element. It introduces a a *tromp-l'oeil* effect while destabilizing notions of authorship and authorial genius. As we saw in the previous chapter, Barry's collage aesthetic evokes the Pattern and Decoration movement that emerged in the United States in the 1970s.[129] Valorizing handicrafts often denigrated as feminine and domestic, artists such as Miriam Schapiro, Joyce Kozloff, Robert Kushner, among many others, created works based on the repetitive patterns of wallpaper and household fabrics and incorporated techniques connected to textile, from printing to stitching.[130] Barry's collages, especially in *One Hundred Demons*, similarly incorporate textiles and repeat drawn and collaged motifs. The "free" and often childlike drawing style also participates in a politics comparable to that of the Pattern and Decoration artists by drawing attention to ignored forms of creation. In Barry's case, childish and girly elements strike the dominant notes in lieu of feminine and domestic features. Her patterns and motifs are often clearly handmade and prone to unevenness, in contrast to the often perfectly regular patterns created by Kozloff or Schapiro. Her practice, as we saw in the previous chapter, is also more democratic and accessible since it unfolds in a book instead of in the museum space.[131]

---

[126] Assmann, *Cultural Memory*, 377.
[127] Chute and Barry, "Lynda Barry," 76.
[128] Chute, *Graphic Women*, 110.
[129] Chute, *Graphic Women*, 110.
[130] For more on Pattern and Decoration see Anna Katz, ed., *With Pleasure: Pattern and Decoration in American Art, 1972-1985* (MOCA and Yale University Press, 2019).
[131] Michael, "Scrapbooking Caravaggio's *Medusa*."

Parallel to the active reworking of photographic and archival elements in the collages, Barry also mentions her childhood practice of transforming pictures in magazines into monsters.[132] This is one of the relatively rare autobiographical moments in *Picture This*. On a page in blue and gray tones, surrounded by ghostly faces and reworked photographs, Lynda recalls how she was chastised by her mother for destroying the magazine. When Lynda points out that her mother had already thrown the magazine away and that she had fished it out from the garbage, Lynda's mother insists: "Do not ruin the garbage! When I put something in the garbage I want it to stay there!" Even the reanimation and metamorphosis of garbage comes with its own perils and unpredictable outcomes, including new, unexpected lives and reactions.

The acts of drawing over introduce new textures, personalizing and transforming existing works. They also recall another avant-garde practice, that of *détournement* or the misappropriation of images, famous examples of which include Marcel Duchamp's painting of a moustache over a copy of the *Mona Lisa*, which he rebranded as *L. H. O. O. Q* (1919) or Asger Jorn's equally childlike distortion from 1962 of a young bourgeois girl's portrait from the nineteenth century, found at a flea market. In uneven letters imitating chalk and spread all over the somber background of the portrait, Jorn writes defiantly, "*L'avant-garde se rend pas*" (The avant-garde does not surrender), which became the reworked painting's new title. Two doodles in the same white paint as the text confirm the connection to children's worlds and childish rebellion. Of course, these two avant-garde examples, just like the collage practice, which the critic Clement Greenberg hailed as revolutionary in 1959, acquire a completely different status and new connotations in Barry's books.[133] What all these works share is the engagement with, and reconsideration of, existing material, a testing and even transformation of value systems. At the center of Barry's practice is the experience of the image, not only the act of visualizing, as she clarifies in an interview, but the experience that is transmitted by making marks.[134]

The final section of this chapter returns to Barry's specific brand of life writing, autobifictionalography. While autobifictionalography modulates

---

[132]Barry, *Picture This*, 53.
[133]Clement Greenberg, "Collage," in *Art and Culture: Critical Essays* (Beacon Press, 1989), 70–83.
[134]Chute, "Lynda Barry," 76.

the presence and absence of Barry and her memories, the collages expand these concerns to a collective scale. Unfolding in the marginal medium of comics and also intervening in the unstable mode of life writing in comics, Barry's collages, by transposing the paradoxical art of cutting and pasting to comics, become a means of materially questioning and stretching the limits of the comics form, a form which, with its grid-like, schematic structure is, to a certain extent, inherently self-conscious. Following the logic of authorial presence and absence characterizing collages, the next section argues that Barry creates stories that mediate between the personal and the collective acquiring a truthfulness through sustaining a reality that resonates on both individual and collective levels.

Life Writing

This fourth and final section on life writing builds on the archival elements introduced through collages to elaborate on the memory-making dimensions of Barry's comics. It expands on the diaristic and the notebook-keeping practice introduced in Chapter 1 through insights on comics autobiographies. These are enhanced by understandings of how specific materialities in Barry's comics contribute to a dialogic, even playful and not always reliable, authentification.

It will not come as a surprise that the first chapter of Elisabeth El Refaie's book on autobiographical comics opens with Barry's portrayal of herself in *One Hundred Demons* as she questions the degree of truth required to distinguish autobiography from fiction. El Refaie turns to life writing scholar Sidonie Smith's observation that autobiography was traditionally dominated by the "tyranny of the arid 'I', which obscures through a gray and shapeless mist everything colorful that lies within its vision."[135] As countless scholars, including El Refaie, have deftly shown, comics autobiography is anything but gray, even when it shuns color. In Barry's case, the autobiographies are visually and thematically colorful, maintaining a degree of unreliability while not shying away from sharing or

---

[135]Elisabeth El Refaie, *Autobiographical Comics: Life Writing in Pictures* (Jackson, University Press of Mississippi, 2012), 11. El Refaie refers to Sidonie Smith's *Subjectivity, Identity and the Body: Women's Autobiographical Practices in the Twentieth Century* (Indiana University Press, 1993). See also Kunka, *Autobiographical Comics*.

even oversharing, much in the tradition of underground comics. Unlike the pioneering underground artist, Aline Kominsky-Crumb and many other female graphic novelists, Barry's obsessions often surround her creative activities and her childhood. And, apart from the "Head Lice" demon in *One Hundred Demons* and the several guest appearances by her husband, Kevin Kawula, we often encounter her present self as a creator reflecting on the role of the past on the present.

We have already seen how Barry portrays her own creative anxieties in her manuals to introduce exercises and potential solutions to creative blocks. In reprints of older works, such as *The Greatest Marlys* and *Everything*, Barry also incorporates brief comics reflecting on how she made certain works. While in the introductory comic for *The Greatest Marlys*, as we saw above, Barry interweaves a childhood memory, in *Everything*, she offers more detail into her artistic influences and artistic choices, avoiding the heavier, autobiographical episodes that we encounter in *What It Is* and in the margins of *Picture This*.

Concerning the abrupt end of her first comic, *Two Sisters*, for instance, Barry explains how the comic very quickly became an artistic dead-end for her:

> After several months of drawing the "Two Sisters" comics I felt trapped by the characters and the drawing style I'd been so sure about. In my sketchbooks things were changing but I didn't know how to change things in "Two Sisters." So I ended it suddenly and abruptly and in a way that was very harsh for 1979. People who liked "Two Sisters" were very mad at me but I was a smart-ass punk by then. And it was a smart-ass time.[136]

The comics that Barry made following *Two Sisters* were the *Girls and Boys* (later *Ernie Pook's Comeek*) strips, a collection of which was published in 1981 and discussed in the previous chapter. Under a picture showing Barry signing the book for a child and his mother and above an excerpt from her 1984 datebook listing the book signing party on October 11, 1981, Barry recalls aspects she was unaware of at that time:[137] these include her continuing to draw comics and more specific elements such as the

---

[136] Barry, *Everything*, 108.
[137] Barry, *Everything*, 114.

"*unshakeable* and *strong*" traces left by the first drawings she had copied, how her drawing and writing would alternate between bitter and sweet styles, and that the feeling-change she was striving to create through her comics entailed a hybrid form that could not be conveyed through drawing or text alone.

Everything revisits the "comics from around 1979-1981" announced in the title while reworking scraps from the numerous notebooks, datebooks, scrapbooks, and sketchbooks Barry had filled over the years. As Barry explains at the beginning of the book, she does not have any childhood drawings of her own "but I remember scribbling, the feeling of it being so alive and unpredictable and also surprising. I'm told I really liked drawing potatoes."[138] This observation, handwritten on a notebook paper is peppered with diverse potato forms. It appears underneath one of Barry's brother's drawings when he was four and those of a godson when he was five, which are already more figurative. But we also see a small black-and-white photo of a two-year-old Barry smiling in the snow. A sober, neat caption in pencil, a more transient instrument than an ink pen, gives a date and a name to the place: "Richland Center, WI 1958" the town Barry was born in. Two pages earlier, next to the Campbell's soup can drawing by a fourteen-year-old Barry mentioned in Chapter 1 (Figure 1.3), there is also a small school portrait of Barry from 1972, the same year as the drawing. Although this drawing by Barry and her portrait metonymically confirm the presence of the young hand behind the drawing, Barry's second picture as a toddler has no direct connection with the children's drawings, which are also drawn by slightly older pairs of hands; the potatoes are drawn by Barry as an adult in the absence of actual drawings and in memory of what she had been told she liked to draw as a child.

Just like in the previous section, the collage introduces physical and connotational layers and plays on a dialogic relationship between absences and presences, pasts and present, while also highlighting the transformed remains of a life or the Derridian *restance* mentioned above. This ambiguity is especially tangible in the replacement drawings Barry includes to counter the absence of her missing childhood drawings. [139]

In no other graphic novel do we find as many photographs of Barry and her brothers as in *Everything*. The vast majority of these photographs are

---

[138] Barry, *Everything*, 4.
[139] Barry, *Everything*, 6–7.

noticeably not reworked, but pasted almost untouched, giving the pages surrounding the republished early comics the appearance of a family album or a diary. In *One Hundred Demons,* in contrast, photographs of the young Barry are heavily reworked and sparingly included in the autobifictional comic. Photographs only appear on five counts, two of which are variations of photographs published earlier in the book. Barry, then, only offers three photographs from her childhood, intervening and framing them within the intricate visual and narrative mesh of *One Hundred Demons.* For Nancy Pedri, Barry's inclusion of her photographs in juxtaposition to the many traumatic stories reflect the disjunction between inner and outer expressions of the self.[140] Pedri adds that repetition, of photographs, themes and motifs, in the graphic narrative

> also serves as a re-examination and reworking of an experience which has already been remembered and portrayed, visually and verbally, but that has not been fully or satisfactorily understood. Repetition is a highly self-reflexive narrative technique that complicates the original representation with variation, adjustment, expansion, in short, with interpretation. It not only points towards a need to add layers of meaning to the initial representation, but also to a dissatisfaction with or an incompleteness of that which is on the page.[141]

The first photograph that we encounter is small and recurs three times, appearing in the collage for "Common Scents" and later, in the collage for "Lost and Found."[142] In the first instance, Barry colors her younger self's hair a bright red, adds an enormous nose and sandwiches her face between "sensitive" and "nose." Red emanata in the form of quick, short red lines, add an aura of comic importance to the portrait. The photograph is placed on a large green piece of fabric. It is surrounded by an elaborate frame comprising silver studs, a green braid, topped by an orange flower and other cut-out scraps. In "Lost and Found," the same portrait appears against a different background and frame. The section at the bottom with "nose" has been cut off and only "sensitive" remains, alluding to the emotional reactions Barry had to popular music and the stories she imagined around

---

[140] Pedri, "Traumatic Layering of Self," 3.
[141] Pedri, "Traumatic Layering of Self," 8.
[142] Barry, *One Hundred Demons,* 50, 207.

Figure 3.8 Chapter separator for "Resilience," from *One Hundred Demons*, 62. Copyright Lynda Barry. Used with permission from Drawn & Quarterly.

classified ads. The portrait reappears with a more colorful, collaged frame at the bottom right end of the blank green page following the conclusion of "Lost and Found," the last story in *One Hundred Demons*. Throughout the book, Barry uses this space to reiterate a theme or protagonist of the demon-story. Long after the story has been concluded, Barry's small portrait looks at us, smiling under the alterations and reinforcing the connection between herself and "sensitive," encouraging the readers to approach the stories told with care and understanding.

The second photograph is the largest of the three and appears on the collage page for "Resilience," which ends with Lynda's abuse as a very young girl by a stranger (fig. 3.8). Barry is once again smiling and even younger than in the previous photograph. A semi-translucent orange tape is drawn across her eyes and colorful spirals decorate the white background. Additional collage elements spill into the white space of the photograph. The confident joy of this photograph contrasts starkly with the drawn, older Lynda looking out of a window, into the rain, with the words "(c)an't remember, can't forget" alluding to the traumatic events that will follow. Once again, Barry sprinkles the collage with fabrics, colors and numerous elements alluding to the world of childhood. In "Resilience," Barry tries to recall when she became a teenager, knowingly giving in, like her classmates, to self-destructive behavior, refusing in the process to draw a clear line between childhood and adolescence. Barry directly addresses "(t)his ability to exist in pieces" which adults mistake for resilience.[143] As Pedri shows, the collages and the scattered photographs also manifest the fragmentary nature of existence and identity.

The third and final photograph appears on the collage page for "Magic," with "hello" scribbled on the top, next to a drawn panel showing an older Lynda looking thoughtfully at the photograph.[144] The photograph reappears incorporated into the final panel of the story, where we learn that the photograph of Barry and the younger EV had been taken in a booth at a Woolworth's store.[145] The two had been best friends until Barry turned thirteen and became embarrassed by having a younger friend. "Magic" traces the turbulent, inexplicable behavior of adolescence, of self-despair and retrospective regret. All of this contrasts with the sheer joy diffused by the photograph. It is the only photograph in which the faces are untouched and the preteen Barry smiles widely at the camera, hugging a more reserved but also smiling EV. In this final panel, the photograph becomes a message in a bottle, intended for EV but with no certainty as to whether EV will ever see it: "EV, if you're reading this, hello, it's me."[146] In this instance, Barry fully identifies with and incorporates the childhood photograph, perhaps because it preserves a cherished friendship, now lost and limited to the black-and-white photo. The photograph of past joy evokes mixed feelings of recalled happiness and regret for ending a friendship only out of shame for the two-year age difference. This blend of familiar, uncomfortable feelings exemplifies the emotional power of Barry's comics.

Elaborating on the specific role of scrapbooking photographs in *One Hundred Demons*, Pedri points out how Barry's incorporation of collages in her autobifictional life writing acquires a specific "form that leaves the introductory reflection on the distinction between real and imaginary unresolved and the fraught interplay between inner and outer self open."[147] For this, Pedri continues, Barry uses scrapbooking techniques to "speak to a divided, multiple, perhaps unknowable and unrepresentable, but unique self."[148] As mentioned previously, Barry's mode of life writing is not

---

[143] Barry, *One Hundred Demons*, 70.
[144] Barry, *One Hundred Demons*, 98.
[145] Barry, *One Hundred Demons*, 108.
[146] Barry, *One Hundred Demons*, 108.
[147] Pedri, "Traumatic Layering of Self," 10.
[148] Pedri, "Traumatic Layering of Self," 11.

concerned with facts and it is all too aware of the unreliable workings of memory. Factual details are consequently replaced by an emotional and narrative sense of the past, which acquires a fluidity comparable to the ink Barry works with, and wants us to work with, changing form with each stroke and each new look. The collage work is central to this fluidity, as are the multiple constructions of the self within the collages but also in the panels, in the drawn, photographed and reworked iterations of Barry's younger and older selves.

As Susan Kirtley points out, Barry's mode of life writing is comparable to what Charles Hatfield considers the "working-class strain of autobiography" characterizing both underground comix and the alternative comics that followed them.[149] Hatfield connects this "new type of graphic confessional" to "the activist end of comic book culture" where "autobiographical comics have flourished, overturning the corporate comics hero in favor of the particularized and unglamorous common man or woman."[150] Building on Janet Varner Gunn's emphasis that autobiographical truth is situated in the relational essence of autobiography, dependent on the connections established between the story and the reader,[151] Hatfield suggests that the interactive essence of alternative comics, which directly implicate the reader in (re-)constructing a truth is a means of "ironic authentication."[152] Comics by Daniel Clowes, Robert Crumb, and Gilbert Hernandez, for instance, "invite us to play this game: our input is solicited and our skepticism is flattered, by their refusal to be simply 'honest'—that is fictitious." [153]

Barry's work unfolds in a different strain than most alternative comics, since the kind of irony described by Hatfield is not as central to her comics, and even traditional comics tropes recede into the background. Instead, it is the process of remembering, constructing and sharing which becomes a form of interaction that strives toward a certain honesty by asking questions, sharing doubts and laying bare the process of reconstructing a life story. As suggested above, this kind of self-construction that simultaneously deconstructs is convincingly reflected in Tolmie's use of "rememorying" for autobiographical comics, which emphasizes the self-

---

[149]Kirtley, *Girlhood*, 149. Hatfield, *Alternative Comics*, 111.
[150]Hatfield, *Alternative Comics*, 111.
[151]See Janet Varner Gunn, *Autobiography: Towards a Poetics of Experience* (University of Pennsylvania Press, 1982).
[152]Hatfield, *Alternative Comics*, 125. See also Kirtley, *Girlhood*, 159–60.
[153]Hatfield, *Alternative Comics*, 125.

reflective, the processual and the involvement of the reader.[154] Rachel Trousdale observes that already the non-autobiographical *Ernie Pook's Comeek* "comics examine the intersection of the literal life event and the act of interpretation, representing not so much Barry's actual experience as the process of life writing itself."[155] For Trousdale the assumption of autobiography associated with Barry's comics (even when they are not branded as such, as is the case with *Ernie Pook's Comeek*) lies in her comic's allusions to "tropes of autobiography in their structure, their combination of analysis and nostalgia, and their emphasis on how the incidents illuminate the inner lives of the characters involved." [156]

In a recent interview, Barry clarifies: "I'm not trying to work on the tough stuff of my life, but the tough stuff of my life gets worked on."[157] "Trouble," as we saw in the previous chapter and as Chute reminds us,[158] lies at the heart of Barry's graphic narratives, which contrast starkly with the light-hearted and humorous clichés associated with the comics form. Trouble also clashes with what is usually allowed for child figures, which abound in Barry's books and comics. The messy selves that Barry creates of herself, including her child and teenage selves, and fictional characters, embody trouble through their anxious and vivid imagination. They coexist within and through the unsteady textures of collaged elements and Barry's autobifictionalography. Exemplifying the fragmented essence of life writing in comics and comics-like hybrid forms, Barry's books also activate "ugly" aesthetics such as untutored drawings and uncomfortable memories.

Making room for trouble and messy forms is not only an expressive or aesthetic act, it also has social and critical implications as we will see in the next and final chapter: it is through conveying different kinds of trouble, for instance, that Barry draws attention to the darker, often unsaid or ignored features of marginalized childhoods, and the potentialities of the comics form.

---

[154]Tolmie, "Brief Introduction," 3–4.
[155]Trousdale, "Autobiography," 113.
[156]Trousdale, "Autobiography," 113.
[157]Barry and Marchese, "Genius Cartoonist."
[158]Chute, *Graphic Women*, 96.

CHAPTER 4
SOCIAL AND CULTURAL IMPACT

Adults think that kids playing is some nothing thing. . . . But play is a different state of mind, and it can help us do so many things if we just allow ourselves to get back to it.[1]

Lynda Barry (interview with David Marchese)

Barry's above words from a recent interview show how it is not only the representation of children that dominates her work but also childhood worlds, emotions, and modes of creation. These themes have already been introduced and discussed in the previous chapters and this final chapter of the guide begins by focusing on the role of intersectional concerns, especially class, childhood, and girlhood.

The first section shows how Barry elaborates a form of storytelling that is intersectional, almost pre-dating Kimberlé Crenshaw's introduction of the term in 1989.[2] Building on Chaney's discussion of the relevance of the comics child and how "the child also configures lost ways of knowing"[3] mentioned in the previous chapter, this chapter expands on how children in comics acquire new forms and significance in Barry's works. We have seen in previous chapters how Barry's books often embrace the material forms of childhood culture, ranging from the illustrated book (*The Good Times Are Killing Me*) to the composition notebook (*Syllabus* and *Making Comics*). Further, Barry's more recent publications, which move away from autobifictionalographies toward the drawing manual, advocate for a return to the more hybrid use of images and words that young children are accustomed to and that older children and adults are discouraged to use.

---

[1] Barry and Marchese, "Genius Cartoonist."
[2] Kimberlé Crenshaw, "Demarginalizing the Intersection of Race and Sex: A Black Feminist Critique of Antidiscrimination Doctrine, Feminist Theory and Antiracist Politics," *University of Chicago Legal Forum* 1989, no. 1 (1989): 139–67.
[3] Chaney, *Reading Lessons*, 91.

Lynda Barry

The second section of this chapter turns to Barry's pedagogical inspirations, from children's drawings and from teachers in diverse creative fields, to enumerate the key tenets of her exercises.

Barry's comics manuals are communicative, sprinkled with autobiographical moments sharing the personal relevance of certain exercises with their reader-makers. While part of the relevance often lies in how the proposed exercises and tips boost Barry's own creativity, others offer insight into the genesis of certain visual motifs. In *Picture This*, for instance, above a page full of meditating monkeys, Barry recalls the emergence of the serial drawings, adding, at the bottom of the page, a suggestion of their potential healing relevance for the reader: "when a friend of mine died I started drawing this monkey a lot . . . I have drawn thousands of this helpful Monkey. Why not try it?"[4] This moment of sharing and creative advice confirms that the model reader of many of Barry's comics is not only a confidant, keeping within the conventions of autobiographical writing,[5] but is also willing to indulge in creative acts themselves. The final section of this chapter elaborates on how Barry's comics offer different possibilities for connecting and how, as a result, they chart new frontiers for the potential of comics.

Intersectional Comics

In 1989, legal and critical race studies scholar Kimberelé Crenshaw introduced the prism of intersectionality to highlight the imbrication of racial, economic, and gender-related factors in perceptions, power relationships, and policy. Intersectionality has now entered everyday discourse to draw attention to the complex, multifaceted functioning and lasting impact of inequality. This section turns to how Barry represents her own and fictional children's experiences growing up in a working-class neighborhood and facing everyday racism or bullying for being different.

The multilayered spaces Barry creates for representing childhood often thematize the clash between idealized childhoods and the dark realities of growing up, without leaving out moments of joy and even humor. This bittersweet mix complements the hybrid forms of Barry's works. Building

---

[4] Barry, *Picture This*, 122.
[5] Philippe Lejeune, *On Autobiography*, trans. Katherine Leary (University of Minnesota Press, 1989).

on Sara Richardson's discussion of shame in memoir comics, this section also elaborates on Barry's transposition of shame to the realm of childhood.[6] It traces Barry's empathy generation strategies and how she conveys a sense of honesty and authenticity to open up a space for understanding.

Scholars have frequently categorized Barry as a feminist cartoonist,[7] with Melinda Luisa de Jesús including her under a growing group of peminists (Filipina American feminists).[8] Girls and women and their lives are often the main concerns of Barry's comics and their politics often combines the dismantling of gender-based hegemonies alongside mainstream aesthetic and cultural ones. Kirtley points out that Barry's aesthetic, especially in her early weekly strips is one inscribed in, and contributing to, "a shared culture of destruction and authenticity."[9] She adds that Barry's distinctive serialized comic strips worked to "constitute a community of punk—an audience that simultaneously sought to destroy mainstream notions of what a comic strip 'should' be, while positing something more authentic, more real in its wake."[10]

Already Barry's diaries—both fictional, such as *Cruddy* and *The Good Times Are Killing Me*, and autobiographical, such as *One Hundred Demons* and the personal memories seeping through *What It Is* and *Picture This*—activate a deliberately feminine form. Emphasizing how diary-keeping is a feminine activity, Rebecca Hogan adds that it is also a paratactic form that allows for different readings.[11] Paratactic forms rely on juxtapositions instead of conjunctions. Comics too are paratactic since panels are essentially connected and disconnected through the white space of the gutter. Barry's way of writing, in her illustrated books and comics, is especially paratactic, rapidly moving from one instant to another. And, as shown in the previous chapter, her collages are both paratactic and unabashedly feminine.

Hogan transposes feminist scholar, Naomi Schor's question, "Is the detail feminine?"[12] to the diary. The femininity of detail unpacked by Schor

---

[6]Richardson, "'Perseveration on Detail,'" 149–58.
[7]See, for instance, Melinda L. de Jesús' chapter, "Liminality and Mestiza Consciousness."
[8]de Jesús, "Of Monsters and Mothers: Filipina American Identity and Maternal Legacies in Lynda J. Barry's *One Hundred Demons*," *Méridians: feminisms, race, transnationalism* 5, no. 1 (2004): 1–26, 2.
[9]Kirtley, *Typical Girls,* 107.
[10]Kirtley, *Typical Girls,* 114.
[11]Rebecca Hogan, "Engendered Autobiographies: The Diary as a Feminine From," *Prose Studies* 14, no. 2 (1991): 95–107, 103–4.
[12]Hogan, "Engendered Autobiographies," 95. See also Naomi Schor, *Reading in Detail: Aesthetics and the Feminine* (Routledge, 2007).

Lynda Barry

finds an echo in Barry's rich collages, and even a literal echo in the girly collages of *One Hundred Demons*. For Hogan, "the diary, which valorizes the detail in both the realms of ornament and everyday, can also be seen as feminine."[13] Barry's blend of ornament and the everyday extends to her comics manuals, which are carefully decorated, with pulled lines and numerous other visual components, textures, and colors. Chapters 2 and 3 drew parallels with the Pattern and Decoration movement but there is another form of less contained detail that also persists in Barry's comics.

Alicia Chase has convincingly shown how visual artist Carolee Schneemann's words from her *Interior Scroll* (1975) performance resonate strongly in graphic memoirs by female artists:[14]

> the personal clutter
> the persistence of feelings
> the hand-touch sensibility
> the diaristic indulgence
> the painterly mess
> the dense gestalt
> the primitive techniques[15]

This excerpt from Scheemann's *Interior Scroll* adapts the opening lines from her film, *Kitsch's Last Meal* (1973–7), when a structuralist filmmaker lists the reasons why he cannot see films by women.[16] Although Chase focuses on the diaries of Phoebe Gloeckner, Debbie Dreschler and Julie Doucet, clutter and the willingness to share personal moments also play a prominent role in Barry's graphic novels, especially *One Hundred Demons*. Tactility, emotionality, messiness, sharing and even oversharing feature in all of Barry's comics, even non-autobiographical ones. Although Barry does not openly voice political, feminist ambitions, the techniques she uses, like those of the Pattern and Decoration artists, like the "flaws" listed by Schneeman's filmmaker,[17] are closely connected to the feminine.

---

[13]Hogan, "Engendered Autobiographies," 96.
[14]Chute, *Graphic Women*, 96.
[15]Carolee Schneemann, "Text from Interior Scroll, 1975," *Carolee Schneemann Foundation*, accessed December 5, 2024, https://www.schneemannfoundation.org/writing/interior-scroll.
[16]See also Victoria Horne, "'the personal clutter . . . the painterly mess . . .' Tracing a History of Carolee Schneemann's *Interior Scroll*," *Art History* 43, no. 5 (2020): 984–1006.
[17]Miriam Schapiro was one of the founders of the Feminist Art Program at CALARTS in 1971.

Barry activates the everydayness, the intimacy and emotionality of these techniques to portray childhood worlds, sad and even traumatic memories and splintered, wavering constructions of the self.

Michael offers a particularly sophisticated reading of Barry's approach and highlights its "feminist reparative potential," something which, as Michael points out, Cvetkovich does not do, despite mentioning *What It Is* as one of the creative antidotes to fighting depression.[18] For Michael, as we saw in Chapter 2, the hybrid and fluid, unassuming essence of Barry's comics allows for effective, even radical political engagement by offering new, accessible alternatives for such engagement:

> conflating Blake's (illuminated writing) tradition with female/childish amateur processes, the graphic memoir refuses to remain restricted within matrilineal circles and oscillates between distinct categories constantly undermining them and foregrounding their permeability.[19]

The different declinations of Medusa, which encompass Caravaggio's self-portrait as the Medusa, the mythical figure it refers to, Lynda's encounter with it through a monster film, Barry's cartoony iterations of the figure, later re-worked into the cephalopod and Sea-Ma, and the parallels drawn with the abusive mother, evoke Hélène Cixous' iconic essay, "The Laugh of the Medusa," an impassioned call for women to write themselves in a form of embodied writing or *écriture feminine*.[20] As mentioned in Chapter 1, Michael shows how the young Lynda learns to face the terrifying power of the Medusa and transform it into a creative source incarnated by the magic cephalopod and the Sea-Ma.[21] For Michael, these reworkings are closely connected to Cixous' understanding of women's writing, its visceral connections and othered bodiliness.[22] Barry seems to follow Cixous' call to face the Medusa who, instead of transfiguring the looker into stone, will reveal her beauty and laugh back. Michael points out how "(i)t is this gaze at the maternal monster that Barry's text performs because it also

---

[18] Cvetkovich, *Depression*, 203–11.
[19] Michael, "Scrapbooking."
[20] Hélène Cixous, "The Laugh of the Medusa," trans. Keith Cohen and Paula Cohen *Signs* 1, no. 4 (1976): 875–96.
[21] Michael, "Excavating Childhood," 557–61.
[22] Michael, "Excavating Childhood," 560–1.

revises patriarchal discursive formations of the terrifying *vagina dentata* and intervenes in the artistic history of the female monster, both high and low, to introduce a feminist take on it."[23] Elsewhere, Michael notes how the unsettling of boundaries between high and low arts and between art and life, extends to Lynda's gendering, who generally appears as a tomboy, and one who is drawn in a childish style: "it is precisely this childish perspective on the body with its omission of bodily characteristics that could demarcate one's gender and sex that facilitates the representation of Lynda as embodying gender undecidability."[24]

Barry does not focus so much on womanhood as on childhood and girlhood. The focus on children imbues her fictional and autobifictional diaries with a degree of uncontrollability and even volatility, which is evident in the stream of conscious, wildly unpredictable flow of *Cruddy* and persists in *One Hundred Demons*, where the colorful collages are not a simple celebration or affirmation of childhood but incorporate varying shades of dark undertones, matching the stories told.

Theresa Tensuan compellingly observes that *One Hundred Demons* adheres to the tendency in Barry's comics to offer "an ongoing critique of the forms of discursive violence that structure and modulate day-to-day life."[25] Tensuan considers *One Hundred Demons* and Marjane Satrapi's *Persepolis* as forms of loitliterature. Coined by Ross Chambers, loitliterature is a broad genre encompassing narratives that are "wayward," incorporating techniques of deferral and digression, espousing episodic forms over coherent, linear ones.[26] In being deliberately wayward, loitliterary forms can shed light on systemic blindness, modes of exclusion and offer new ways of knowing and critiquing.[27] To illustrate such loitliterary workings, Tensuan turns to the "Lost and Found" and "Girlness" episodes in *One Hundred Demons*. In the former (discussed in Chapter 1) Barry recalls her childhood love for classified advertisements and the emotional stories she wove around them. In a self-reflexive twist, the fragmented form of the advertisements

---

[23]Michael, "Excavating Childhood," 561. *Vagina dentata* (toothed vagina) refers to the myth, taken up in Freudian psychoanalysis and reflected in the Sea-Ma (556).
[24]Michael, "Scrapbooking."
[25]Theresa M. Tensuan, "Comic Visions and Revisions in the Work of Lynda Barry and Marjane Satrapi," *Modern Fiction Studies* 52, no. 4 (2006): 947–64, 948–9.
[26]Tensuan, "Comic Visions," 951. See also, Ross Chambers, *Loitliterature* (Nebraska University Press, 1999).
[27]Tensuan, "Comic Visions," 951.

page is reflected in the comics form and in the episodic structure of *One Hundred Demons*. The collaged separator for this story juxtaposes Barry's drawn versions of her younger and older selves, a reworked photograph, the famous opening line of fairytales, "once upon a time," numerous torn out classified ads and lists of essential telephone numbers.[28] These readings, just like Lynda's preference for the middlebrow *Reader's Digest* stories, contrast starkly with "enshrined childhood literary classics,"[29] of which Barry mentions here, and in *What It Is*, that she possessed very few.[30]

In providing "alternative practices for imagining and inscribing stories," Barry sheds light on ignored childhoods, excluded from the mold of idealized childhood.[31] Scholars of childhood such as Patricia Crain and Carolyn Steedman have shown how, from the nineteenth century onwards, childhood was conflated with an interior, bourgeois space.[32] The childhood interior spaces in Barry's books are often cramped with limited room for the typical objects of childhood such as toys and books. Instead of comfort and childhood paraphernalia, Barry details the smells imbuing her house when her grandmother moved in. Smells which she couldn't smell but which were considered markers of her otherness by the children of her neighborhood, with a girl explaining why she couldn't visit Lynda anymore: "My mom says your people fry weird food and save the grease and also that you boil pig's blood which is the reason for the smell . . . the smell gets on my clothes, makes my mom sick."[33] The girl's mother was an avid user of air freshener and disinfectant. The penultimate page to this story incorporates a critique of consumer culture, much in the vein of Barry's early comics, listing the vast range of air freshening products and pointing out their ridiculousness by imagining new variations such as "cherry pop-up fried liver," "tropical passion aroma therapy cat box," or "piney woods pig's blood stew breakdown."[34] "Common Scents" is one of several stories in *One Hundred Demons* pointing to the casual, everyday

---

[28]Barry, *One Hundred Demons*, 206–7.
[29]Tensuan, "Comic Visions," 961.
[30]Barry, *One Hundred Demons*, 213. Barry, *What It Is*, 27.
[31]Tensuan, "Comic Visions," 961.
[32]Patricia Crain, *Reading Children: Literacy, Property and Dilemmas of Childhood in Nineteenth-Century America* (University of Pennsylvania Press, 2016), 2–4. See Steedman, *Strange Dislocations*.
[33]Barry, *One Hundred Demons*, 55.
[34]Barry, *One Hundred Demons*, 58.

racism encountered by Barry. As we saw in Chapter 2, race was the central concern in *The Good Times Are Killing Me*, erecting an insurmountable barrier between the white Edna and the African American Bonna.[35] *Cruddy* similarly wields strong social critique against different kinds of marginalized childhoods.[36]

"Hate" in *One Hundred Demons* begins as a familiar story of childhood exclusion and hypocritical adult morality which forbids the children to use the word hate even when it accurately describes their feelings. It is only toward the end of the story that a substitute teacher explains the different kinds of hate to Lynda's class, one rooted in prejudice, which led to a boy calling Lynda ugly and pushing her, and the other a reaction to violent acts. While Lynda's mother and other parents do not subscribe to the teacher's logic, the young Lynda thanks the teacher with a card and the words, "I. Love. You," adding "sincerely."[37] This appreciation is for the space opened up by the teacher for the children to react emotionally and to express their anger and frustration at being the targets of violence.

Other comics stories in *One Hundred Demons* thematize differences in social class that continue to haunt Barry well into adulthood, as illustrated by the two conversations Lynda has with other writers in "Lost and Found":[38] claiming to be a cartoonist, Lynda distances herself from literary writers with whom she does not share what Pierre Bourdieu has famously called cultural capital.[39]

In "Girlness," Barry explicitly ties expressions of girlhood with class and the possibility of buying beautiful, "girly" objects. The collage announcing the demon of girlness reintroduces the portrait of a pensive Arna pasted next to the table of contents. Here the portrait is adorned with a white cloth flower on one end and lace at the opposite end, around a pink dial showing a dancing boy and girl mouse. Girlness, as mentioned earlier, imbues many of the rich, colorful collages in *One Hundred Demons*. But it is only toward the end of the book that the theme is addressed as a demon. The collage page opposite the title page for "Girlness" (Figure 4.1) reinforces the theme through numerous elements: a miniature crochet dress, a rabbit ballet

---

[35] See Kirtley, *Lynda Barry*, 187–8.
[36] See Rachel Luria, "Confusions So Horror-Bright: Class and Gender in Lynda Barry's *Cruddy*," in *Contagious Imaginations*, 143–53.
[37] Barry, *One Hundred Demons*, 84.
[38] Barry, *One Hundred Demons*, 212–15.
[39] Bourdieu, *Forms of Capital*.

Social and Cultural Impact

Figure 4.1 "Girlness" chapter separator from *One Hundred Demons*, 182. Copyright Lynda Barry. Used with permission from Drawn & Quarterly.

dancer (a figure that also reappears in Barry's other graphic novels), more lace and flowers printed on fabric or made of fabric and the repetition of "girl, girl," "girlness" and a printed "it's a girl" announcement. Nevertheless the drawn portrait on this page is not of a girl, but a peevish-looking dog, Oola, introduced in the preceding story, "Dogs": as a puppy Oola had been thrown out of a window leading to a broken leg and behavioral problems. The collaged page draws parallels between Oola's "trouble" and Lynda's own "trouble" as a young girl and the contrasting pedagogical approaches to it: showing extra kindness and attention as Mrs. Lesene did, allowing Lynda to draw during recess or refusing to show any flexibility like the third-grade teacher who followed Mrs. Lesene.[40] Barry interweaves these episodes from the past where Lynda is often crying, or being yelled at by her mother for wasting stationary (which the young Lynda replicates before her surprised dog), with the adult Lynda trying to train Oola according to the rules established by "dog books," which rely on asserting dominance. Ultimately, it is kindness that helps Oola, just like it had helped the young Lynda. The juxtaposition of Oola's portrait, against a dark background that

---

[40] Barry wrote an essay on the kindness of a teacher Claire LeSane (see Kirley, *Lynda Barry,* 17), on whom Mrs. Lesene is probably based.

is comparable to Barry's portrait of her younger self in *What It Is* discussed earlier,[41] adds a somber note to the otherwise exuberant collage.

The first two panels of "Girlness" introduce the contrast between the tomboys on Barry's street and the many "girlish girls" from a nearby, more affluent neighborhood.[42] Admitting that there must be more scientifically grounded explanations for the differences, Barry sums them up as follows: "clothes, toys, *and* hair. The girlish girls *had* a lot of *these* things."[43] And adds: "Even *their* dolls had pretty clothes, teeny toys *and* long, combable, *fixable* hair. *If* I had these things would I have *been* a girlish girl too?"[44]

We then learn that Lynda's mother was extremely feminine even though she refused to dress up Lynda in a similar way or let her grow her hair, convinced that it would not suit her. While Lynda's mother manicures her nails, she recalls her childhood in a war-torn Philippines and Lynda reminds us that her mother was only seven when the Second World War broke out. Her mother's femininity and war trauma are interconnected as Melinda de Jesús suggests: it is the extreme deprivation of the war that Lynda's mother compensates for by constructing femininity through active consumerism for herself; she denies this possibility to her daughter, for whom she refuses to buy Barbies or clothes in girlish colors.[45] The complex factors of psychological trauma, race and class become entangled in Barry's exploration of girlness.

Barry then introduces the polar opposite to her, Mariko, a beautiful Japanese-Mexican girl, "who had all the girlness the rest of us *were* missing."[46] While Mariko's mother allows her daughter to keep long hair, acquire beautiful dresses and dolls, she is as overbearing and proscriptive as Lynda's mother, banning her daughter from playing on the street. "Girlness" finds a resolution when the adult Lynda shops with Norabelle, a thirteen-year-old girl visiting her. Lynda allows Norabelle to buy all the girly items she wants and, encouraged by Norabelle, even buys a stationery set for herself. Lynda adds: "I loved *her* sense of girlness. If you could *have* taken me *and* Mariko and *mixed* us together stirring until our *mothers* dissolved,

---

[41] Barry, *What It Is*, 2.
[42] Barry, *One Hundred Demons*, 184.
[43] Barry, *One Hundred Demons*, 185.
[44] Barry, *One Hundred Demons*, 185.
[45] de Jesús, "Of Monsters," 18.
[46] Barry, *One Hundred Demons*, 188.

you would have gotten Norabelle."⁴⁷ Norabelle reconciliates the different, starkly opposed girlhoods presented by Lynda and Mariko and imposed by their mothers. Barry also creates room for trying to understand her mother's cruelty, both through the parallel with Mariko's mother and through the harsh circumstances of the war. In a panel showing Lynda looking in the mirror, she wonders whether her mother would have been "a more momish mom if *the war* had *never* happened? Would I have *been* a more *girlish* girl? Or would we have both *turned* out *the* way *we* were anyway?"⁴⁸ Like many of the questions in *One Hundred Demons* and *What It Is*, this one is unanswerable. In incorporating these questions in her autobifictional stories, Barry emphasizes the malleability of the past, the absence of fixed narratives and the necessity to question. In Barry's comics, childhood is the locus of such questions.

In her article on shame and the graphic memoir, which focuses on Alison Bechdel's *Fun Home* and Art Spiegelman's *Maus*, Sarah Richardson observes the following: "Barry recounts childhood shame around class, race, and creative ability. Her textual avatar exhorts the reader to reject this kind of self-consciousness and return to a purer state of innocence and confidence."⁴⁹ Childhood shame strikes a dominant note in Barry's books and while her manuals encourage a return to a state of making without judging (discussed in further detail in the next section), the resolution of racial and class-based shame lies elsewhere. Richardson recalls Silvan Tomkin's, and more recently, Elspeth Probyn's suggestions "that the interrogation of shame can render it productive" and emphasizes the need to read beyond the therapeutic aspirations underlining the confessional mode.⁵⁰ In contrast to Bechdel's and Spiegelman's graphic memoirs, *One Hundred Demons*, is about the therapeutic process of automatic painting and its results. The demons are not confessions. Instead, they open possibilities toward understanding disparate, key moments in Barry's life. The shame represented here is often connected to being different, of stemming from a mixed-race family, where the "other," Filipino side was the most present and welcoming. It is also connected to the issue of being poor and not having enough, highlighted by the very first story,

---

⁴⁷Barry, *One Hundred Demons*, 191.
⁴⁸Barry, *One Hundred Demons*, 188.
⁴⁹Richardson, "Shame and Confession," 149.
⁵⁰Richardson, "Shame and Confession," 149, 153–4.

"Head Lice and My Worst Boyfriend," which starts with Lynda being called a "little cootie girl," not because she actually had lice but because she was racially different (even in a mixed-race environment, Lynda was too different) and came from an impoverished family.[51] The only time in her childhood when she found it easy to make friends was during a summer visit to the Philippines, where her red hair and white skin were a source of fascination and an example of idealized Western beauty. Lynda only encountered a louse (for which she uses the Filipino word *kuto*), and head lice, when she was in an unbalanced relationship with a man from an affluent background who made little effort to understand who she was. In the penultimate panel, Lynda realizes that her boyfriend, in his lack of empathy and outright denigration of her, closely resembles her mother. The everyday cruelties of the relationship are represented through the lens of irony and humor, which acquire grotesque proportions toward the end when her boyfriend literally metamorphoses into her mother. Humor is a powerful tool that comics wield to counter and even subvert harsh realities, such as racism and socio-economic struggles in Henry Yoshitaka Kiyama's *The Four Immigrants Manga* (1931), the first Asian American migrant graphic novel.[52] While Barry's humor is a far cry from generic modes of humor, such as slapstick, she inserts humorous moments and grotesque caricature to attenuate the harshness of painful situations.

In harnessing the numerous possibilities of expression offered by the comics form's blend of word and image and combining it with other fragmentary techniques such as collage, Barry shares multiple nuanced and moving "life moments" (which is how the demons are described on the backflap of the book) from her childhood and adulthood. In the process, sources of shame and embarrassment become spaces of social critique. Both class and racial biases play a prominent role in this critique. Barry carefully traces the contours of her mixed-race identity, sharing both the prejudices stuck to it and the richness of the heritage transmitted through her mother's family, especially through her loving grandmother, as we saw in Chapter 1.

---

[51] de Jesús, "Liminality and Mestiza Consciousness," 80.
[52] Monica Chiu, "Coming to America, 'Land of the Free': Asian American Representations in the Graphic Novel," in *The Cambridge Companion to the American Graphic Novel*, ed. Jan Baetens, Hugo Frey, and Fabrice Leroy (Cambridge University Press, 2023), 226–41, 239. The full title of the comic is *The Four Immigrants Manga: A Japanese Experience in San Francisco between 1904 and 1924*.

Observing how the rich, colorful visuality of *One Hundred Demons* "are an integral part in the process of self-creation,"[53] Melinda L. de Jesús writes:

> The Filipino American history of disarticulated racial grieving finds its form in Barry's work; indeed, it is this tension between racial grieving (Filipino American identity crisis) and hope (mestiza consciousness) that gives Barry's vision its agency: testifying to the reality of pain and confusion caused by colonization and forgetting, her comics underscore our agency in the maintenance or dismantling of these systems.
>
> *One Hundred Demons* refutes the idea of Filipina American "unrepresentability," because its form (aesthetic/artistic) and themes link mestiza consciousness to decolonization. It points out the real demons in Filipino America, encouraging us to own and confront them.[54]

Here, de Jesús transposes Gloria Anzaldúa's affirmative understanding of mestiza consciousness as "a new way of being and seeing that transcends the oppositional forces/narratives that would divide her."[55] As we already saw in Chapter 1, Barry's demons and other comics, going back to her earliest works, repeatedly mock oppressive and destructive systems, including consumer culture, which promise happiness through incessant consumption, and adult prejudices, which are reproduced in children's games and daily interactions.

Barry's focus on detail and on specificities is another way of both understanding and offering hope, of overcoming the pain wrought by the numerous demons. In sharing intimate details from her childhood and her past and present anxieties, Barry paves the way toward empathic identification. This is especially striking in her powerful portrayals of children's worlds. As Rachel Trousdale demonstrates in her article, "Autobiography and the Empathic Imagination in *Ernie Pook's Comeek*," Barry's portrayal of children's inner worlds effectively channels empathic connections. In the "About the Author" note in *The Greatest of Marlys*, Barry explains how Marlys' childhood was very different from hers and how

---

[53] de Jesús, "Liminality and Mestiza Consciousness," 76.
[54] de Jesús, "Liminality and Mestiza Consciousness," 90.
[55] de Jesús, "Liminality and Mestiza Consciousness," 78.

Marlys helped Barry understand and even express certain things, becoming her most cherished imaginary friend in the process. Trousdale suggests that this note's "discussion of the line between fiction and autobiography also sheds light on the comic's treatment of how the narrative framing of memory can become an act of empathy—for others and for the past self—and of self-defense."[56] The role of child characters and children's worlds, of imaginatively remembering and reworking—rememorying—is crucial.

Tamaryn Bennett observes how in *One Hundred Demons* and *What It Is*, "Barry's questions and invocations periscope into the inner life of children, a place that more chronological approaches to reconstruction of childhood gloss over."[57] Bennett cites Jeanne Cooper for whom "by retrieving the everyday discards of conversation and experience and mixing in remnants of her personal life, Barry has created a found art of children's souls, one than can veer from harrowingly poignant to wildly funny and never go off course."[58] Of the many children Barry has portrayed, ranging from her younger selves, the children she grew up with to the diverse fictional children, all are flawed and believable. We understand these children and even empathize with them. Part of this is connected to how children evoke interiority, which was introduced in Chapter 2. Carolyn Steedman suggests that children "gained their enormous affective power" and were seen "as extensions of the adult self" through a "process [. . .] of personification."[59] This contributes to the emotional hold of the figure of the child, which Steedman explains through evoking Raymond Williams' famous concept of structure of feelings, which can reveal shared cultural patterns at a particular time: "The figure of the child, released from the many texts that gave birth to it, helped shape feelings, and structure feeling into thought."[60] In other words, the emotions and affects attached to children give rise to certain assumptions and clichés around childhood. The children in Barry's comics excel at both harnessing these affective givens and subverting expectations. As we have seen, Barry's portrayals regularly dismantle conventions associated with narratives around childhood.

---

[56] Trousdale, "Autobiography," 125.
[57] Tamaryn Bennett, "Dancing with Demons: Consciousness and Identity in Lynda Barry's *One Hundred Demons*," in *Picturing Childhood: Youth in Transnational Comics*, ed. Mark Heimermann and Brittany Tullis (University of Texas Press, 2017), 218–33, 221.
[58] Cited by Bennett, "Dancing," 228.
[59] Steedman, *Strange Dislocations*, 18.
[60] Steedman, *Strange Dislocations*, 19.

While many of the children in Barry's works represent unusual paths of growing up, by growing up too quickly and unwillingly, for instance, or refusing to grow up or conform to idealized notions of childhood, Freddie from *Ernie Pook's Comeek* embodies what Kathryn Bond Stockton calls growing sideways. In pointing out how children remain difficult to fully understand and even strange and queer, Stockton draws our attention to the "(e)stranging, broadening, darkening forms of the child-as-idea (. . .) with a keen eye on the ghostly gay child (emblem and icon of children's queerness) as a figure hovering in the twentieth century."[61] She focuses on the concept of "children's delay," "their slow gradual growth, their suggested slow unfolding, which, unhelpfully, has been relentlessly figured as vertical movement upward" and juxtaposes it to the Derridean understanding of delayed meaning during the process of reading a sequence of words.[62]

Freddie personifies Stockton's "ghostly gay child."[63] Constantly bullied and called a fag in the early *Freddie Stories* by his cousin and other bullies, Freddie's loveless, alcoholic mother also taunts him for his queerness, claiming that he is "more of a girl than Marlys is."[64] As we saw in the previous chapter, "The Lost Stories," narrated and even drawn from Freddie's point of view, delve further into Freddie's queerness and the bullying that his difference engenders. These strips introduce additional queer children whom Freddie befriends or tries to help, such as Galvin in the second "lost story" who ends up bleeding in the head after being smashed with a rifle by Freddie's cousin Arnold,[65] and Tony/Hector Delarosa, a Spanish-speaking friend who is also labelled a fag by the school bully because he writes poems and sits with Freddie.

In "One Thing I Have Found Out," the comic about the aftermath of the extra credit report mentioned in Chapter 3, for which Freddie was sent to the counselor's office, Freddie details the repercussions of asking whether he and Hector were fags: "One thing I have found out about fags is it sure makes people freak out!"[66] Hector's mother decides

---

[61] Kathryn Bond Stockton, *The Queer Child, or Growing Sideways in the Twentieth Century* (Duke University Press, 2009), 3.
[62] Stockton, *Growing Sideways*, 4.
[63] Stockton, *Growing Sideways*, 17–22.
[64] Barry, *Freddie Stories*, 65.
[65] Barry, *Freddie Stories*, 138–9.
[66] Barry, *Freddie Stories*, 150.

to immediately transfer her son to a Catholic school. Freddie's mother is less surprised and considers it a family flaw.[67] While Freddie's uneven text narrates these events, the pictures, which are accompanied by brief captions and dialogue imagine another planet to which Freddie flies off to find Hector. The final image shows Hector and Freddie dancing under a smiling sun to music from free records on a free record player.[68] It is in images that Freddie and Hector find the freedom denied to them at school or at home.

Freddie's reputation for emotional problems (echoing Barry's own childhood) stems from his sensitivity and wild imagination.[69] Haunted by the sudden, ridiculous death of his strange classmate, Glenn—who had briefly been friendly toward Freddie before becoming another bully after Freddie's refusal to publicly acknowledge him as a friend—Freddie invents a more plausible reason for Glenn's death: he was murdered by the creature, accompanying Freddie since his birth, who appears in the dark and terrifies Freddie to screams. These screams bring Freddie little relief since his mother insists that Freddie has to "grow up to be a man"[70] and cannot expect his mother to come and comfort him. This specific story reappears in "The Lost Stories," redrawn in Freddie's style.

Other imaginary stories by Freddie in "The Lost Stories" illustrate a strategy of delaying, of avoiding the need to become a man, a state in which no one can comfort him when he gets nightmares. Freddie's elaborate musings on the nature of animals, imaginative interludes, or alternative realities narrativize a strategy of delay. According to Stockton:

> Delay is seen as a friend to the child. Delay is said to be a feature of its growth: children grow by delaying their approach to the realms of sexuality, labor, and harm. The point of delay as a boon to growth is to shelter children from these domains.[71]

Stockton is quick to point out the paradoxical nature of this sheltering, which eventually has to give way to allow the child to grow up.

---

[67]Barry, *Freddie Stories*, 151.
[68]Barry, *Freddie Stories*, 151.
[69]See Barry, *One Hundred Demons*, 176.
[70]Barry, *Freddie Stories*, 67.
[71]Stockton, *Growing Sideways*, 62.

In delaying, Freddie often crosses over into other worlds, not only imaginative ones, such as the planet he invents for Hector and himself but also more ghostly, liminal realms, such as the endless hallucination of burning skulls, or the fantom-like, silent form Freddie adopts to listen to Maybonne who is unable to visit him in the hospital he has been confined to as a disturbed child.[72] The final "Lost Stories" comic, "The Other Side," offers a sideral, sideways ending: Freddie crosses over a mountain, to a dream space or afterworld full of friendly skeletons growing flowers. These skeletons evoke the parade of life that is at the heart of the very first "lost story," "The Parade," composed exclusively of skeletons, just like a Day of the Dead parade. The motif of skeletons and, by implication, death, is recurrent in *The Freddie Stories*. "On the Other Side" ends like an almost familiar child's fantasy as Freddie realizes that the skeleton's "skulls were made of sugar and their breath was fragrant like chocolate, like copal, like the marigolds. . . . Sweet."[73] What makes the story somewhat unsettling is the second-person address, when Freddie talks directly to the reader and explains how the skeletons send their regards and miss, think and dream of "you," the reader.

In the afterword to *The Freddie Stories* Barry recalls how an earlier collection of the stories from the 1990s excluded certain comics because they were deemed "too strange or depressing" or because they did not contribute to the comic's continuity.[74] Both "The Parade" and "The Other Side" can therefore also be read in light of the lapse of time between *The Freddie Stories* collection published by Drawn & Quarterly and the making, and selective printing, of the original stories: Freddie does come back to us from another side, not exactly a death, but a (side)stepping away. He remains locked in perpetual delay with a lost dog that his mother refused to let him keep and who accompanies him in Barry's afterword.

The lost dog parallels Freddie's own sense of being lost, of not fitting into normative, heterosexual categories. Both dog and child, in a makeshift wizard costume (with Marlys' hat) in the afterword, and the related possibilities of magic and creation, in their simultaneous lostness and timelessness, also incarnate qualities of the image that Barry imparts in her manuals. Concluding that "Barry exposes possibilities for comics not

---

[72]Barry, *Freddie Stories*, 150–1, 162–3.
[73]Barry, *Freddie Stories*, 177.
[74]Barry, *Freddie Stories*, 128.

only to represent childhood, but also to actively reconstruct it," Bennett adds that "Barry's praxical comics counter the hopelessness of childhood experiences."[75] Trousdale identifies a similar dynamic of reworking and understanding through child characters.[76]

As we saw previously, Barry's comics manuals strive to retrieve the early childhood joy of unfettered drawing, and turn to "childish" methods and practices to encourage creativity. The next section elaborates further on the pedagogical practices that play such a central role in Barry's graphic novels and their interweaving of techniques from the world of childhood, the experience of drawing like a child and the emotional connections attached to it.

Teaching Comics

As we have seen throughout this guide, Barry's comics do comics and image theory. For Jeanette Roan, the theory of the image Barry shares through her books echoes visual studies concerns of according presence and even life to images.[77] It will not come as a surprise that the majority of the essays collected in the critical anthology, *Contagious Imagination: The Work and Art of Lynda Barry* are about the pedagogical elements of Barry's comics. For Tolmie, Barry "is the embodiment of research-creation," which is also reflected in the close intertwining of fictional and autobiographic storylines and pedagogy in her comics.[78]

Copying, as we already saw, is a central principle of both fine art practice and Barry's teachings. Mike Classon Frangos examines how contemporary Swedish feminist artists incorporate Barry's principles to create norm-critical comics using childish drawing styles, Disney characters as avatars or digital collage to question conventions and power structures.[79] In his afterword to *Contagious Imagination*, Glenn Willmott emphasizes "Barry's commitment to comics as the communication neither of form nor of content but of

---

[75]Bennett, "Dancing," 232–3.
[76]See Trousdale, "Autobiography," in *Contagious Imagination*.
[77]Roan, "What Is An Image?"
[78]Tolmie, "Introduction," in *Contagious Imagination*, 3.
[79]Mike Frangos Classon, "Swedish Norm-Critical Comics and the Comics Pedagogy of Lynda Barry," *The Comics Grid: Journal of Comics Scholarship* 11, no. 1 (2021), https://www.comicsgrid.com/article/id/4042/.

practice—specifically, a reading and writing practice."[80] Recalling Roland Barthes' distinction between readerly and writerly texts, where readerly texts provoke passive consumption while writerly texts encourage readers to recreate the text they are reading, Willmott places Barry's work firmly in the second category.[81] He concludes: "This practice of a writable imagism, which Barry finds rooted in shameless childhood capacities and pursuits, and Barthes finds rooted in play, struggles to escape the commodity form of writing" and makes Barry "one of the most interesting inheritors of modernism, and subversive inventors of what comics can do."[82]

Building on the previous section, this section first elaborates on how the child impacts the forms and styles of Barry's comics and is often at the heart of Barry's teaching philosophy. As we have seen throughout this guide, Barry's comics reflect what Michael Chaney has called "the child as comics" with the child being "a resilient emblem of the comics and its mediation."[83] In Barry's works the child prevails as a source of drawing lessons and inspiration. The section then turns to Barry's comics lessons and teaching philosophies. Drawing lessons were already part of the many lessons already offered in *Ernie Pook's Comeek*, foreshadowing the manuals that Barry is now known for. These exercises, which are often tongue-in-cheek, also determine the form of *Naked Ladies, Naked Ladies, Naked Ladies* which claims to be a coloring book, therefore revindicating a familiar childhood exercise for a picture book that reworks adult visual entertainment and subverts its sexist images.

As we saw earlier, comics-making lessons became the central focus of Barry's books beginning with *What It Is,* her first book with Drawn & Quarterly in 2008. It announces an almost commercial promise on its cover: "Do you wish you could write?" Two years later, *Picture This* asks a question that expresses a creative desire: "Do you wish you could draw?" These promises of creativity involve tackling blocks and drawing anxieties. The two manuals printed in the form of composition notebooks, *Syllabus* and *Making Comics,* also elaborate on Barry's fears about teaching comics and the criticism levied against her work, such as her childish style, the

---

[80]Glenn Willmott, "My Kid," in *Contagious Imagination,* 183.
[81]Willmott, "Afterword: My Kid Could Do That: Lynda Barry and Subversive Writing," 183–7, 186–7. See also Roland Barthes, *S/Z,* trans. Richard Miller (Farrar Strauss Giroux, 1974).
[82]Willmott, "My Kid," 187.
[83]Chaney, *Reading Lessons,* 16.

unconventionally excessive wordiness of her panels and the equally unconventional themes often conveyed through child protagonists.

Barry's collaborations with children are comparable to the works of picturebook authors like Ruth Krauss and the photographer Jill Krementz, both of whom worked closely with children, conducting fieldwork with them and incorporating their feedback.[84] In contrast to the picturebooks, however, Barry's comics speak to an adult audience while donning a childish sheen reflected by the lively figures that break away from the rigid lines of the notebook pages, the bright colors and collages of girly and childish objects, children's drawings from her own and other found archives.

Just like in her other comics and books, Barry accords a central place to the world of childhood in her manuals: encompassing children's drawings and writing, drawing techniques associated with children's art classes such as bright colors, crayons and coloring books and, perhaps most importantly, childhood experiences of creation. Early in *Syllabus*, Barry points out how "the languages of music and drawing and pictures" precedes the ability to talk and write and how "(e)very baby old enough to hold a crayon can already use and understand these 3 languages. Sometimes all at once."[85] The text is accompanied by a dancing, singing, drawing toddler. A ghost-like image, with a tree inside it, and branches for arms, floats in a balloon from an abstract drawing that the toddler has just completed, animating the notion of the abstract, mental image that Barry subscribes to. Ghostly forms appear repeatedly in Barry's comics, embodying the amorphous nature of images and reflecting their fluidity and ability to transcend the material confines of the page. In the "Two Questions" section in *What It Is*, it is a ghostly cephalopod who eventually encompasses Barry's body and guides her hand.[86] The creature has the words "Don't Know" inscribed three times across its body, and it reappears at the bottom of the page, behind a drawing child. It is this feeling of unknowingness, of allowing "something *alive take shape*" that is central to creation, closely connected to childhood experiences and the physical movement of the hand.[87] As mentioned in the preceding chapters, Barry's conceptualization of the

---

[84] Marah Gubar, "Risky Business: Talking about Children in Children's Literature Criticism," *Children's Literature Association Quarterly* 38, no. 4 (2013): 450-457
[85] Barry, *Syllabus*, 14.
[86] Barry, *What It Is*, 135.
[87] Barry, *What It Is*, 135.

image is not limited to visual manifestations and is comparable to W. J. T. Mitchell's and other art historians' anthropological understandings of the image as both abstract and alive. Referring to *What It Is*, Willmott describes Barry's image as "a volatile, dynamic *process* of sensing, feeling, remembering, and thinking; it is even a ghostly or shadowy kind of living thing."[88]

Barry confirms this understanding on the page opposite the drawing baby who sings and dances at the same time: "By image I don't mean a visual representation. I mean something that is more like a ghost than a picture; something <u>which feels somehow alive, has no fixed meaning and is contained and transported by something</u> that is not alive (. . .) anything we call an 'art form.'"[89] She immediately links this understanding of images to childhood experience:

> Images are also contained by certain objects that young children become deeply attached to, like a certain blanket a certain child can't stand to be without (. . .) <u>The blanket has come to contain something the child interacts with as if it were alive</u>. How did this 'it' come to be located in the blanket? (. . .) Why do we have an innate ability to have a sustained and interactive relationship with an object/image well before we are able to speak?[90]

Could art, a small bat wonders in four panels on the same page, fulfill a biological function? The stakes of image-making could not be higher: it becomes a necessity, a means of surviving, something which Barry has already underscored in her autobiographical comics. Reading, writing and drawing offer not only escape but also a means of understanding and exploring; such understanding often entails recollecting childhood experiences. In a homework exercise from spring 2013, Barry asks her students to focus on a difficult period from childhood, how they dealt with it and how it continues to affect them. Most importantly, the students have to think what role images might have played in helping them get through the difficult period.[91] Encouragements to indulge in this kind of "time

---

[88] Willmott, "My Kid," 184.
[89] Barry, *Syllabus*, 15.
[90] Barry, *Syllabus*, 15. Emphasis in the original.
[91] Barry, *Syllabus*, 173.

travel" appear intermittently in *Syllabus* and are sources of autobiographical material and, ideally, different ways of being and looking at the world.[92] At the same time, to complexify the nature of autobiography itself, Barry also reinstates the difference between fiction and non-fiction, problematized in *One Hundred Demons,* as an exercise where students have to list seven types of fiction and non-fiction and consider an unanswerable question: "Is a dream autobiography or fiction?"[93]

In a later description of the Unthinkable Mind course for spring 2013, understanding the biological function of the arts appears as one of the aims of the course.[94] Although artistic talent and experience is not a requirement, students should have an interest in "the physical structure of the brain, how memory, pictures and stories work, the relationship between using our hands and insight."[95] Assignments include regular writing, picture making and memorizing exercises and one of the course outcomes is "a handmade book."

In *Picture This,* Barry asks:

> if I keep
> my pen or brush in motion
> something happens between the inside and the outside
> do images need some motion to come into being?[96]

Moving hands is so central that Barry uses two pages in *Syllabus* to explain a repetitive folding exercise.[97] The resulting folds are means of training hands and creating boxes within which drawings can be made and contained.

"Kids speak image," writes Barry in *Making Comics,* as mentioned earlier in the guide,[98] emphasizing the need to re-acquire this language to effectively communicate with comics: "This language is what I'm trying to teach in my comics classes. This language moves up through your hand and into your head. Young children are native speakers."[99] Here and elsewhere

---

[92]See for instance, Barry, *Syllabus,* 123.
[93]Barry, *Syllabus,* 167.
[94]Barry, *Syllabus,* 37.
[95]Barry, *Syllabus,* 35.
[96]Barry, *Picture This,* 120.
[97]Barry, *Syllabus,* 98–9.
[98]Barry, *Making Comics,* 8.
[99]Barry, *Making Comics,* 8.

in Barry's comics, image-making is described as a physical activity, connecting motricity, the movement of the hand, with specific sections of the brain that adults are not accustomed to using but that children activate automatically. In *Syllabus*, the slur of childish drawing is used as an example to question the notion of "bad drawing" and to teach a new way of looking at and appreciating images. Adapting the car drawing exercise from Ivan Brunetti's *Cartooning* book, Barry asks her students to draw Batman in one or two minutes. The time constraint entails rapid drawing without thinking and while the outcomes are disappointing for the students, Barry shows how the exercise can result in "a natural kind of picture."[100] She adds:

> what if the way kids draw—that kind of line that we call "childish"— what if that is what a line looks like when someone is having an experience by hand? A live wire! There is an aliveness in these drawings that can't be faked, and when I look at them, that aliveness seems to come into me. I'm glad to see them and feel them.[101]

We have already explored the central role of animation in the previous chapter and how numerous elements—diverse archives, the line itself, monsters—are brought to life in Barry's works. In one of her posters for the Making Comics course Barry animates an amorphous "bad drawing" which converses with its maker, a playfully reworked version of Brunetti's cartoon figure with rounded head and curved arms, but with circles or wheels for legs.[102] The figure asks whether he will be allowed to attend the course even though he is unable to draw. The drawing answers that the only requirement is a willingness to draw. The figure eventually realizes that the drawing was "the last unself-conscious drawing" he made before stopping drawing altogether, to which the drawing responds, "Draw me some more!" The comic does not end there. Barry adds "to be continued . . ." under the strip suggesting that the interaction will continue in the course itself.

The (meta-)connections established through children's drawings and childish styles work on several levels. They destabilize cultural legitimation impulses and media dynamics and challenge the simplicity associated with comics by pushing untutored, childish drawing into the limelight. Further,

---

[100] Barry, *Syllabus*, 50.
[101] Barry, *Syllabus*, 31.
[102] Barry, *Syllabus*, 37.

the imitation or recuperation of childish drawing can also be seen as a polygraphic gesture, a notion introduced by Thierry Smolderen to explain the different connotations channeled by graphic styles in light of their historical and contextual use (Smolderen, 2014). Childish drawing styles are often used for humorous purposes and to fully immerse the reader in the child's world, examples of which range from Cham's *Misunderstood Genius* to the comics drawn by Lester in Jeff Lemire's *Essex County*.[103] In the early twentieth century, artists famously turned to art brut or untutored forms of art, including children's drawings, for inspiration.[104] Barry's use of children's drawings is comparable to the modernists' search of unfettered modes of creation. But Barry's engagement with, and incorporation of, children's drawings, and the stuff of childhood in general, is more involved and constant, encompassing all kinds of childish drawings, including those made by adults. Such incorporation extends from pasting the drawings in her graphic novels to copying them, following the paths taken by untutored hands in attempts to replicate the communicative energy of the drawings.

The importance of children's drawings to Barry's work is especially obvious in *Making Comics*, where Barry connects the power of untutored drawings with children's drawings. She begins with an example of her favorite kind of drawing which "shows up in the very first drawings we do as a class (. . .) The line is unpracticed, even a little timid, it's the line of someone who quit drawing. It's impossible to fake and difficult to copy" (Figure 3.3)[105] While this drawing is by an adult, Barry likens its aliveness to a four-year-old's unsteady writing discussed in the previous chapter, and the seemingly abstract, colorful image drawn by a two-year-old which acquires meaning when the child talks about the content.[106] Both the aliveness and immediacy of an image are thematized in Barry's afterword to *The Freddie Stories*. "Comic strip time is different," in comparison to our memory, especially childhood memories, which Barry likens to ghosts.[107] She reflects on how both Freddie and a stray dog he befriends will continue to live,

---

[103] For more on the interactions between comics and children's drawings see Maaheen Ahmed and Benoît Crucifix, eds., "Children's Drawings in Comics/Les dessins d'enfance dans la bande dessinée," *Comicalités* (2023), https://doi.org/10.4000/comicalites.8374.
[104] See, for instance, Jonathan Fineberg, *The Innocent Eye: Children's Art and the Modern Artist* (Princeton University Press, 1997).
[105] Barry, *Making Comics*, 4.
[106] Barry, *Making Comics*, 6.
[107] Barry, *Freddie Stories*, 127.

Social and Cultural Impact

possessing "a certain aliveness that feels to be on-going."[108] The afterword is a meditation on memory and the persistence of images. It also reflects on comics temporality and relationality: "The *when* in a comic strip is always *now*. The same *now* you are in this instant."[109] Being in the moment is one of the states of being that Barry's exercises—think of the meditative spiral exercise, for instance—try to inculcate.

While the previous chapter discussed aliveness in connection to the animation of images, aliveness can also be read in light of the "sticky," affective quality of children's drawings and untutored styles in general.[110] As Barry often reminds us, such styles are reminiscent of the drawings all of us made at some point. They point to the possibility of drawing that many adults deny themselves and to a specific past and mode of experiencing through creation that is alienated from adult life.

As we have seen throughout this guide, Barry's interest in teaching has been a persistent feature of her comics. It is already discernible in the do-it-yourself, "punk" elements of Barry's earliest comics and the playful "how-to comics" mentioned in Chapter 2.[111] It is, therefore, not surprising that the very first comic reproduced in *Everything: Comics from Around 1978-1981* is a mix between a mock-drawing exercise and a mock-advertisement for the Lynda de Bari Fine School of the Artistic.[112] The headline, with each word written in a different style, announces: "You May Have Hidden Artistic Talent!" The advertisement continues in a broken, spoken idiom, promising a "development," a surefire method of drawing that is tested by copying Betty, a poorly drawn, smiling cow, recognizable only through its disproportionate udders. "So many have tried our development and the money is flow like rain and good luck to them" the advertisement continues, promising a handsomely paid alternative to "a stupid job" that the target audience might be struggling with.

The traits of oral language play, humor and even social critique were drawn out earlier in this guide. Underneath the humor, there are also vestiges of Barry's techniques and penchants that she shares in her later graphic novels: the encouragement to copy and the large blank panel for

---

[108]Barry, *Freddie Stories*, 128.
[109]Barry, *Freddie Stories*, 129.
[110]See Sara Ahmed, "Happy Objects," in *Affect Theory Reader*, ed. Melissa Gregg and Gregory J. Seigworth (Duke University Press, 2010), 29–51.
[111]Kirtley, *Typical Girls*, 117–18.
[112]Barry, *Everything*, 14.

readers to make their own drawing. While these early comics are more exercises in humor instead of comics-making, the tasks Barry proposes in her graphic novels, beginning with *One Hundred Demons*, are no longer pastiches but exercises to put into practice. The later graphic novels, *What It Is*, *Picture This*, *Syllabus* and *Making Comics* offer concrete step-by-step instructions. While humor is still present, often through the commenting figures, the instructions and tips are serious.

Barry inscribes her manuals in a diverse line of artistic and creative teaching philosophies. In *Syllabus*, Barry thanks three influences and "critical friends": Dan Chaon, who taught courses on creative writing, Ivan Brunetti and Marilyn Frasca.[113] Frasca's influence was already discussed in Chapters 1 and 2. Barry thanks her college art teacher on several occasions for imparting a more holistic understanding of the image and image-making that goes beyond judging and evaluating. As we saw earlier, it was in Frasca's class that Barry began keeping notebooks. Frasca's aim to teach students about "being present and seeing what's there" and "listening to images" resonates through all of Barry's manuals. Situating Barry's teaching practice in the educational and art theories of D. W. Winnicott, Marion Milner and Frasca, Allan Pero explains Barry's understanding of the image as

> the psychic reality of an object that can be conjured and sustained through an unconscious intermingling of memory, play, and a yielding to formlessness. This yielding is simultaneously a means of invoking and coping with anxiety (. . .) a playful distinguishing of subjects from objects, and the creation of transitional objects.[114]

Following Winnicott, "transitional objects create a neutral space of experience."[115] Pero emphasizes the connection between play and work in Barry's comics and how this connection has to be devoid of any productive expectations in order to be, paradoxically enough, creatively fruitful.[116]

In *Syllabus*, Barry incorporates several exercises from Brunetti's manual, *Cartooning*, where instructions to make figures out of simple shapes appear

---

[113]Barry, *Syllabus*, 6–7.
[114]Pero, "Orbit of the Cephalopod," 99.
[115]Pero, "Orbit of the Cephalopod," 104.
[116]Pero, "Orbit of the Cephalopod," 101.

very early in the book.¹¹⁷ Barry continues to insert Brunetti figures with large round heads, triangle torsos and curving limbs throughout the book even when the exercises are not from his book. The simple and quick figure drawing creates a common ground for her classes of students with diverse artistic capabilities. She likens this to "the starting place we all share: our first drawings of people made when we were little," once again drawing a connection to childhood.¹¹⁸ Barry later adds, next to a series of geometric versions of herself robbing a bank, that such simple forms offer an easy solution to visualizing action and constructing scenes.¹¹⁹

Like Brunetti, Barry incorporates several exercises based on different kinds of constraints, ranging from temporal ones to using diverse drawing tools, different drawing sizes, and even drawing with the non-dominant hand. Significantly, Barry portrays herself reading *Cartooning* and doing an exercise from it based on repeating the same motif in shorter and shorter periods of time (the final one being thirty seconds).¹²⁰ She adds drawings of castles to illustrate the contrasts and similarities between the first castle, made in three minutes and the final castle, made in five seconds: the idea of the castle is clearly present in both and the simplicity, and uniqueness, of the rapidly drawn castle makes it even more interesting and original than the more time-consuming castle which, in its details, reproduces all-too-familiar elements.¹²¹ Through copying exercises based on increasingly brief time constraints, Barry highlights how the limited time entails reducing the copy to the essentials.¹²² This exercise also highlights the centrality of motricity and rhythm to an image: "Copying helps you with timing the pace and rhythm of moving your hands and fingers in a way that leaves lines and shapes."¹²³

In making her students follow variations of Brunetti's stylized character drawing exercises, Barry shows how individual styles emerge, even when drawing the exact same shapes. She also adapts Brunetti's four-by-four exercise, which encourages mixing and rearranging panels.¹²⁴ Unlike

---

[117] Barry, *Syllabus*, 17.
[118] Barry, *Syllabus*, 17.
[119] Barry, *Syllabus*, 71.
[120] Barry, *Syllabus*, 94–7.
[121] Barry, *Syllabus*, 95.
[122] Barry, *Syllabus*, 97.
[123] Barry, *Syllabus*, 97.
[124] Barry, *Syllabus*, 120.

Lynda Barry

Brunetti, however, Barry encourages less stylized drawing and her constraints do not incrementally lead to creating a comics page: characters are allowed to emerge and page layouts are almost irrelevant.

Barry's manuals place a strong emphasis on writing and not only drawing, as is the case with the x-page exercise, which involves writing out images from memories and constructing a story around them. Explained across six pages, against a background of carefully pulled lines in color, this task helps address the hesitation of facing a blank page. Recalling the accusation of wasting paper that Barry's mother often directed at her, Barry adds a light, reassuring note: "Don't worry about 'wasting' paper our comp-books don't mind being used up."[125] The x-page offers a first inspiration for a new story and for this Barry recites a poem while the students start making spirals and then write down ten memories connected to a random word she selects. One of those memories forms the central image of the story and is used for the title. Students fill the page with rapid answers connected to the image in order to flesh out the story and eventually draw images around it. The x-page reappears in *Making Comics* where, in one instance, it is used to structure a "memory jam" of three minutes around a familiar walk.[126] The x form creates an organizational space to structure ideas, while highlighting their physical presence and connections on the page. The x-page also appears in the workbook section of *What It Is* with the instruction to "stay inside the image" and to use the different segments as points of orientation to fully "write" the image.[127]

In *Syllabus*, Barry incorporates a quote from social worker and organizational behavior specialist, Mary Parker Follet's *Creative Experience* (1924), under a series of parallel inked lines to explain the importance of manually doing activities to understand drawing, instead of theorizing it.[128] There is, however, one theory of the mind that Barry introduces in *Syllabus*: just like with Brunetti's *Cartooning*, Barry portrays herself reading literary scholar and psychiatrist Iain McGilchrist's book, *The Master and His Emissary: The Divided Brain and the Making of the Western World*. For Barry it is "the book that made me want to teach this class."[129] Her portraits of her reading selves confirm this implication and attachment to the readings she assigns. Gilchrist suggests that human beings comprise two hemispheres that actually

---

[125]Barry, *Syllabus* 76.
[126]Barry, *Making Comics*, 156.
[127]Barry, *What It Is*, 153.
[128]Barry, *Syllabus*, 72.
[129]Barry, *Syllabus*, 49.

collaborate despite working in oppositional ways. Students only have to read the introduction where McGilchrist explains his central argument that each hemisphere represents two opposed ways of apprehending the world and consequently, two very different realities, both of which contribute to the construction of the world as we know it. While the right hemisphere focuses on wholes, the left hemisphere focuses on details. McGilchrist transposes Nietzsche's story, in which the right hemisphere of the brain, commonly associated with creativity, is the master, while the left is the emissary and acquires the upper hand. This dominance reduces possibilities to engage with the world to the most rational ones. Barry's image-making classes encourage more intuitive modes of perceiving and understanding the world and unlearning rational modes of thinking and seeing.

Barry also reads and incorporates the ideas of psychologist and artist Marion Milner's book *On Not Being Able to Paint* (1950) explicitly in *What It Is* and *Syllabus* and implicitly throughout her manuals. For Emilia Halton-Hernandez, the image in *What It Is* showing Barry reading Milner's book with a bird and a smiling spider, within a frame that could be both a gift-wrapped window or a cage, suggests that the "book guides Barry to an experience of an alive creative subjectivity."[130] Trained in Freudian psychoanalysis, Milner had a strong interest in children's art and was an advocate of free drawing, what such drawings can reveal about the person making them while also transforming that person. Milner was particularly interested in the kinds of consciousness such instances of drawing activated and how they could bring about temporary effacement of self-consciousness. Barry strives for a similar state of creation in which forms and comics characters emerge through the act of drawing itself and are not pre-conceived. Just like with the introduction to *The Greatest of Marlys*, Barry explains the genesis of the characters in *Syllabus* as follows:

> I was drawing nothing in particular, practicing something I call 'my line,' watching the way the ink went into the paper, letting one shape lead to the next, and letting a skating feeling take over—one smooth line and another and there they were.[131]

Milner's ideas complement the constrained drawing and writing exercises that Barry adapts from Brunetti's *Cartooning*: both free and constrained

---

[130]Haltan-Hernandez, "Milner in the Comic Frame," 150.
[131]Barry, *Syllabus*, 144.

drawing coexist to make a coherent comic that also remains meaningful, on a personal level, for the artist, and on a dialogic level, for the reader and viewer. Making art, Barry's manuals often remind us, is closely connected to self-understanding. This is why the composition notebook, which *Syllabus* and *Making Comics* adopt the form of, is a central element of Barry's comics pedagogy. While keeping diaries and sketchbooks is a common practice for all kinds of artists, including Brunetti, who emphasizes the importance of keeping a sketchbook, the composition notebook forming the core of Barry's classes combines the different activities of sketching, journaling, and jotting down ideas.[132]

The notebook comprises one-third of the final grade and is intended to accompany the students throughout the semester and even outside the comics class.[133] The diaries should be filled with "everything."[134] Toward the end of *Syllabus*, Barry emphasizes the importance of taking notes by hand. Here, and later in *Making Comics,* the composition book is introduced "as a place. The practice of developing a place not a thing."[135] To help students overcome their hesitation of what to jot down, Barry identifies four categories, and adds time constraints ranging from thirty seconds to two and a half minutes for each section: the lists of items the diarist saw and did, phrases they overheard and, finally, a picture drawn on a daily basis.[136] The composition notebook consequently becomes a record of awareness, when the diarists actually become observers of their world, which is a prerequisite for both writing and drawing.

The x-page exercise mentioned above also hones capacities of attention and awareness, for which it begins with a careful, tight spiral, as a means of relaxation and concentration.[137] Pointing out the recurrence of these spirals in *Syllabus*, Szép elaborates on how "(t)he spiral is Barry's most frequent and most easily recognizable indicator of thinking through the body."[138] Szép explains how

---

[132] Ivan Brunetti, *Cartooning: Philosophy and Practice* (Yale University Press, 2007), 13–14.
[133] Barry, *Syllabus*, 60.
[134] Barry, *Syllabus*, 60.
[135] Barry, *Syllabus*, 194; Barry, *Making Comics,* 35.
[136] Barry, *Syllabus*, 61, 63.
[137] Barry, *Syllabus*, 76–7, 143.
[138] Szép, *Comics and the Body,* 66.

(i)n the gesture of the spiral, Barry unites movement and contemplation, and uses this form to mark physically, on the surface of the page, that the process of image making has begun. The spiral tracks reaching the desired creative state of mind via the movement of the hand. Ultimately, the spiraling line is a visual imprint of the already mentioned temporality of creation, the meanwhile temporality.[139]

Paying attention is a central tenet of Barry's courses, inspired from her painting classes with Frasca. Paying attention to images is only possible when we do not try to classify images under the labels of good or bad drawings. It also extends to observation and experience in general, as Barry notes on a collaged page in *Syllabus*: "Not liking or disliking: but learning to pay patient attention to things as they are. Liking/disliking = blinders."[140] The same page includes a note concerning story structure which "is about how people are, not about how stories are." At the left bottom of the page, under a crumpled piece of gold foil with a cloud-like shape, Barry adds: "It's about following something small carefully and—sincerely."[141] In light of the insights Barry shares in the *Syllabus* and her other manuals, the "it" to be followed refers to both the story and the image itself, both of which are inextricably connected. This connection is also reflected in Barry's holistic intertwining of writing and drawing that contributes to the comicity of her works.

In order to enhance her students' abilities to focus, Barry incorporates numerous memory exercises, beginning with an Emily Dickinson poem for her first Unthinkable Mind class.[142] Later in the comic, after a sequence of comics fill-in-the-blanks, Barry explains the relevance of poems in what can be best described as a self-reflexive poetry comic (Figure 4.2).[143]

Poems reveal the possibilities of the world while also opening new worlds. The protagonist of this comic is a figure following Brunetti's formula. Flying with a jet pack and a horn or a loudspeaker, the figure evokes the angels adorning the first cover of *The Good Times Are Killing Me*. Its horn does not emit words but squiggly lines that were already introduced in *Picture This*

---

[139] Szép, *Comics and the Body*, 66.
[140] Barry, *Syllabus*, 168.
[141] Barry, *Syllabus*, 168.
[142] Barry, *Syllabus*, 53.
[143] Barry, *Syllabus*, 180.

Figure 4.2 "Poems can make you see," from *Syllabus*, 180. Copyright Lynda Barry. Used with permission from Drawn & Quarterly.

(see Chapter 3). Playful and dynamic, these doodles eventually form the dense sphere on the verge of swallowing the protagonist. This partially open sphere at the corner of the poetry comic plays with notions of panels and temporality, trading the sequentiality of the panels for a tabular aesthetic that approaches the entire page as a composition.[144]

Speaking through the multi-eyed sea monster, Barry explains in the "Mood Doodles" section in *Picture This*: "Doodle is a name I dislike for a kind of drawing I love." Further below, on the same page, she adds, "Some people call it mindless drawing and there are times when a certain frame of mind is exactly what I want less of."[145] "Mood Doodles" begins with an epigraph by Marion Milner on contemplative action, a method of free

---

[144] On the tension between linear and tabular reading, see Pierre Fresnault-Deruelle, "From Linear to Tabular (1976)," in *The French Comics Theory Reader*, ed. Ann Miller and Bart Beaty (Leuven University Press, 2014), 121–38.
[145] Barry, *Picture This*, 124. My insertion in parentheses.

Social and Cultural Impact

Figure 4.3 "My Favorite Doodles," from *Picture This*, 124. Copyright Lynda Barry. Used with permission from Drawn & Quarterly.

drawing: contemplative emphasizes the thoughtfulness implied by the process and action refers to the moving hand, both of which are concretized by the doodles and by Barry's teachings at large.[146]

Barry offers a large set of doodles (Figure 4.3), many of which decorate her graphic novels: different forms of "branching" spirals, "circle in circle," "amoeba with food vacuoles," "bacilli," "spirilla" and even a game called "electric shocker" in which two people draw lines that repeatedly halve the page, without touching each other because touching results in electrocution. Barry proposes doodles as a way of waiting between ideas for pictures and stories. Admitting that repetitive drawings like doodles often result in decorative images, she explains that "they are more like a clock or a motion metronome that helps me not think until the story starts up again

---

[146]Marion Milner, *On Not Being Able To Paint* (Routledge 2010), 163.

187

on its own."¹⁴⁷ Barry inserts this text between a portrait of herself, labelled "out side" and another portrait of the near-sighted, smoking monkey under the words "in side." The monkey becomes a visualization of her creative self and is connected to the sea monster who provides an additional tip for doodles at the bottom of the same page, encouraging readers to work with a vast range of marks.

Just like doodles, copying and coloring, which are also considered childish, unartistic practices, play an important role in Barry's lessons. In addition to proposing "[c]oloring things in by hand as study aid" in *Syllabus*,¹⁴⁸ as we saw in Chapter 2, Barry adds that "[c]opying is good for you because it takes time and—it requires a certain sort of sustained concentration that invites a different sort of thinking."¹⁴⁹

Color is introduced early in *Syllabus*, where the agenda for the first day includes "crayons and hard-core coloring assignments first thing. Build hands up, use color and somewhat frustrating materials that take time."¹⁵⁰ Barry includes samples of different kinds of paper that has been colored on and encourages testing different supports. She also asks students to each select and fill in three coloring book pages from the numerous options she hangs on the wall.¹⁵¹ This is comparable to the numerous pages, often with Marlys and the Near-Sighted Monkey, inviting the reader to color in *Picture This*. While *Picture This* also introduces different palettes, *Syllabus* focuses on the more psychological aspect of coloring, and how adult students are embarrassed to indulge in it.¹⁵² Barry transforms this embarrassment into a site of interrogation. *Syllabus* turns to one of the less malleable tools associated with childhood, crayons: students learn how how to color and to organize their crayons according to usage to understand their color preferences.¹⁵³

Syllabus introduces different kinds of tools: the crayons are followed by watercolors, the non-photo blue pencil and, eventually, the uni-ball pen.¹⁵⁴ For this, Barry suggests a copying exercise comprising lines for which

---

[147] Barry, *Picture This*, 127.
[148] Barry, *Syllabus*, 3.
[149] Barry, *Syllabus*, 184.
[150] Barry, *Syllabus*, 38.
[151] Barry, *Syllabus*, 66.
[152] Barry, *Syllabus*, 68.
[153] Barry, *Syllabus*, 84–5.
[154] Barr, *Syllabus*, 155.

students have to focus on their breathing and time the drawing of each line to an exhalation. The gradual introduction of tools in *Syllabus* and *Making Comics* contrasts with the "What's Inside Your Art Box?" page in *Picture This*, which includes a variety of items, including snippets of color, collage tools of scissors and glue, a large block of ink, an ink reed pen and even a ruler.[155]

Certain principles of collage work are also present in the manuals, such as spontaneous juxtaposition, enabled through the use of word bag prompts for an exercise in drawing oneself in four panels in *Syllabus*.[156] Barry introduces a more elaborate "comics kit" in *Making Comics,* which comprises six bags: word bag, picture bag, scene bag, camera angle bag, character bag and setting bag.[157] We have a classic Barry mix: practical tools for making comics, a range of constraints and much that is ultimately left to chance; the latter shares connections with the surrealist practices of automatic creation and the possibilities of free drawing, allowing images and connections to emerge.

As this section has tried to show, Barry's manuals are quintessentially collaborative, urgently calling for reader responses. They also impart a broader understanding of comics that is rooted in telling stories through combining words and images. The next section elaborates on both of these aspects, which inform Barry's expansion of the comics form, through testing its material and physical affordances and through highlighting its communicative potential.

Expanding Comics

This fourth and final section elaborates on the collaborative features of Barry's comics, unfolding through the different collective and redrawing exercises that she assigns to her students, drawings that are sometimes made with two or more artists and Barry's own copies of diverse kinds of drawings, including those by the children and college students she teaches. Such exercises emphasize how image-making is a collaborative activity and how it is possible to appreciate a broad spectrum of drawings and to learn

---

[155]Barry, *Picture This*, 4.
[156]Barry, *Syllabus*, 151.
[157]Barry, *Making Comics*, 189–95.

from them. Barry's comics mediate between the personal and the collective, often through the very act of drawing but also through creative techniques, especially the collages, as discussed above.

In *Projections: Comics and the History of Twenty-First Century Storytelling*, Gardner mentions a crucial difference between cinema and comics that persists despite their concurrent emergence and their close interactions: "comics (. . .) continue to explore the unique affordances of a form that depends inevitably and irrevocably on a participatory relationship to its readers."[158] Gardner considers the advent of autobiographical comics as the moment which drastically transformed the nature of reader participation, reducing, for instance, the weight of readers' letters that had the power to change the course of serial narratives.[159] Within the form of the graphic novel or memoir, reader participation is often limited to engaging with the stories being told. Barry's "writerly" comics, especially her manuals, offer alternative forms of participation that accord importance to creative expression. Such participation differs from Henry Jenkins' famous concept of participatory culture, which relies heavily on social media platforms.[160] While making and sharing creative content is also one of the components of the participatory culture theorized by Jenkins, the possible sharing proposed by Barry's books unfolds on a far more personal scale. It also extends beyond the artist and the reader to a broader group of artists, children, students, and teachers who have contributed to Barry's comics, ultimately extending to encompass the readers themselves. While this sharing is comparable to that of autobiographical comics and remains personal, even in the collages, its scope is much broader.

As Emma Tinker points out, Barry's "how-to" comics and instructions are a means of forming a vast, comics-making community: "DIY aesthetics also reflects a commitment to inclusiveness."[161] Kirtley links this inclusiveness, which establishes a rapport of equality with the reader, with the feminist methods proposed by anthropologist Susan Harding to dismantle hierarchies to provide a shared critical framework.[162] Kirtley

---

[158] Jared Gardner, *Projections: Comics and the History of Twenty-First Century Storytelling* (Stanford University Press, 2012), xiii.
[159] Gardner, *Projections*, 127.
[160] Henry Jenkins, *Textual Poachers: Television Fans and Participatory Culture* (Routledge, 2012).
[161] Tinker, "Selfhood," 124.
[162] Kirtley, *Typical Girls*, 116.

concludes: "This participatory bent is key to Barry's work and ethic: she compels the reader to join in, to play a part in the community, an *agora* marked by rebellion against the establishment."[163] In extending this observation to Barry's later work, the *agora* is grounded in creativity instead of political rebellion. Barry's recollection of posting comics and zines to Matt Groening and Gary Panter confirms her understanding of comics as a community-building tool: "it was more fun to make something when you had someone to send to."[164] As suggested in the section on invisible images in Chapter 3, Barry's comics images—just like the words and stories that accompany it—have an intersubjective, communicative function for the maker and the viewer.

On the final page of the Batman drawing exercise in *Syllabus*, for instance, Barry mentions that all the rapidly drawn variations of Batman have been made by her adult students. Adding how she colored in the drawings that her students did not want to keep, Barry then addresses her readers: "You power them on."[165] The many Batmen, iterations of an iconic comics figure, acquire multiple, often anonymous authors, and new lives in the eyes of each new reader-viewer.

As we saw previously, Barry's comics manuals emphasize the dependence of drawing on the viewer, the interactions that can unfold through drawings and how the aliveness of drawing is dependent on both the artist and the viewer. This aliveness establishes a connection between the artist and viewer. Drawing together, making collective drawings, or copying drawings are other possibilities of connection offered by Barry's manuals. *Syllabus*, for instance, compiles numerous student drawings, including the drawings submitted with applications for the course, the attendance card drawings, responses to exercises and materials that students did not want to take with them and that Barry keeps.

Next to an example of a four-panel diary entry in which the images and the text do not have to match, Barry elaborates on the impact her students' drawings had on her and how she "loved to try drawing some of their characters," adding that she had never drawn flying characters before encountering students' art in her spring 2013 Making Comics class.[166] Just

---

[163] Kirtley, *Typical Girls*, 132. See also Samanci, "Lynda Barry's Humor."
[164] Barry, *Everything*, 111–12.
[165] Barry, *Syllabus*, 33.
[166] Barry, *Syllabus*, 188.

like in the opening pages of *Making Comics* discussed above, Barry mentions her fascination for "what feels like a bad drawing to the person who made it" and how she finds it very difficult to copy drawings by unpracticed hands.[167] Tracing and copying, which form a key component of *Picture This*, become means of building creative connections, of sharing forms, giving them a new life and finding new modes of implication. Copying other students drawings is also a classroom exercise. In *Making Comics*, Barry explains how tracing the lines of children's drawings give her a specific feeling: "I'm on the path their hand took—it's a walking pace that gives me a different view of the *image*. Now MY HAND is *involved*."[168]

The significance and space Barry accords to copying, by hand, also offers an illustration of how problematic it is to conflate Marion's concept of graphiation with an original, personal style, because all style is an outcome of several levels of negotiations, between tutored and acquired styles, styles that are deemed appropriate for certain subjects and genres and styles that remain communicative.[169] Elaborating on Marion's concept of graphiation, Baetens emphasizes how the trace at the heart of the visual form of comics is "a reflection, a symptom, an index of the subjectivity of the narrator (. . . which is) never studied in itself but in its relationship with the narratee." [170] He adds: "The way the visual form of a comic is established and transformed throughout a work is then interpreted in the light of an ongoing dialogue between narrator and narratee."[171] Graphiation is, like the trace, built on a dialectic of presence and absence, whereby graphiation is perhaps most present in the preparatory sketches of a comic;[172] a dialogic relationship between artist and reader consequently lies at the heart of the comics form. A similar emphasis on the relationality of comics and their dependence on the viewer can be found in one of Barry's answers in an interview with her former student and comics researcher Leah Misemer: "where's the comic? The comic is somewhere between the person who made it and the person who's looking at it. It's a relationship."[173] As we have seen in Chapter 3 and throughout this guide, Barry does not hesitate in collaging her sketchbook

---

[167] Barry, *Syllabus*, 138.
[168] Barry, *Making Comics*, 13.
[169] Baetens, "Revealing Traces," 152.
[170] Baetens, "Revealing Traces," 145.
[171] Baetens, "Revealing Traces," 145.
[172] Baetens, "Revealing Traces," 147.
[173] Misemer, "Teaching the Unthinkable Image with Lynda Barry," 168–85, 174.

drawings, going as far back as her high school notebooks in *Everything*. While such collages reject a clear storyline or even a chronology, they offer us a glimpse into a curated selection of Barry's early visual worlds.

The relationality of the works by Barry and the numerous anonymous artists is powerful through their coexistence as collaged elements forming a vast collaborative and intersubjective space. It is also a found space, like the many student drawings and random images Barry rescues from the trash can. This recuperation of trash, of refusing to throw away is a recurrent practice layering most of Barry's graphic narratives. Barry's storing of her students' unwanted drawings, or her recuperation of a schoolteacher's archive in *What It Is*, are ways of preserving and reinforcing connections with people, especially students, both her own and anonymous ones. The relationality of these diverse, coexisting images, as indicated earlier, also has an affective, "sticky" quality, especially when the images are untutored drawings. Such relationality is characterized by a certain open-endedness, which presses for a response from the reader.

Tellingly enough, the role of hands in Barry's works is not limited to multiple, collective and sometimes unidentifiable authorship. Hands are also a recurrent visual motif and an imprint. One of the first tasks Barry connects to composition notebook keeping in *Making Comics* is tracing one's hand on the first page, adding one's date of birth and the date the notebook was started.[174] The hand is also introduced early in *Syllabus* (Figure 2.11) to emphasize the importance of making by hand. Here, the aim of the Unthinkable Mind course is summed up on the palm: "A semester of writing and drawing by hand until we arrive at the *unthinkable* and put it in a book."[175] That the aim of the course is anchored in the palm of the traced hand confirms the centrality of both the aim and the hand in the teachings and aesthetics of the comics manuals. Later in *Syllabus*, a hand looms over an assignments page and comes alive through the diverse labels on the thumb and fingers, with a "visitor" at the center of the hand announcing and blowing "from the unthinkable mind" into the index finger. The index finger emanating "I C U 2!" becomes, as we saw in Chapter 1, an image

---

[174]Barry, *Making Comics*, 35.
[175]Barry, *Syllabus*, 8.

that is not only seen but also sees.[176] Barry makes the hand come alive and communicate, just like the hand-drawn images.

Hands in Barry's comics are loaded with meaning beyond their primary function as sources of drawn marks and creativity. They visualize the importance Barry accords to using our hands and making things with them. They also capture the emotional connections enabled by art, the imprint of the creator and the possibility for everyone to create. The traced hands that appear in Barry's works are ways of leaving traces in perhaps the most humanly connected way: they reproduce a shape that is shared by all humans with a gesture that is easily reproducible. These hands concretize the possibility of touching, bypassing fleshy membranes through drawing, forms and textures.

Rebecca Scherr transposes film scholar, Laura Marks' concept of haptic visuality to Joe Sacco's *Palestine* to emphasize the transformative potential of comics journalism in challenging the dynamics of othering and shedding light on "a corporeal politics of pain and the circulation of images of pain in an international context."[177] Underscoring how "the handshake is a statement of corporeality, as touch is a primary body sensation," Scherr concludes that

> this gesture calls attention to the fact that the comics genre is in many ways as much of a haptic form as it is visual; in order to process the image-text relationship, readers must draw on various sensory and cognitive modalities that render the reading experience as physically intimate.[178]

Just like the handshake, Barry's traced hands can "be read as a visual metonym for the process of haptic readership."[179] These traced hands carry the implication of using hands and generating handedness, of reaching out to touch and affect a readership, and further, to move them to use their own hands and follow the gestures carefully broken down and detailed in the comics manuals.

---

[176]Barry, *Syllabus*, 157. On the double, self-conscious and animated roles incarnated by Barry's images, see Chute, *Graphic Women*, 127–8.
[177]Rebecca Scherr, "Shaking Hands with Other People's Pain: Joe Sacco's *Palestine*," *Mosaic: An Interdisciplinary Critical Journal* 46, no. 1 (2013): 19–36, 21.
[178]Scherr, "Shaking Hands," 21.
[179]Scherr, "Shaking Hands," 21.

Building on Yaël Schlick's observation that the coexistence of multiple authors, alongside the sharing of creative exercises, is "a democratized creative process,"[180] Szép emphasizes that Barry's "fluid image lives in collaboration, in the reworking, rethinking, and reformulation of works by others."[181] She adds that "the line is born not only out of movement and out of a state of mind, but also out of exploring one's vulnerability."[182] This observation connects with the emphasis on process in Barry's comics manuals, which also lies at the heart of the comics form, from its sequentiality to the essence of the drawn line itself.

Tim Ingold has famously proposed the line as the ultimate form of connection

> since there is no life that is not social—that does not entail an entwining of lines—in a world of blobs there could be no life of any kind. In fact, most if not all life-forms can be most economically described as specific combinations of blob and line, and it could be the combination of their respective properties that allows them to flourish. Blobs have volume, mass, density: they give us materials. Lines have none of these. What they have, which blobs do not, is torsion, flexion and vivacity. They give us life. Life began when lines began to emerge and to escape the monopoly of blobs. Where the blob attests to the principle of territorialisation, the line bears out the contrary principle of deterritorialization.[183]

Just like Barry's comics, lines are open-ended, creating new possibilities, monsters, worlds and, above all, seeking and establishing new connections. In *Making Comics,* Barry explains the possible connections activated by a drawing, from the act of seeing it to finishing a copying of it:

> A drawing may come from you but exists apart from you, in both matter and meaning to others. . . . When I look at a drawing . . . I'm meeting something. And it's also meeting me, if I can stand it. . . . When I copy a drawing, I'm meeting it in a different way—it's a sort of

---

[180]Schlick, "Selves and Texts," 41.
[181]Szép, *Comics and the Body,* 60.
[182]Szép, *Comics and the Body,* 68.
[183]Tim Ingold, *Life of Lines* (Routledge, 2015), 4.

teleportation of that something which comes in through my eye and out through my hand.[184]

Just after the "Two Questions" sequence in *What It Is*, Barry explains how her students taught her how to teach and "become convinced about the aliveness of images and the aliveness we feel when we experience them."[185] She ends with a question that is once again an invitation to create: "Will you help them (the images) cross over?"[186] All of these questions, from the unanswerable, major questions in *What It Is*, or the questions ending demon-stories like "Magic Lanterns" where Barry asks whether the lost panda she could not throw away might be the reader's,[187] move the reader from a passive position to a contemplative and reflexive one. They draw us in, compelling us to participate, even if it's through a thinking exercise.

The ideas, teachings, and possibilities shared by Barry similarly remain open-ended and co-dependent on their reader's involvement and willingness to transition from the role of the reader to a maker. Can there be any better way of understanding a form than engaging with it directly?

---

[184]Barry, *Making Comics*, 102.
[185]Barry, *What It Is*, 136.
[186]Barry, *What It Is*, 136. My insertion in parentheses.
[187]Barry, *One Hundred Demons*, 156. Reading a Proustian intertext into this episode, Yaël Schlick suggests that the magic lantern is "a place where the narrative articulates the relations of texts to selves and to self-formation and theorizes it." Schlick, "Selves and Texts," 36.

CONCLUSION

> To be capable of being in uncertainties.[1]
>
> Lynda Barry, *Picture This*

The above quote appears in a vertically oriented strip on the table of contents page for the spring issue in *Picture This*. While the contents, as discussed in Chapter 2, focus on ways of seeing, this sentence appears next to a panel showing Freddie's cousin Arnold burning magazines in a fireplace. Fire is an element of fascination and uncontrollable destruction in *The Freddie Stories*. It is also present in the children's stories retold in *Making Comics* (Figure 3.4). It is difficult not to draw connections between the fire Arnold is stoking in the hearth and the uncertainties mentioned in the above quote. Through the power of collaged juxtaposition, it is possible to extend these uncertainties to the variations of seeing forming the table of contents in *Picture This*.[2] As we have seen throughout this guide, Barry's comics manuals, just like her comic strips and autobiographical graphic novels, are more about probing into uncertainties than providing certainty. It is about "seeing things," "finding" creatures and characters, about visual explorations and possibilities, moving images (to recall Benjamin's moving script), instead of fixed ones.[3]

This probing, meta- and self-referential questioning makes Barry's creative work provide the ideal lens from which to interrogate and explore the medium of comics and its limits. Crafting fictional, autobiographical and pedagogical storylines, Barry encourages us to explore further, to delve into very the nature of creativity. Barry's comics are often self-conscious and meta-reflexive, laying bare the inner workings of the form itself. At the same time, her work is also *relational*, establishing connections with readers and creating strong empathic bonds. In the page from *Syllabus* below (Figure 5.1), Barry connects this relationality to comics characters. She animates a

---

[1] Barry, *Picture This*, 95.
[2] Barry, *Picture This*, 95.
[3] Barry, *Making Comics*, 10.

Conclusion

Figure 5.1 "Why do we make comic characters?" from *Syllabus*, 142. Copyright Lynda Barry. Used with permission from Drawn & Quarterly.

creature linked to temporality, to taking time and keeping time who had appeared a few pages earlier to personify reflections on timing, including the temporality of copying photographs and how copying creates a different temporality, creative space and experience.[4] Szép coins the term "meanwhile temporality" to describe the specific sense of temporality propitious for creation that Barry proposes and tries to activate through her exercises.[5]

To questions on the above page concerning what comics characters want and do, Barry gives an almost mystical answer emphasizing the need to "believe in them in a certain way." This belief is necessary to unleash the magic of creation.

Barry details numerous prompts and exercises to awaken our own slumbering sea monsters and magic cephalopods, encouraging readers to

---

[4]Barry, *Syllabus*, 129–31.
[5]Szép, *Comics and the Body*, 58–9.

cross over the threshold of passive reading to active creation by making marks and forming words, lines and shapes until characters and stories emerge and acquire a life of their own. This is, of course, anything but straightforward, as Barry reminds us repeatedly by sharing her own moments of creative despair and anxiety and by offering tips on how to tame our inner critical voices and demons.

The starting point of any creative act, as we saw earlier, is mark-making. In her numerous exercises seeking to make hands move and remember what it was like to draw, Barry breathes life into marks and the drawn line. Jared Gardner recalls Tim Ingold's observation that "the literal making of lines, once understood to be central to all arts, had become associated not with the artist but with the artisan, and specifically with the printer."[6] As manifested by the vast body of comics scholarship since Gardner's "Storylines" article, the once ignored drawn line of comics has received more attention than ever before, even taking the center stage in the transmission of not only narrative but also memories and embodied traces.[7] Comics are both embodied but also very bodily, with the book itself metonymically representing a body;[8] the line is a key mediator of corporeal elements, permitting representation, incorporation and interaction. Elaborating further on the haptic visuality of Joe Sacco's comics, Rebecca Scherr suggests that his comics activate elements of the medium that "allow readers to experience the narrative in a powerfully *visceral* manner."[9] In *Footnotes in Gaza,* for instance, readers not only encounter Palestinians but they are made to listen: "Because Sacco's cartoon avatar is positioned as the reader's filter as we navigate this landscape of crisis, we too are positioned as listeners as much as we are positioned as spectators."[10] Readers, Scherr emphasizes, become "active participants in the gathering and hearing of testimony; our engagement with the material is corporeal, physical, intimate."[11] Comparable synesthesia, unfolding in moments of crisis—both individual and collective—that are difficult to contain or fully express

---

[6] Gardner, "Storylines," 128.
[7] See, for instance, Chute, *Graphic Women* and *Disaster Drawn*; Marion, *Traces en cases*; and Szép, *Comics and the Body*.
[8] Miller, "Diary as Body."
[9] Rebecca Scherr, "Framing Human Rights: Comics Form and the Politics of Recognition in Joe Sacco's *Footnotes in Gaza*," *Textual Practice* 29, no. 1 (2015): 111–31, 115.
[10] Scherr, "Framing Human Rights," 115.
[11] Scherr, "Framing Human Rights," 115.

Conclusion

can also be discerned in Barry's graphic narratives: the collaged layers are necessary because we can only peel off or grasp fragments of a specific trauma or loss at a time. Most of these traumas are traced back to real and fictionalized childhood experiences. Childhood is also the locus of both the beginning and the end of unfettered creativity.

As we have seen throughout this guide, Barry's comics delineate a vast terrain around mark-making, sharing its variety, potential and possibilities in a highly original way, through blending autobiography, comics work, and comics manuals, for instance, or through the incorporation of messy, non-linear forms, such as the collage. This messiness draws our attention to a third aspect that makes Barry's comics stand out: the attention to detail, which is impossible to escape in the heavily textured collages and which also seeps through in the careful breaking down of the comics form to its basic components. As we saw at the beginning of Chapter 4, Naomi Schor's identification of the detail as essentially feminine finds a prime example in Barry's comics, which are about detail and close, careful reading and unpeeling, just as they are about drawing attention to the tragedies and magic of the quotidian, the margins and marginalized. From the earliest comic strips with trouble in them to the recent, elaborate graphic narratives, the unconventionality, emotionality and alternating styles and textures of Barry's comics demand careful attention. They draw in their readers, involving them in a process of understanding and, ideally, creating.

By teasing the limits of the subject matter, styles and the very scope associated with the comics form, Barry's comics expand the vast comics archive, providing alternative, intuitive and messy modes of collaged curation and archiving.[12] Her comics highlight and confirm the centrality of children to the comics form, from giving space to ignored, non-normative childhoods to elaborating on the power of children's art, outsider art and other forms that are often denied the status of art. In this way, Barry's comics are both a gateway into the rich, ever-changing world of comics and a means of accessing and sharing creativity at large.

This guide, beginning with the historical and biographical contexts, and moving through key texts, major themes and the social and cultural impact of Barry's works, has striven to approach a vast and diverse

---

[12]See Crucifix, *Drawing*.

Conclusion

corpus through unpacking the potentialities of drawing and other visual techniques, the image and storytelling theories Barry conveys through her graphic narratives, while paying special attention to the close interplay of personal and fictionalized narratives. The complexity of autographics or graphic memoir is fully tested and played with in Barry's oeuvre.

Throughout its four chapters, this guide has fleshed out central concepts, often in a circular movement, comparable to the meditative spirals in Barry's manuals, building on ideas introduced in the preceding chapters. The first chapter introduced troubled childhood and diary-keeping, interaction with and distance from conventional comics forms, merging of art and comics worlds, covering diverse genres such as bittersweet humorous comics, the how-to manual, autobiography and fiction.

As we saw in the second and third chapters, the imbrication of autobiography and fiction in autobifictionalography is also reflected in the importance Barry accords to journaling, for her own practice and in her courses, emphasizing the personal facet of making art. There are then at least two kinds of awareness Barry transmits through her works: self-awareness, but also awareness of an image as an image that goes beyond visible appearances by being animated and acquiring a life of its own. As we saw in the third chapter, these images also have different degrees of presence, depending on the maker and the viewer and the context in which they find the images. We have encountered numerous ghostly images in Barry's books with different degrees of transparency and resurrection, which are connected to a rogue archival process. One of Barry's preferred alternative archival techniques, the collage, is also a comicitous form, in its hybridity and reliance on multiple reading trajectories. Next to the seemingly anonymous gesture of the collage, Barry also insists on the importance of using one's hands, of folding, cutting, tracing, copying, coloring in and writing by hand.

The final chapter returned to the troubled childhoods and elaborated on the collaborative elements of Barry's comics and how her very specific use of the form tests and expands the limits of comics. Barry's self-conscious and participatory comics teach us about the potentialities of the medium and its ability to channel different possibilities of expression, which are honest, authentic without necessarily being factual, moving, affective but also funny. The uniqueness of Barry's body of work reflects, in many ways, the medium specificity of comics, its possibilities of conveying complex emotions and

Conclusion

stories. In Barry's comics, the artistic gesture of braiding (*tressage*) and the readerly act of weaving (*tissage*) unfold on an equal plane.[13] Through offering works that are accessible, frank, and moving, Barry blurs the lines between readerly and writerly texts,[14] involving readers while encouraging them to look and read for more and, perhaps, even make.

---

[13]Groensteen, *System of Comics,* 144–53; Postema's complementary concept of weaving translates into *tissage* in French. See *Narrative Structure in Comics,* 112–13.
[14]See Willmott, "My Kid," in *Contagious Imagination,* 183; Barthes, *S/Z.*

BIBLIOGRAPHY

Primary Sources

Barry, Lynda. *Girls and Boys*. Real Comet Press, 1981.
Barry, Lynda. *Big Ideas*. Real Comet Press, 1983.
Barry, Lynda. *Naked Ladies Naked Ladies Naked Ladies*. Real Comet Press, 1984.
Barry, Lynda. *Everything in the World*. Harper Perennial, 1986.
Barry, Lynda. *The Fun House*. Harper Perennial, 1987.
Barry, Lynda. *Cruddy: An Illustrated Novel*. Simon & Schuster, 2000.
Barry, Lynda. "Two Questions." In *McSweeney's Quarterly Concern* no. 13, edited by Chris Ware, 60–5. McSweeney's, 2004.
Barry, Lynda. *What It Is*. Drawn & Quarterly, 2008.
Barry, Lynda and Kevin Kawula (guest water colorist). *Picture This: The Near-Sighted Monkey Book*. Drawn & Quarterly, 2010.
Barry, Lynda. *Everything: Comics From Around 1978-1981*. Drawn & Quarterly, 2011.
Barry, Lynda. *The Freddie Stories*. Drawn & Quarterly, 2012.
Barry, Lynda. *Syllabus: Notes from an Accidental Professor*. Drawn & Quarterly, 2014.
Barry, Lynda. "Coping With Stress." In *The Complete Wimmen's Comix*, edited by Trina Robbins, 363. Fantagraphics, 2016.
Barry, Lynda. *The Greatest of Marlys*. Drawn & Quarterly, 2016.
Barry, Lynda. "Seven Deep Psychological Problems." In *The Complete Wimmen's Comix*, edited by Trina Robbins, 295. Fantagraphics, 2016.
Barry, Lynda. *The Good Times Are Killing Me*. Drawn & Quarterly, 2017.
Barry, Lynda. *One Hundred Demons*. Drawn & Quarterly, 2017.
Barry, Lynda. *Making Comics*. Drawn & Quarterly, 2019.
Barry, Lynda. "Menopositive." In *Menopause: A Comic Treatment*, edited by M. K. Czerwiec, 11–16. Pennsylvania State University Press, 2020.

Secondary Sources

Abate, Michelle Ann. *No Kids Allowed: Children's Literature for Adults*. Johns Hopkins University Press, 2020.
Ahmed, Maaheen. *Openness of Comics: Generating Meaning within Flexible Structures*. University Press of Mississippi, 2016.

Bibliography

Ahmed, Maaheen. *Openness of Comics: Generating Meaning Within Flexible Structures* University Press of Mississippi, 2016.

Ahmed, Maaheen. "Tracing the Invisible: Lynda Barry's Comics." *Mediascapes* 22, no. 2 (2023): 35–51. https://rosa.uniroma1.it/rosa03/mediascapes/article/view/18635/17685.

Ahmed, Maaheen and Benoît Crucifix, eds. "Children's Drawings in Comics/Les dessins d'enfance dans la bande dessinée." *Comicalités* (2023). https://doi.org/10.4000/comicalites.8374.

Ahmed, Sara. "Happy Objects." In *Affect Theory Reader,* edited by Melissa Gregg and Gregory J. Seigworth, 29–51. Duke University Press, 2010.

Assmann, Aleida. *Cultural Memory and Western Civilization: Functions, Media, Archives.* Cambridge University Press, 2011.

Assmann, Aleida. "Forms of Forgetting." *Herengracht 401: Research, Art, Dialogue.* https://h401.org/2014/10/forms-of-forgetting/7584/.

Baetens, Jan. "Revealing Traces: A New Theory of Graphic Enunciation." In *The Language of Comics: Word and Image,* edited by Robin Varnum and Christina T. Gibbons, 145–55. University Press of Mississippi, 2001.

Baetens, Jan and Hugo Frey. *The Graphic Novel: An Introduction.* Cambridge University Press, 2014.

Ball, David M. and Martha Kuhlman, eds. *The Comics of Chris Ware: Drawing Is a Way of Thinking.* University Press of Mississippi, 2010.

Barnholden, Neale. *From Gum Wrappers to Richie Rich: The Materiality of Cheap Comics.* University Press of Mississippi, 2024.

Barthes, Roland. *S/Z.* Translated by Richard Miller. Farrar Strauss Giroux, 1974.

Beaty, Bart. *Fredric Wertham and the Critique of Mass Culture.* University Press of Mississippi, 2005.

Beaty, Bart. *Comics Versus Art.* University of Toronto Press, 2012.

Beaty, Bart. "Some Classics." In *The Cambridge Companion to the Graphic Novel,* edited by Stephen E. Tabachnik, 175–91. Cambridge University Press, 2017.

Beaty, Bart. "Chris Oliveros, Drawn and Quarterly, and the Expanded Definition of the Graphic Novel." In *The Cambridge History of the Graphic Novel,* edited by Jan Baetens Hugo Frey and Stephan E. Tabachnik, 426–42. Cambridge University Press, 2018.

Bechdel, Alison. *Are You My Mother? A Comic Drama.* Mariner Books, 2012.

Beckett, Sandra L. *Crossover Fiction: Global and Historical Perspectives.* Routledge, 2009.

Beineke, Colin. "On Comicity." *Inks: The Journal of the Comics Studies Society* 1, no. 2 (2017): 226–53.

Benjamin, Walter. "The Storyteller: Reflections on the Work of Nikolai Leskov." In *The Storyteller Essays,* edited and introduced by Samuel Titan. Translated by Tess Lewis. NYRB, 2019.

Bennett, Tamaryn. "Dancing with Demons: Consciousness and Identity in Lynda Barry's *One Hundred Demons*." In *Picturing Childhood: Youth in Transnational Comics,* edited by Mark Heimermann and Brittany Tullis, 218–33. University of Texas Press, 2017.

Bourdieu, Pierre. *Forms of Capital.* Translated by Peter Collier. Polity, 2021.

Bibliography

Brown, Kieron. "Play and Playfulness in Lynda Barry's *What It Is*." *Eludamos: Journal for Computer Game Culture* 12, no. 1 (2021) : 127–48. https://doi.org/10.7557/23.6366.

Brunetti, Ivan. *Cartooning: Philosophy and Practice*. Yale University Press, 2007.

Bukatman, Scott. *Poetics of Slumberland : Animated Spirits and the Animating Spirit*. University of California Press, 2012.

Cardinal, Roger. *Outsider Art*. Studio Vista, 1972.

Carrier, David and Joachim Pissaro, *The Margins of Aesthetics: Wild Art Explained*. Pennsylvania State University Press, 2019.

"Celebrate Seminal Seattle Publisher Real Comet Press on March 10!" *Fantagraphics Blog,* February 28, 2012. Accessed December 4, 2025. https://blog.fantagraphics.com/celebrate-seminal-seattle-publisher-real-comet-press-on-march-10/.

Chambers, Ross. *Loitliterature*. Nebraska University Press, 1999.

Chaney, Michael A. *Reading Lessons in Seeing: Mirrors, Masks and Mazes in the Autobiographical Graphic Novel*. University Press of Mississippi, 2017.

Chiu, Monica. "Coming to America, 'Land of the Free': Asian American Representations in the Graphic Novel." In *The Cambridge Companion to the American Graphic Novel*, edited by Jan Baetens, Hugo Frey and Fabrice Leroy, 226–41. Cambridge University Press, 2023.

Chute, Hillary L. *Graphic Women: Life Narrative and Contemporary Comics*. Columbia University Press, 2010.

Chute, Hillery L. *Disaster Drawn: Visual Witness, Comics and Documentary*. Bellknap Press, 2016.

Chute, Hillary L. and Lynda Barry. "Lynda Barry." In *Outside the Box: Interviews with Contemporary Cartoonists*, 57–79. University of Chicago Press, 2014.

Cixous, Hélène. "The Laugh of the Medusa." Translated by Keith Cohen and Paula Cohen. *Signs* 1, no. 4 (1976): 875–96.

Classon, Mike Frangos. "Swedish Norm-Critical Comics and the Comics Pedagogy of Lynda Barry." *The Comics Grid: Journal of Comics Scholarship* 11, no. 1 (2021). https://www.comicsgrid.com/article/id/4042/.

Crain, Patricia. *Reading Children: Literacy, Property and Dilemmas of Childhood in Nineteenth-Century America*. University of Pennsylvania Press, 2016.

Crenshaw, Kimberlé. "Demarginalizing the Intersection of Race and Sex: A Black Feminist Critique of Antidiscrimination Doctrine, Feminist Theory and Antiracist Politics." *University of Chicago Legal Forum* 1989, no. 1 (1989): 139–67. https://chicagounbound.uchicago.edu/cgi/viewcontent.cgi?article=1052&context=uclf.

Crucifix, Benoît. *Drawing from the Archives: Comics Memory in the Contemporary Graphic Novel*. Cambridge University Press, 2023.

Cummings, E. E. "A Foreword to Krazy." In *Arguing Comics: Literary Masters on a Popular Medium*, edited by Jeet Heer and Kent Worcester, 30–4. University Press of Mississippi, 2004.

Cvetkovich, Ann. *Depression: A Public Feeling*. Duke University Press, 2012.

Bibliography

de Jésus, Melinda L. "Of Monsters and Mothers: Filipina American Identity and Maternal Legacies in Lynda J. Barry's *One Hundred Demons.*" *Méridians: Feminisms, Race, Transnationalism* 5, no. 1 (2004): 1–26.

de Jésus, Melinda L. "Liminality and Mestiza Consciousness in Lynda Barry's *One Hundred Demons.*" In *Multicultural Comics: From Zap to Blue Beetle*, edited by Frederik L. Aldama, 73–94. University of Texas Press, 2010.

De Kosnik, Abigail. *Rogue Archives: Digital Cultural Memory and Fandom.* MIT Press, 2016.

Debord, Guy. *Society of the Spectacle.* Translated by Ken Knabb. AK Press, 2005.

Derrida, Jacques. *Limited Inc.* Translated by Samuel Weber. Northwestern University Press, 1988.

Derrida, Jacques. *Of Grammatology.* Translated by Gayatri Chakravorty Spivak. Johns Hopkins University Press, 1998.

Derrida, Jacques, Daniel Bougnioux, and Bernard Stiegler. *Trace et archive, image et art suivi de hommage à Jacques Derrida.* INA, 2014.

Drucker, Johanna. *The Century of Artists' Books*, Granary Books, 2004.

Eichhorn, Kate. *Adjusted Margins: Xerography, Art and Activism in the Late Twentieth Century.* MIT Press, 2016.

El Refaie, Elisabeth. *Autobiographical Comics: Life Writing in Pictures.* Jackson, University Press of Mississippi, 2012.

Felski, Rita. *Hooked: Art and Attachment.* University of Chicago Press, 2020.

Fineberg, Jonathan. *The Innocent Eye: Children's Art and the Modern Artist.* Princeton University Press, 1997.

Flowers, Ebony. "On Copying." In *With Great Power Comes Great Pedagogy: Teaching, Learning and Comics*, edited by Susan Kirtley, Antero Garcia, Peter E. Carlson, 85–91. University Press of Mississippi, 2020.

Fresnault-Deruelle, Pierre. "From Linear to Tabular (1976)." In *The French Comics Theory Reader*, edited by Ann Miller and Bart Beaty, 121–38. Leuven University Press, 2014.

Gardner, Jared. "Autobiography's Biography (1973-2007)," *Biography* 31, no. 1 (2008): 1–26.

Gardner, Jared. "Storylines." *SubStance* 40, no. 1 (2011): 53–69.

Gardner, Jared. *Projections: Comics and the History of Twenty-First Century Storytelling.* Stanford University Press, 2012.

Gaudreault, André. *From Plato to Lumière: Narration and Monstration in Literature and Cinema.* Translated by Timothy Barnard. University of Toronto Press, 1997.

Genette, Gérard. *Narrative Discourse: An Essay in Method.* Translated by Jane E. Lewin. Cornell University Press, 1980.

Genette, Gérard. "Introduction to the Paratext." Translated by Marie Maclean. *New Literary History* 22, no. 2 (1991): 261–72.

Gilbert, Roger. "Four-Panel Epiphanies: The Art of Lynda Barry." *Northwest Review* 34 (1996): 78–96.

Gilmore, Leigh. *Autobiographics: A Feminist Theory of Women's Autobiography.* Cornell University Press, 1994.

Bibliography

Greenberg, Clement. "Collage." In *Art and Culture: Critical Essays*. Beacon Press, 1989.

Grennan, Simon. *A Theory of Narrative Drawing*. Palgrave, 2017.

Grennan, Simon. *Thinking about Drawing: An Introduction to Themes and Concepts*. Bloomsbury, 2022.

Groensteen, Thierry. *The System of Comics*. Translated by Bart Beaty and Nick Nguyen. University Press of Mississippi, 2007.

Gubar, Marah. "The Teflon Kid." *Public Books,* January 5, 2015. Accessed September 24, 2024. https://www.publicbooks.org/the-teflon-kid-how-annie-enables-apathy-about-inequality/.

Guibert, Xavier and Charles Burns. "The Interior Worlds of Charles Burns." *du9*, January 2016. Accessed September 24, 2024. https://www.du9.org/en/entretien/the-inner-worlds-of-charles-burns/.

Gunn, Janet Varner. *Autobiography: Towards a Poetics of Experience*. University of Pennsylvania Press, 1982.

Haltan-Hernandez, Emilia, "Milner in the Comic Frame: Lynda Barry and Alison Bechdel's Autobiographical Cures." In *The Marion Milner Method: Psychoanalysis, Autobiography and Creativity*, 150–73. Routledge, 2023.

Harris, Miriam. "Cartoonists as Matchmakers: The Vibrant Relationship of Text and Image in the Work of Lynda Barry." In *Elective Affinities: Testing Word and Image Relationships*, edited by Catriona MacLeod, Véronique Plesch, and Charlotte Schoell-Glass, 129–46. Rodopi, 2009.

Hatfield, Charles. *Alternative Comics: An Emerging Literature*. University Press of Mississippi, 2005.

Hirsch, Marianne. "Editor's Column: Collateral Damage." *PMLA* 119, no. 5 (2004): 1209–15.

Hogan, Rebecca. "Engendered Autobiographies: The Diary as a Feminine Form." *Prose Studies* 14, no. 2 (1991): 95–107.

Hollindale, Peter. *Signs of Childness in Children's Books*. Thimble Press, 1997.

Horne, Victoria. "'the personal clutter… the painterly mess…' Tracing a History of Carolee Schneemann's *Interior Scroll*." *Art History* 43, no. 5 (2020): 984–1006. https://doi.org/10.1111/1467-8365.12529.

Ingold, Tim. *The Life of Lines*. Routledge, 2015.

Jenkins, Henry. *Textual Poachers: Television Fans and Participatory Culture*. Routledge, 2012.

Justin Seattle. "31 Years Later, Celebrating the 'Seminal' Alternative Press Spawned by the Comet Tavern." *Capitol Hill Seattle Blog. Community News for all the Hill*, March 4, 2012. Accessed December 2, 2024. https://www.capitolhillseattle.com/2012/03/31-years-later-celebrating-the-seminal-alternative-press-spawned-by-the-comet-tavern/.

Karasik, Paul and Mark Newgarden. *How to Read Nancy: The Elements of Comics in Three Easy Panels*. Fantagraphics, 2017.

Kashtan, Aaron. *Between Pen and Pixel*. Ohio State University Press, 2018.

Katz, Anna, ed. *With Pleasure: Pattern and Decoration in American Art, 1972–1985*. MOCA and Yale University Press, 2019.

Bibliography

Keen, Suzanne. "On Narrative Empathy." *Narrative* 14, no. 3 (2006): 207–36.

Key, Ellen. *The Century of the Child*. G. P. Putnam's Sons, 1909. Project Gutenberg, 2018, https://www.gutenberg.org/cache/epub/57283/pg57283-images.html.

Kirtley, Susan. *Lynda Barry: Girlhood through a Looking Glass*. University Press of Mississippi, 2012.

Kirtley, Susan. *Typical Girls: The Rhetoric of Womanhood in Comic Strips*. Ohio State University Press, 2021.

Kukkonen, Karin. "Metalepsis in Comics." In *Metalepsis in Popular Culture*, edited by Karin Kukkonen and Sonja Klimek, 213–31. De Gruyter, 2011.

Kunka, Andrew J. *Autobiographical Comics*. Bloomsbury, 2018.

Kwa, Shiamin. "Life Writing in Comics." In *The Cambridge Companion to Comics*, edited by Maaheen Ahmed, 185–203. Cambridge University Press, 2023.

Kwa, Shiamin. "Making Magic: Comics and the Ekphrastic Art of Almost There." In *The Routledge Companion to Art and Literature*, edited by Neil Murphy, W. Michelle Wang and Cheryl Julia Lee, 290–306. Routledge, 2024.

Lehoczky, Etelka. "Cartoonist Lynda Barry: 'Drawing Has To Come Out of Your Body.'" *npr.org,* November 17, 2019. Accessed September 23, 2024. https://www.npr.org/2019/11/27/782921983/cartoonist-lynda-barry-drawing-has-to-come-out-of-your-body.

Licari-Guillaume, Isabelle. "Ambiguous Authorities: Vertigo and the Auteur Figure." *Authorship,* no. 2 (2017). https://doi.org/10.21825/aj.v6i2.7700.

"Lynda Barry." *MacArthur Foundation*. Accessed December 2, 2024. https://www.macfound.org/fellows/class-of-2019/lynda-barry#searchresults.

"Lynda Barry: Award-Winning Author and Artist." *Steven Barclay Agency*. Accessed December 2, 2024. https://www.barclayagency.com/speakers/lynda-barry.

"Lynda Barry: Comics Deserve To Be Taken Seriously." *Faces of Evergreen,* May 1, 2012. Accessed December 4, 2024. https://www.evergreen.edu/faces-evergreen/lynda-barry.

Manovich, Lev. "Database as Symbolic Form." *Convergence* 5, no. 2 (1999): 80–99.

Marchese, David. "A Genius Cartoonist Believes Child's Play is Anything But Frivolous." *New York Times (Online)*, September 5, 2022. Accessed September 18, 2024. https://www.proquest.com/blogs-podcasts-websites/genius-cartoonist-believes-child-splay.

Marion, Philippe. *Traces en cases: travail graphique, figuration narrative et participation du lecteur. Essai sur la bande dessinée*. PhD dissertation. Université catholique de Louvain, 1993.

McCloud, Scott. *Understanding Comics: The Invisible Art*. HarperPerennial, 1994.

Michael, Olga. "Excavating Childhood: Fairy Tales, Monsters and Abuse Survival in Lynda Barry's *What It Is*." *a/b: Auto/Biography Studies* 32, no. 3 (2017): 541–66.

Michael, Olga. "Scrapbooking Caravaggio's *Medusa*, Reconfiguring Blake: *What It Is*, *One! Hundred! Demons!* and Lynda Barry's Feminist Intervention in the (Male) Artistic Canon." *ImageText* 9, no. 2 (2017). https://imagetextjournal.com/scrapbooking-caravaggios-medusa-reconfiguring-blake-what-it-is-one

-hundred-demons-and-lynda-barrys-feminist-intervention-in-the-male-artistic-canon/.

Michael, Olga. "Graphic Autofiction and the Visualization of Trauma in Lynda Barry and Phoebe Gloeckner's Graphic Memoirs." In *Autofiction in English*, edited by Hywel Dix, 105–24. Palgrave, 2018.

Miller, Rachel R. "Keep Out, or Else: Diary as Body in *The Diary of a Teenage Girl* and *Cruddy*." In *Comics Memory: Archives and Styles*, edited by Maaheen Ahmed and Benoît Crucifix, 101–19. Palgrave, 2018.

Milner, Marion. *On Not Being Able to Paint*. Routledge, 2010.

Miodrag, Hannah. *Comics and Language: Reimagining Critical Discourse on the Form*. University Press of Mississippi, 2013.

Misemer, Leah. "Teaching the Unthinkable Image with Lynda Barry." In *With Great Power Comics Great Pedagogy: Teaching, Learning and Comics*, edited by Susan E. Kirtley, Antero Garcia, and Peter E. Carlson, 168–85. University Press of Mississippi, 2020.

Mitchell, W. J. T. *Iconology: Image, Text, Ideology*. University of Chicago Press, 1986.

Mitchell, W. J. T. *What Do Pictures Want: The Lives and Loves of Images*. University of Chicago Press, 2005.

Ngai, Sianne. *Ugly Feelings*. Harvard University Press, 2007.

Nyberg, Amy. *Seal of Approval: The History of the Comics Code*. University Press of Mississippi, 1998.

Parkinson, Gavin, ed. *Surrealism, Science Fiction and Comics*. Liverpool University Press, 2015.

Pedri, Nancy. "Re-Visualizing the Map in Guy Delisle's *Pyongyang*." *Arborescences*, no. 4 (2014): 99–114. https://doi.org/10.7202/1027434ar.

Pedri, Nancy. "Traumatic Layering of Self: Scrapbooking Personal Photographs in *One Hundred Demons*." *Polysèmes* 19 (2018). https://journals.openedition.org/polysemes/3460.

Pizzino, Chistopher. "The Doctor versus the Dagger: Comics Reading and Cultural Memory." *PMLA* 130, no. 3 (2015): 631–47.

Pizzino, Christopher. *Arresting Development: Comics at the Boundaries of Literature*. University of Texas Press, 2016.

Postema, Barabara. *Narrative Structure in Comics: Making Sense of Fragments*. RIT Press, 2013.

Powers, Thom and Lynda Barry. "Cartoonist Lynda Barry Teaches us How to Silence Our Inner Critic and Draw Like a Child." Q with Tom Power. *Canadian Broadcasting Centre*, November 25, 2019. Accessed December 2, 2024. https://www.youtube.com/watch?v=2CfmeTPQHLE.

Powers, Thom and Lynda Barry. "The Lynda Barry Interview – Part 2." *The Comics Journal*, January 2, 1989. Accessed September 23, 2023. https://www.tcj.com/the-lynda-barry-interview/2/.

Rath, Jay. "Comic Genius: Lynda Barry's New Book is a How-to Book and Much More." *Isthmus*, February 27, 2020. Accessed September 18, 2024. https://isthmus.com/arts/books/making-comics-book-lynda-barry/.

Bibliography

Richardson, Sarah. "'Perseveration on Detail': Shame and Confession in Memoir Comics." In *Cultural Excavation and Formal Expression in the Graphic Novel*, edited by Jonathan C. Evans and Thomas Giddens, 149–58. Brill, 2013.

Roan, Jeannette. "'What is an Image?' Art History, Visual Culture Studies, Comics Studies." In *Seeing Comics through Art History*, edited by Maggie Gray and Ian Horton, 247–68. Palgrave, 2022.

Root, Maria P. P. "Reconstructing the Impact of Trauma on Personality." In *Personality and Psychopathology: Feminist Appraisals*, edited by Laura S. Brown and Mary Ballou, 229–65. Guildford Press, 1992.

Sabin Roger. *Adult Comics: An Introduction*. Routledge, 1993.

Samanci, Özge. "Lynda Barry's Humor: At the Juncture of Private and Public, Invitation and Dissemination, Childish and Professional." *International Journal of Comic Art* 8, no. 2 (2006): 181–99.

Scherr, Rebecca. "Shaking Hands with Other People's Pain: Joe Sacco's *Palestine*," *Mosaic: An Interdisciplinary Critical Journal* 46, no. 1 (2013): 19–36.

Scherr, Rebecca. "Framing Human Rights: Comics Form and the Politics of Recognition in Joe Sacco's *Footnotes in Gaza*." *Textual Practice* 29, no. 1 (2015): 111–31.

Schmitt, Arnaud. "Avatars as the raison d'être of Autofiction." *Life Writing* 19, no. 1 (2022): 15–26.

Schneemann, Carolee. "Text from Interior Scroll, 1975." *Carolee Schneemann Foundation*. Accessed December 5, 2024. https://www.schneemannfoundation.org/writing/interior-scroll.

Schor, Naomi. *Reading in Detail: Aesthetics and the Feminine*. Routledge, 2007.

Singer, Marc. *Breaking the Frames: Populism and Prestige in Comics Studies*. University of Texas Press, 2019.

Smith, Sidonie and Julia Watson. *Reading Autobiography Now: An Updated Guide for Interpreting Life Narratives*. University of Minnesota Press, 2024.

Smolderen, Thierry. *The Origins of Comics: From William Hogarth to Winsor McCay*. Translated by Bart Beaty and Nick Nguyen. University Press of Mississippi, 2014.

Steedman, Carolyn. *Strange Dislocations: Childhood and the Idea of Human Interiority, 1780-1930*. Harvard University Press, 1998.

Stockton, Kathryn Bond. *The Queer Child, or Growing Sideways in the Twentieth Century*. Duke University Press, 2009.

Szép, Eszter. *Comics and the Body: Drawing, Reading and Vulnerability*. Ohio State University Press, 2020.

Tensuan, Theresa M. "Comic Visions and Revisions in the Work of Lynda Barry and Marjane Satrapi." *Modern Fiction Studies* 52, no. 4 (2006): 947–64.

Thorn, Jesse and Lynda Barry. "The Sound of Young America: Lynda Barry, Author of *Picture This* and *What It Is*." *Bullseye*, hosted by *Maximum Fun*, January 3, 2011. Accessed December 4, 2024. https://maximumfun.org/episodes/bullseye-with-jesse-thorn/lynda-barry-author-picture-and-what-it-interview-sound-young-america/.

Tinker, Emma. "Selfhood and Trauma in Lynda Barry's Autobiofictionalography." In *Identity and Form in Alternative Comics, 1967-2007*, 106–35. PhD Thesis.

University College London, 2008. Accessed September 24, 2024. https://emmatinker.oxalto.co.uk/downloads/barry.pdf.

Tolmie, Jane, ed. *Drawing from Life: Memory and Subjectivity in Comic Art.* University Press of Mississippi, 2013.

Tolmie, Jane, ed. *Contagious Imagination: The Work and Art of Lynda Barry.* University Press of Mississippi, 2022.

Tucker, Susan, Katherine Ott, and Patricia Buckler, eds. *The Scrapbook in American Life.* Temple University Press, 2006.

VanderMeer, Jeff and Lynda Barry. "Amazon's Omnivoracious Interview with Lynda Barry." *Drawn & Quarterly,* November 30, 2010. Accessed December 2, 2024. https://drawnandquarterly.com/press/amazons-omnivoracious-interviews-lynda-barry/.

Vasari, Giorgio. *The Lives of the Artists.* Translated by Julia Conaway Bondanella and Peter Bondanella. Oxford University Press, 1998.

Ware, Chris. "On Charles Burns' Paired Photographs." *Virginia Quarterly Review: A National Journal of Literature and Discussion* (Winter 2007): 105–7.

Whitlock, Gillian. "Autographics: The Seeing 'I' of Comics." *Modern Fiction Studies* 52, no. 4 (2006): 965–79.

Wiesenthal, Christine, Brad Bucknell, and W. J. T. Mitchell. "Essays into the Imagetext: An Interview with W. J. T. Mitchell." *Mosaic: An Interdisciplinary Critical Journal* 33, no. 2 (2000): 1–23.

INDEX

Note: Page numbers followed by 'n' indicate note numbers; page numbers in *italics* refers to figures.

affect   7, 18, 32, 107, 126, 168, 175, 179, 194, 201
Ahmed, Sara   179 n.110
Alcott, Louisa May   113
aliveness   7, 11, 22, 88–9, 101, 107, 120, 177–9, 191, 196
animate/animation   22, 103, 105, 107, 117–19, 122, 123, 142, 177, 179
animatedness (Ngai)   107, 118–20, 122, 123
archive   6, 10, 12, 28–30, 35, 51, 107, 119, 123, 136–8, 141, 174, 177, 193, 200
art brut   178
artists' books   1–5, 14–20, 22, 28, 29, 33, 35, 36, 40, 41, 43, 45–7, 49, 53, 58, 59, 64, 66, 69, 80, 81, 83, 84, 89, 91, 93, 100–14, 123, 125, 134, 141, 144, 147, 158, 160, 167, 172, 176, 178–81, 183, 184, 188–93, 199, 200
Assmann, Aleida   137, 141, 142, 144
autobifictionalography   12, 13, 67, 80, 145–6, 153, 155, 201
autobiography   6, 7, 32–4, 46–7, 53
autoclasm   54
autographics   33, 201
automatic drawing   11, 42, 49, 94, 105, 108, 114; *see also* free drawing
avatar   2, 4, 4 n.8, 20, 27–8, 37, 49, 91, 165, 172, 199

Baetens, Jan   111–13, 192
Barnholden, Neale   136
Bart Beaty   3
Barthes, Roland   173
Baudelaire, Charles   138; *see also* chiffonnier
Bauman, Zygmunt   138
Beaty, Bart   3, 46–7

Bechdel, Alison   1, 32
Beckett, Sandra L.   68 n.43, 78 n.78
Beineke, Colin   28
Benjamin, Walter   9, 10, 24, 126, 138, 197
Bennett, Tamaryn   168, 172
Big Ideas (Barry)   43, *44*, 55, 61–2, *62*
biocularity   78 n.78
braiding (Groensteen)   17, 108, 116, 117, 139, 141, 202
Briggs, Clare A.   2
Brown, Kieron   21–2, 113
Brunetti, Ivan   2, 41, 98, 100–2, 177, 180–5
Bukatman, Scott   118
bumpiness   81, 144
Burns, Charles   40
Bushmiller, Ernie   57

Cardinal, Roger   23
Carrier, David   40
Cartooning (Brunetti)   2, 98, 101, 177, 180–4
cephalopod   14, 14 n.15, 20–1, 25, 79, 89, 119, 139, 140, 159, 174, 198
Chambers, Ross   160
Chaney, Michael   114–15, 129, 155, 173
Chaon, Dan   41, 100–1, 180
Chase, Alicia   158
The Chicago Reader   43
chiffonnier (Baudelaire and Benjamin)   138
child/children   7, 9, 13, 26, 27, 29, 30, 32, 34–40, 43, 49–51, 54–67, 155–6, 167–70, 174–9, 183, 189–90, 192, 197, 200
childhood   7, 9, 11–13, 16, 18, 20–33, 37, 45, 48, 53–5, 64–86, 95, 101, 106–8, 113–17, 123, 127, 129, 133–4, 138, 140, 145–78, 181, 188, 200, 201

Index

Christian, Barbara 143
Chute, Hillary L. 6, 11, 31, 58, 74, 81, 95, 105, 115, 124, 126–7, 129, 135, 153
Cixous, Hélène 159
collage 3, 7, 8, 12, 13, 18, 21–3, 25, 28, 30, 34, 39–40, 48, 49, 51, 53, 55–7, 59, 67, 69, 80–2, 85, 90, 92, 100, 103, 105, 108, 113–20, 123, 124, 127, 135–53, 157–8, 160–4, 166, 172, 174, 185, 189, 190, 193, 197, 200, 201
color/coloring 23–5, 28, 31, 34, 43, 56–7, 70, 79, 83, 90–3, 95–8, 101, 115–17, 122–3, 126, 133–5, 137, 140, 146, 149–50, 158, 160, 162, 164, 167, 174, 178, 182, 188–9
Comet Tavern 43
comicity/comicitous (Beineke) 28, 78, 117, 124, 141, 142, 185, 201
Comics Code 115, 131–2
composition notebooks 48, 101, 155, 173–4, 184, 193; *see also* exercise books; *Making Comics* (Barry); sketchbooks; *Syllabus* (Barry)
contemplative action (Milner) 186–7
Cooper Point Journal 42
"Coping with Stress for Under One Dollar" 38, 39
copying 3, 11, 28, 59–60, 79, 89, 91, 93–5, 98, 102, 108, 133, 135, 172, 178, 179, 181, 188, 191, 192, 195, 198, 201
"The Creation of the World" (Barry) 62, 62–3
Crenshaw, Kimberlé 155, 156; *see also* intersectionality
crossover fiction 68, 68 n.43
Cruddy (Barry) 7, 45, 49, 53, 72–8, 80, 82, 91, 125, 157, 160, 162
cummings, e. e. 58
Cvetkovich, Ann 81, 159

database aesthetic 141
Debord, Guy 49
de Jesús, Melinda L. 157, 164, 167
delay (Stockton) 169–71
Derrida, Jacques 107, 110, 111, 124, 135
détournement 145
diary 4, 26, 27, 49, 53, 67–78, 84, 98, 100, 113, 115, 125–6, 149, 157–8, 191, 201

Dickinson, Emily 185
disegno 135
doodle 17, 18, 97, *109,* 141, 145, 185–8
Drawn & Quarterly (D&Q) 4 n.9, 12–14, 16, 17 n.30, 33, 35, 39, 44–6, 50, 55, 56, 59, 62, 67, 71, 86, 87, 92, 96, 99, 109, 116, 121, 122, 128, 131, 139, 150, 163, 171, 173, 186, 187, 198

Eco, Umberto 141
El Refaie, Elisabeth 146
emotion 6, 7, 18, 34, 36, 40, 53, 66, 82, 117, 118, 121, 149, 151–2, 155, 162, 168, 170, 194, 200, 201
Ernie Pook's Comeek (Barry) 9, 12–13, 25, 30, 42–5, 53, 55, 58, 61, 64–6, 127, 136, 147, 153, 167, 169, 173
Esquire 38
Evergreen State College in Olympia, Washington 41–2
Everything: Comics from Around 1978-81 (Barry) 7, 9, 18, 26, 29–30, 35, 55–7, 65–6, 82, 112, 136–7, 141, 147–8, 179, 192
Everything in the World (Barry) 30, 34, 62, 64
exercise books 23, 27, 55, 100
exercises 3, 5, 8, 23, 26, 27, 55, 70, 91, 93–7, 100, 147, 173, 176, 180, 196, 198, 199
 chicken in winter exercise 94
 copying exercise 188
 drawing exercises 2, 11, 53, 98, 102, 108, 124, 177, 181, 183, 189, 191
 demon-making exercise 78–80, 83, 119
 memory exercise 185
 spiral exercises 97, 100, 179, 182
 x-page exercise 182, 184

Fangos, Mike Classon 172
Fantagraphics 43
feeling-change 18, 36, 58, 65, 66, 148
Feiffer, Jules 44
feminism 36, 39, 55, 81, 144, 157–60, 164, 172, 190, 200
Fleener, Mary 112–13
Flowers, Ebony 89–90, 94
Follet, Mary Parker 182
four-by-four exercise 181–2
Frasca, Marilyn 21, 41–2, 84–9, 140, 180, 185

213

Index

The Freddie Stories (Barry) 45, 129–30, 169, 171, 178, 197
free drawing 3, 23, 30, 101–2, 183, 186–7, 189; *see also* automatic drawing
Fun Home (Bechdel) 79, 106
The Fun House (Barry) 30, 38, 62, 64

Gardner, Jared 9, 32, 78, 112, 126, 141, 190, 199
Gaudreault, André. 106–7
ghost 15, 31, 76, 92, 103, 109–10, 130, 139–42, 145, 169, 171, 174–5, 178, 201
Gilbert, Roger 58–9
Giotto (Giotto di Bondone) 87–9
Girls and Boys (Barry) 6, 9, 13, 43, 53, 55–7, *59*, 61, 64, 66, 136, 147
The Good Times Are Killing Me (Barry) 5, 7, 31, 44–6, 53, 67–72, 77, 81, 155, 157, 162, 185
Graham, Kenneth 27
graphiation (Marion) 19, 106–7, 111–12
graphie (Derrida) 111, 121, 124
Greenberg, Clement 145
Grennan, Simon 3 n.5, 20
Groening, Matt 40, 42, 44, 100, 191
Groensteen, Thierry 17, 116, 139
growing sideways (Stockton) 169
growing up 7, 9, 11–32, 43, 53, 64, 68, 115, 156, 169

Halton-Hernandez, Emilia 183
hand 2, 15, 17–20, 174, 176–8, 181, 184, 185, 187, 188, 192–4
handwriting 9, 15, 19, 98, 124, 126
haptic visuality (Marks) 194, 199
Harding, Susan 190
Harper Perennial 38, 45
Harris, Miriam 37, 66–7
Hatfield, Charles 152
Herriman, George 37–8, 58, 125
Hillenbrand, Cathy 43; *see also* Real Comet Press
Hirsch, Marianne 78, 78 n.78
Hogan, Rebecca 157–8
horror vacui 23
Huggan, Graham 76
imagetext (Mitchell) 10, 19
Ingold, Tim 195, 199
interiority 70, 168
intersectional comics 156–72

Jenkins, Henry 190
Jorn, Asger 145

Kabakov, Ilya 144
Karasik, Paul 57
Kashtan, Aaron 48
Kathryn Bond Stockton 169
Keister, John 42
Kirtley, Susan 5–6, 10–11, 30, 45, 55, 65, 69, 73, 82–4, 113, 125, 152, 157, 190–1
Knighton, Ryan 100
Kominsky-Crumb, Aline 147
Kozloff, Joyce 81, 144
Krauss, Ruth 174
Krazy Kat (Herriman) 38, 58, 125
Krementz, Jill 174
Kunka, Andrew J. 4 n.8, 146 n.135
Kushner, Robert 81, 144
Kwa, Shiamin 103, 107, 118

L. H. O. O. Q (Duchamp) 145
Lewis, C. S. 27
Life in Hell (Groening) 40, 42
life writing 4 n.8, 6, 7, 12, 20, 35, 67, 78, 103, 105–6, 118, 144–53; *see also* autobiography; autofiction
Little Nemo in Slumberland (McCay) 63, 118
loitliterature (Chambers) 160
Luke, Gary 45

MacArthur Fellowship 1
Madden, Matt 2
Madonna and Child (Giotto) *87*, *88*, 88–9
Making Comics (Barry) 2, 7, 27, 48, 54, 72, 84, 94, 98, 101, 107, 119–24, 127, 133, 136, 155, 173, 176–8, 180, 182, 184, 189, 191–5, 197
Manovich, Lev 141
manuals 1–2, 7, 11, 14 n.15, 15, 18, 20, 22, 23, 26, 38, 40–2, 45, 48, 50, 53, 61, 64, 70, 78, 79, 84, 91, 93, 95, 97, 98, 100, 103, 108, 119, 124, 125, 129, 133, 135, 147, 155, 156, 158, 165, 171–4, 180–5, 189–94, 197, 200, 201
maps 76–8, 81
margin 17–18, 40, 86, 143, 200
Marion, Philippe 19, 22, 106, 111, 113, 135, 192

Index

Marks, Laura   194; see also haptic visuality
The Master and His Emissary (McGilchrist)   182–3
materiality   7, 10, 23, 48, 57, 78, 81, 98, 143
McCay, Winsor   118
McCloud, Scott   2, 108
McGilchrist, Iain   182–3
McSweeney's Quarterly Concern   45, 83
mediagenius (Marion)   113
3500 Meisterzeichnungen (Werkner)   47
memory   28, 29, 31, 34, 48, 67, 72, 77, 78, 80, 82, 83, 85, 95, 100, 103, 106, 108, 117, 120, 127, 129, 133, 137–8, 141–8, 152–3, 157, 159, 168, 176, 178–80, 182, 185, 199
"Menopositive" (Barry)   31, 129
metalepsis(-es)   73, 118, 129
Michael, Olga   25–6, 81, 159–60
Milner, Marion   26, 180, 183, 186–7
Miodrag, Hannah   6, 37–8, 125
Misemer, Leah   192
A Misunderstood Genius (Cham)   132, 178
Mitchell, Doris   119, 137–8, 140
Mitchell, W. J. T.   10–11, 19, 22, 89, 120, 175
Modern Romance   38
Monstration (Gaudreault)   107
Morgenthaler, Walter   23
Moriarty, Jerry   103
Morrison, Toni   143
moving script (Benjamin)   9, 197
Naked Ladies, Naked Ladies, Naked Ladies (Barry)   5, 43, 95, 115, 173
National Lampoon   36
Newgarden, Mark   57, 112–13
Ngai, Sianne   107, 118
notebooks   26, 27, 31, 35, 47, 48, 55, 68, 69, 72, 91, 98, 100, 101, 103, 121, 136, 137, 139, 140, 143, 146, 148, 155, 173, 174, 180, 184, 193

Oliveros, Chris   45; see also Drawn & Quarterly (D&Q)
One Hundred Demons (Barry)   3–4, 4, 6, 7, 9, 12, 14, 20, 24–31, 36, 45, 46, 48, 53, 58, 59, 61, 64, 67, 78–85, 91, 96, 100, 105, 107, 108, 115–19, 124, 126–7, 134, 139–50, 157–68, 176, 180
outsider art   23, 200; see also art brut; wild art

Panter, Gary   112, 191
paratactic   157
paratext (Genette)   69
peritext (Genette)   69
participatory culture (Jenkins)   190–1
Pattern and Decoration   81, 144, 158
Peanuts (Schulz)   58
Pedri, Nancy   76–7, 149, 151
pentimento   103
Pero, Allan   119, 180
photograph   24, 34–5, 82–3, 115–17, 140, 145, 148–52, 161, 198
Picture This (Barry)   2, 3, 9, 11, 14–21, 24–8, 48, 50, 54, 55, 57, 59, 79, 82, 84–6, 89–10, 114, 133–7, 143, 145, 147, 156, 157, 173, 176, 180, 185–9, 192, 197
Pissaro, Joachim   40
Pizzino, Christopher   54, 132–3
polygraphy (Smolderen)   178
Pomian, Krzysztof   137
"Poodle with a Mohawk" poster (Barry)   43, 44
Porcellino, John   118
Postema, Barbara   17, 116, 139
pulled lines   100–1, 121, 158, 182

readerly texts (Barthes)   173, 202; see also writerly texts
Reader's Digest   4, 27, 161
Real Comet Press   43–4, 55, 57, 68
relationality   6, 10, 40, 113, 128, 179, 192–3, 197
rememorying   119, 142–3, 152–3, 168
restance (Derrida)   135, 148
Richardson, Sarah   106, 157, 165
Roan, Jeanette   120–1, 172
Root, Maria P. P.   36–7

Sacco, Joe   194, 199
Sasquatch Books   45
Satrapi, Marjane   115, 160
Schapiro, Miriam   81, 144, 158 n.117
Scherr, Rebecca   194, 199
Schlick, Yaël   31, 84, 85, 194, 196 n.187
Schmitt, Arnaud   4 n.8
Schneemann, Carolee   158
Schor, Naomi   157–8, 200
scrapbook   6, 7, 26, 29–30, 34, 35, 82–3, 98, 141, 143, 148, 151

215

Index

sea monster/Sea-Ma   14, 24–6, 64, 79, 80, 83, 94, 100, 117, 133–4, 139, 140, 143, 159, 186, 188, 198–9
"Sear's Portrait of Marlys" (Barry)   96, 96–7
Seattle Sun   43, 65
semiophor (Pomian)   137
short stories   24–5, 31
Situationists (Debord)   49
sketchbooks   147, 148, 184, 192; *see also* composition notebooks; exercise books; notebooks
Smith, Sidonie   20, 78 n.78, 146
Smolderen, Thierry   178
Sousanis, Nick   2
Spiegelman, Art   105, 106, 135, 165
spirals   11, 97, 100, 139, 150, 179, 182, 184–5, 187, 201
Spivak, Gayatri Chakravorty   111
Steedman, Carolyn   70, 161, 168
Stevenson, Robert L.   143
sticky/stickiness (S.Ahmed)   130, 179, 193
Stockton, Kathryn Bond   169, 170
Subitzky, Ed   36
Syllabus (Barry)   2, 9, 11, 22, 26–8, 41–2, 48, 54, 72, 84, 86, 91, 94, 98–102, 123, 124, 136, 173, 174, 176–7, 180–5, 188–9, 191, 193, 197–8
Szép, Eszter   3 n.5, 6, 11, 20, 22, 79–80, 84, 114, 126, 184–5, 194–5, 198

temporality   101, 115, 179, 185, 186, 198
Tensuan, Theresa M.   160
Tinker, Emma   190
Tolmie, Jane   6, 143, 152–3, 172
trace   106, 107, 110–11, 124, 135, 192
trash   102, 107, 136, 137, 193; *see also* waste/wasting
trauma   7, 14 n.15, 31, 36–7, 78, 164, 200
Treasure Island (Stevenson)   143

trouble   53, 58, 61, 66, 132, 153, 163, 200
Trousdale, Rachel   153, 167–8, 172
"Two Questions" (Barry)   45, 83–4, 123, 174, 196
Two Sisters (Barry)   53, 65, 136, 147

underground comics   10, 30, 33, 36, 54, 69, 147

VanderMeer, Jeff   90
Vasari, Giorgio   135; *see also* disegno
The Village Voice   44
Voss, Jan   47

Ware, Chris   45, 134
Warhol, Andy   34
waste/wasting   7, 18, 28–9, 81, 110, 123, 136–8, 141–4, 163, 182
Watson, Julia   20
weave/weaving (Postema)   17, 45, 108, 139, 202
Werkner, Arthur   47
Wertham, Fredric   131, 132
What It Is (Barry)   2, 3, 6, 9–11, 17, 19–29, 41, 45, 48, 50, 54, 59, 70, 82–91, 97–101, 108, 113, 119, 123, 127, 137–41, 143, 144, 147, 157, 159, 161, 164, 165, 168, 173–5, 180, 182, 183, 193, 196
Whitlock, Gillian   33
wild art   40
Williams, Raymond   168
Willmott, Glenn   172–3
Wilson, Gahan   36
Wimmen's Comix   33, 38, 39, 49
Winnicott, D. W.   21, 180
Wölfli, Adolf   23
writerly texts (Barthes)   173, 190, 202; *see also* readerly texts